STONE
in the GARDEN

STONE
in the GARDEN

Inspiring Designs and Practical Projects

Gordon Hayward

Illustrations by Gordon Morrison

W. W. Norton & Company
NEW YORK • LONDON

To Mary, my muse

The text of this book is composed in Garamond

Composition by Susan McClellan
Manufacturing by R.R. Donnelley & Sons
Book design by Susan McClellan
Cover photograph by Richard W. Brown
Illustrations by Gordon Morrison

Library of Congress Cataloging-in-Publication Data

Hayward, Gordon.
    Stone in the garden: inspiring designs and practical projects /
Gordon Hayward.
        p. cm.
    Includes bibliographical references (p.) and index.
    ISBN 0-393-04779-2
    I. Stone in landscapegardening. I. Title.

SB475.5 .H39 2001
717–dc21

00-069945

W. W. Norton & Company, Inc., 500 Fifth Avenue, New York, NY 10110
www.wwnorton.com
W. W. Norton & Company Ltd., 10 Coptic Street, London WC1A 1PU

1 2 3 4 5 6 7 8 9 0

ACKNOWLEDGMENTS

ANY GARDEN BOOK IS A COLLABORATION AMONG THE AUTHOR, editors, illustrator and photographers. I would like to thank all of them for their guidance, patience, good will and for all that I have learned from them over the years. Beyond the professionals are all those in the background. Thanks to all the men and women with whom I installed gardens over nearly twenty years. Thanks also to all my past and present clients who had and have faith in my work. And thanks also to the people who have extended their hospitality as I visited many, many parts of the country in support of this book. I would especially like to thank the following:

John Barstow and Helen Whybrow, editors and friends who knew how to keep me on the right path; Gordon Morrison, such a very skilled illustrator and good man; Susan McClellan, book designer, who has the same clear vision as her photographer/husband, Richard W. Brown; Pamela Ader, client, friend and passionate painter of the natural world; Peter and Theodora Berg, friends and clients; Richard Bergmann, architect in New Canaan, Connecticut; Andre Bernier, stone mason; Patrick Chassé, mentor and friend; Tom Cooper, editor at *The Garden*, who launched me as a garden writer twenty-two years ago in the pages of *Horticulture* magazine; Helen Dillon, fellow lecturer and garden designer from Dublin; Stan and Cheryl Fry, friends and clients; Fran Judd, quarrier; Judy Juracek, author and photographer of stone surfaces; Dieta Matthiesen, purveyor and installer of fine stone garden ornaments; George and Janet Scurria, clients who became fast friends; Nan Sinton, garden designer and symposia organizer for *Horticulture* magazine; Tim Smith, architect, who has offered me such rewarding work over the years; Dan Snow, friend, and the best dry stone waller I've ever worked with; Mac and Catherine Taylor, friends and the most gracious of hosts in Portland; Nick and Joan Thorndike, past clients and friends; Nancy Waterhouse, assistant; Barry and Elsa Waxman, close friends and clients; Jim Williams and Dennie Freshee, architects and builders

And to the students in the Longwood Gardens Graduate Program who first encouraged me to speak about the uses of stone in the garden at their 1997 symposium "Sticks and Stones," especially to Linda Jones, Julia Lo and Lizzy Butler. Your idea started me on the path to this book. Many thanks. And, finally, and again, thanks to all the photographers who were so very patient and cooperative. Without you, this book would not have been possible.

CONTENTS

INTRODUCTION   9

PART ONE   INSPIRING USES FOR STONE

CHAPTER ONE   Garden Walls – Freestanding and Retaining   14

CHAPTER TWO   Stone Underfoot – Paths and Steps, Terraces and Patios   44

CHAPTER THREE   Boulders and Bedrock   78

CHAPTER FOUR   Water and Stone   90

CHAPTER FIVE   Standing Stones and Benches   116

PART TWO   WORKING WITH STONE IN THE GARDEN

CHAPTER SIX   Dry-Laid Walls   136

CHAPTER SEVEN   Laying Paths and Terraces   152

CHAPTER EIGHT   Boulders and Bedrock   170

CHAPTER NINE   Building Pools and Fountains   180

CHAPTER TEN   Setting Sculptures and Benches   192

CHAPTER ELEVEN The Geography of Stone   200

GLOSSARY   212

APPENDICES
    A. *Sources of Stone Across North America*   214
    B. *Sources of Stone Benches, Sculpture, Garden Ornaments and Details*   216
    C. *Associations*   218
    D. *Types of Stone from Across North America for Walls, Paving and Standing Stones*   219
    E. *Sources for Pool Liners and Stones, Real and Faux*   220

BIBLIOGRAPHY   221

PHOTOGRAPHY CREDITS   221

INDEX   222

INTRODUCTION

T
wenty years ago, when I started designing gardens here in the Northeast, stone supplies were limited to very few choices. At stone supply yards, I would see a few pallets of cut bluestone over in the corner and a pile of costly granite cobble brought up from Boston. Now I visit those same yards, and others across the country, and see rows and rows of cut bluestone, sandstone, and limestone for patios and pathways. Piles of inexpensive granite cobble and lichen-covered boulders on pallets are ready to go, as are rounded river rocks, granite fenceposts to mark garden entrances, cast-stone pavers, stepping-stones, cut-stone benches and garden ornaments, or palletized wall stone from all over the country. Stone yard offices and even garden centers are manned by people conversant with stone being reopened or about new products coming out of old but ever-expanding quarries: round-sawn tabletops; laminated, curved ornamental bridges; 5-foot boulders sliced clean through time and again to create stepping-stones.

Visiting gardens across America, I see all these uses of stone and more: indigenous bedrock in spruce woodland surrounded by planted moss to make the woodland look ancient; great pieces of stone set into the ground to match nearby existing bedrock; boulders standing alone and used for their sculptural effect; granite fenceposts connected by chain swags acting as the spine of a perennial garden; upright stones at the end of long gravel woodland paths to frame a superb view of distant mountains. All this, and stone walls going up everywhere.

I lecture across the country on the uses of stone in the garden. After the lectures, garden owners frequently come up to me to rave about a new sandstone path they've just put down between a pair of mixed borders, or quarry owners tell me about new veins they've just hit that are yielding a lovely beige crushed gravel or pink sandstone. Type "landscaping stone" into your search engine, and the Internet will provide you with many entries that you could visit. Stone is in. And as a result of this increasing interest in stone, the number of highly skilled stonemasons is also growing.

The variety of stone they have to work with is expanding all the time too:

Virtue is like

a rich stone,

best plain set.

Francis Bacon
(1561–1626)

sandstones from the Southwest and mica schists in the Northeast, granite in New Hampshire and marble in Vermont, columnar basalt from Oregon and Lompoc flagging from California, sandstones from Utah and limestones from Indiana. When you really begin to explore stone, you'll come across wonderful names like Rose Granite cobble and Picture Rock pavers, Iron Mountain flagstone and Crab Orchard flagging, Aspen Frost quartzite and Cherokee sandstone, Kootenai Ledge Dry Stack, rusticated granite and random rubble, Sunset Gold and Buckingham Black, Oregon Moss and, in a wonderful flight of fancy, Featherrock.

We in North America are quarrying, shaping, cutting, and gathering rock from all over the country and the world and bringing it into our gardens in both surprising and traditional ways. Combine the booming landscaping industry with the ease of transportation, given today's big rigs and big highways, and you'll find many of these stones are readily available. The problem lies in how to use all of this diversity to proper effect in your garden.

This enthusiasm for stone, combined with our national passion for garden making, inspired me to write this book to help you see how you might include stone in your garden, just as I have done in our 1½-acre garden here in Vermont. When we first moved to our place 18 years ago, we found ourselves in a run-down 200-year-old farmhouse on a neglected acre and a half covered with brambles, saplings, and junk. But as we began to clean up our land during the first year, we discovered remnants of old stone walls, one of which was in a shaded spot under a circle of seven maple trees. We rebuilt the wall to retain soil so that we could create a flat stone-paved outdoor dining area (see figure 7.1) under the shade of those maples, and the 24-inch-high wall acted as both a bench and a sideboard when we were having guests for dinner. No other material could have set that dining area so naturally into the landscape.

Upon discovering the remnants of an abandoned barn foundation, we rebuilt the tumbled walls and found we had an enclosure for a wild garden that had a direct link to the past of our place. To define a slight rise in the land as we were developing a perennial garden, we used big flat stones that we'd found to build steps up and onto a paved sitting area in the garden (see figure 2.17). As we cleared brambles and saplings, we came upon several 100-year-old granite fenceposts lying on their sides. I set a pair at the beginning of a stepping-stone walkway that led into the woodland garden, and all of a sudden the garden had an entrance; we set others along the length of the woodland path to give structure to the otherwise amorphous garden. And so it goes. Stone gives our garden solidity and weight. It helps to frame views and bring out the colors of the foliage in our plantings; and it provides places to rest and foils for lawn. Used in paths, it shapes how we move through space. Stone artifacts lend a feeling of time and history and often determine the mood and tone of an area. My intent in this book, then, is to show you how stone can do the same for your garden, no matter how big or small, no matter where it is.

My goal here is to present you with ideas that are both inspiring and useful. The first five chapters, rich with color photographs of gardens across North America and England, are designed to encourage imaginative thinking about walls and walkways, stone and water, boulders and bedrock. They are written to appeal to your creative urges and to your willingness to work both inside and outside tradition.

The last six chapters, illustrated with line drawings and photographs, are designed to help you put your ideas into practice. I close the book with helpful lists of stone across North America; sources of quarried and shaped stone, garden ornaments, benches, and tables; and associations to which you can turn for further information.

PART ONE

INSPIRING

USES

FOR STONE

GARDEN WALLS

A gardyn walled

al with stoon

So fair a garden I

nowhere noon

From Snowshill Manor,
Gloucestershire, England

STONE WALLS ARE BUILT IN TWO BASIC FORMS: FREESTANDING and retaining. Freestanding walls are self-supporting fences open on both sides and can be built on flat or sloping ground. Retaining walls are open only on the front side; the other side is buried as it holds soil back, creating a raised, level area in otherwise sloping land. Retaining walls are associated with hilly, rolling terrain, where their work is required.

I bring stone walls into my garden designs for practical as well as aesthetic reasons. Freestanding walls provide a classic, durable background for a mixed perennial and shrub border. At the same time they separate (and therefore clearly define the purpose of) areas of different character: the refined garden from the scruffy meadow; the outer edge of the lawn from the street; the cars in a parking area from the more private garden and path leading to the front door. I also use retaining walls, which create terraces so that previously sloping areas become useful places for sitting and outdoor dining or level gardens or lawns at the front of a house. And flat areas combined with walkways and steps enable me to garden a formerly daunting bank at the back or sides of a house.

I also cast stone walls in any number of other roles in gardens: to increase the feeling of privacy; to trap the sun's heat, thereby creating microclimates; to make de facto benches from the tops of walls. Sometimes I make breaks in existing walls for steps or entrances.

In the process of solving practical problems, such as slopes and lack of separation of spaces in a garden, stone walls also help develop permanent garden structure and framework. As Mirabel Osler writes in *The Garden Wall*, "Walls are the sheet anchor of garden design." They hold shapes, forms, lines, and levels firmly in place and, in doing so, relate lines of the house to lines of the garden. Summer and winter, they provide clean forms and a solid framework, and if skillfully built of indigenous stone, they add the same feeling of age and permanence that so many fine old farm walls

■ FIGURE 1.1 Stone walls can act as the spine of the garden. In the McGourty's garden in northwestern Connecticut, a mortared stone wall runs down the center of a garden, acting as background and foreground for perennials.

hold within them. But then, there are fine walls and not-so-fine walls.

Miles and miles of truly bad stone walls have been thrown up across America, walls that display little or no artistry, little or no craft. Often made of concrete glommed onto irreplaceable stones, they are, in fact, little more than long piles of stone. Many neighborhoods contain more examples of how *not* to build stone walls than examples of how to build them. The purpose of this chapter, then, is to teach you to unerringly see the difference between the two.

Good freestanding walls are carefully proportioned – typically 2 feet wide and 3 feet high, or 3 feet wide and 4 feet high – tapering back on both sides 2 inches per foot of height. The best are not necessarily the most tightly fitted and perfectly aligned; a wall built to perfection can be just as wrong as one sloppily built if it flies in the face of older, more relaxed walls already existing on your property. The best walls are built of local stone in a style and color that match older, existing walls following the traditions of an area. Finally, a wall with stones of too many colors can appear busy and incoherent; walls built of stone with roughly the same color and texture look more pleasing. And the very best walls are dry-laid – gravity holds the stones in place, not mortar.

The same is true of retaining walls – the best are also dry-laid. Good retaining walls do not bulge out because of pressure from behind, and they have skillfully laid cap stones so that anyone could walk on top of the wall and the stones would not shift underfoot. The placement of well-made retaining walls reflects a clear understanding of why the soil had to be level just there in the garden. And like good freestanding walls, they don't have big gaps between the stones. From a few feet away, the wall looks as though it had been built by one person – it feels all of a whole and organically in proportion with its surroundings, almost as if it grew in place. The best walls don't call attention to themselves. Finally, a good retaining wall has a batter, a uniform backward lean of perhaps 2 inches per foot of height so that the wall is literally leaning back against the soil it is meant to retain, the same way you lean into the wind.

Stone walls are either dry-laid or wet-laid. In a dry-laid wall, stones are placed on top of others, and the waller fills the gaps between them with stone chinking or crushed stone. The weight of the stones and the skill with which they are laid give the wall its strength. In a wet-laid wall, the gaps between stones are filled with an inflexible binding mortar that provides the wall with some of its strength. The mortared wall is a single unit.

I don't want to be dogmatic, but I would never have a wet-laid wall built in our garden, though I have to admit I have designed plenty of stone walls for clients that were wet-laid. Even if the mortar is set 2 to 3 inches back behind the face of the stones, even if the gaps between individual stones are thin and little mortar shows, even if, in the parlance of the designers today, they are "laid wet to look dry," over time, the concrete invariably cracks and pulls away from stones. The wall displays its own weaknesses. Dry-laid walls can reflect the skill of wall builders; wet-laid walls can hide their lack of skill.

Wet-laying a wall, which requires that the mason cover all but one side of a stone with mortar, is also disrespectful to the stone itself. Once mortar has dried, those stones are not reusable except as rubble in the interior of future walls. Stone in a dry-laid wall can shift with the movement of the earth underneath it, and if a stone or even a whole section tumbles off the wall during this inevitable movement in a 10- or 20-year period, it can be put back up. Of course there is work involved, but what would you rather do: Spend several hours repairing a fine old wall so that when you are finished, it looks just like it always did? Or hammer and chisel to chip the mortar off – banging the stones all up in the process – get out the cement mixer and trowel to reset the stones, and then, in the end, find that the stones and the mismatching concrete make your repair job stand out like the proverbial sore thumb?

People who construct wet-laid walls are called stonemasons; those who build dry-laid walls are known as dry stone wallers. You would think they have a lot in common. Well, they do, certainly, but only insofar as the purists

FIGURE 1.4 (*above*) **Old stone walls can swoop and dive with the flow of the land, unifying the manmade and natural worlds.**

FIGURE 1.5 In this Hayward-designed garden in Vermont, 24-inch-high freestanding walls enclose the entrance courtyard, a fragrance garden near the screened porch, and a shade garden the length of the house. The position of these walls and the proportions of the gardens stem from the lines and proportions of the house.

versus the pragmatists in any field hold skills in common. If you intend to have a stone wall built, you'll have to choose between these two approaches, and in the end, practical considerations often rule the day. It may well be difficult to find a good dry stone waller. They have skills that are in high demand, and there aren't as many of them around as there are stonemasons. Furthermore, a dry stone waller might well be more costly than a stonemason. If you choose to build your own wall, make it dry-laid; concrete will confound you.

One principle holds for both types of walls: they should appear to grow out of the ground, not balance on it. The base of a wall should be set at least 4 to 6 inches below grade so that you can't see the base of any stones. In this way, the wall feels connected to the ground. Furthermore, if you build the wall with local stone, it will visually settle into the larger landscape.

So what do you do if stone walls are not a tradition in your area and yet you want to construct one? Proceed, by all means, but be sensitive to cues provided by the lines and proportions of your house and gardens, to the lay of the land, and to the color and texture of your local soils and, if they exist, bedrock, boulders, and stone. Plenty of stone walls in new American suburban communities, where no walling tradition exists, look absolutely right for the sites.

But even where walls do have a history, they need to be constructed so that they fit within a local tradition and remain in proportion to the house and garden. I saw a particularly ill-proportioned and badly constructed wall recently in New Hampshire. The 2 to 3 inches of mortar laid with a heavy hand between the stones was one problem, but the greater problem was that the 70-foot-long, 5-foot-high wall, with no gateway in it, stood in front of a new one-story house. The wall, even 50 feet from the house, overpowered it. Had the wall been 24 inches high, with a gateway through it welcoming people to the front door and perhaps a lilac hedge behind it to increase privacy, it would have been in scale with the house and felt right.

I also saw a dry-laid stone wall that was a picture of perfection here in Vermont. Every stone in the wall was within a hair's breadth of the next; the top of the wall was utterly level; the face and ends absolutely plumb. But there in the background were old relaxed stone walls that were in direct contrast to Mr. Perfection out front. The two did not get along. When building new walls on properties where old walls exist, build the new to match, or at least be sympathetic to, the old. Then your whole place is tied together by a unified wall style. It's no good building a tour de force wall if it's going to make all your older walls, which have earned their place on your property over the decades, look terrible.

■ FIGURE 1.6 (*above*) The builder has mortared a long narrow planter atop the wall for such drought-tolerant plants as *Cerastium tomentosum*, *Sedum acre* and others.

■ FIGURE 1.7 (*below*) Tops of walls can give rise to wonderful plantings. Here, geraniums, mosses, lichens and flowering drought-tolerant ground covers creep along the top of the wall.

■ Pricing a Wall

Another consideration limits stone wall construction: cost. Most wall builders charge by the face foot – that is, the square footage of exposed wall – and most can produce between 20 and 30 square face feet per day, depending on the stone and whether it's dry- or wet-laid. (Neither the back of a retaining wall nor the top of a freestanding wall are considered part of the total face-foot figure.) If a freestanding wall, for example, is 2 feet high on both sides and 20 feet long, it would have 2 x 20 = 40 feet of facing on each side, or 80 square face feet. Wall builders charge around $20 to $25 per face foot, so such a wall would cost about $1,800.

Here's an example for an actual wall built in a suburb of New York City, a pricey place to build a stone wall. A retaining wall 18 feet long, 18 inches

GARDEN
WALLS

19

high (and 18 inches wide) has 1.5 x 18 = 27 face feet per side, or 54 square feet of face. The homeowner spent $400 a ton to have 2 tons of stone delivered; the mason who built the wet-laid wall with that stone charged $700 for his labor, with a total cost of $1,500 for 54 face feet, or about $28 per face foot. Given all the variables of type of stone, the region of the country, mason's hourly wages, it would be safe to say that a stone wall could cost anywhere between $20 and $30 per face foot.

There are certainly less costly alternative ways of creating structure, enclosure, and background in the garden: evergreen or deciduous hedges or wooden fencing can replace freestanding walls; concrete or pressure-treated lumber can replace retaining walls. These are less expensive, but what they don't have is the panache, the solidity, or the permanence of stone walls.

On a purely economic level, there is another way to look at this issue of cost, particularly in light of our transient population. Realtors and house appraisers tell me that if you invest in stone walls that border properties or are an integral part of the architecture – walls that retain the back terrace or that enclose an entrance garden – you will likely recoup most of your money under the "amenities" category when you sell your home. Build a little wall out by the vegetable garden, and you probably won't recoup that cost.

But then, if you are going to build the stone walls yourself, and Chapter 6 gives you all the information you'll need, keep one inestimable element in mind: stress reduction. Taking your own sweet time to build your own wall will give you a great deal of absorbing pleasure. (Read John Jerome's *Stone Work: Reflections on Serious Play and Other Aspects of Country Life* for a philosophical and humorous account of his novice wall-building experiences.) Now that we have money out of the way, let's look at what walls can do in your landscape.

FREESTANDING WALLS

FREESTANDING WALLS SOLVE MANY PROBLEMS. IF YOUR HOME IS too exposed to the road or street, a stone wall can form a separation between the two. To increase privacy further, plant shrubs and perennials along the inside of the wall. If that idea involves too much maintenance, consider building a 4-foot-high wooden fence atop a 2-foot-high freestanding wall, as is often done in New England suburbs, so that you completely screen the view of traffic from house and garden and reduce noise. Then you can plant low-maintenance trees or shrubs between your home and the wooden

■ FIGURE 1.9 Plant low perennials in front of a wall, and tall ones behind it
as the McGourtys did in their Connecticut garden, and the wall becomes
a strong structural element running down the center of the garden.

▓ **FIGURE 1.10** (*above, left*) This corner of a finely crafted wall in the Cotswolds provides a place for the fragrant mock orange as well as for *Campanula portenschlagiana*.

▓ **FIGURE 1.11** (*above, right*) At Bourton House Gardens in the North Cotswolds, these perfectly mortared walls come to elegant ends, calling for elegant plantings: topiary boxwood in dark green planters.

fence to settle it into the background. Stone walls can also permanently mark the two side and back boundary lines, thereby establishing a clear line of demarcation between your land and that of your neighbor.

Freestanding walls also divide areas within your property to create outdoor living spaces. It is in such intimate places – the herb garden, the walled perennial garden, the secret garden – that you can truly appreciate the craftsmanship and beauty of walls that enclose space in a warm and lasting way. Stone walls could enclose an entrance garden near the front door or surround a small sitting area off the back of the house. Gaps in freestanding walls create inviting entrances onto walkways into the woods; or to mown lawn paths down through a meadow to the pond; or, formally or informally, into an outdoor dining area. Openings in walls draw people's attention, thereby enabling you to show off a wonderful view from that specific spot; they are also important transition points between one part of the garden and the next.

Several years ago I made a gap in an existing stone wall so that guests can now walk on stepping-stones through the upper end of a perennial garden, through the opening in the wall, and onto a mown path that leads out to a bench under three pin oaks in the meadow. Without that gap and the path, the meadow would have remained virtually inaccessible.

Deciding just where the edges of these many types of freestanding walls will go, as well as the shapes and proportions of the garden space within them, is an important first step in designing walls for enclosure, especially those near a home or outbuilding.

■ Designing Freestanding Walls

Stone walls near buildings need to be built with the proportions, dimensions, and angles of nearby buildings in mind; in that way, building and wall relate to one another. In fact, stone walls are marvelous for linking the garden to the house, as the lines of walls can often be laid out as extensions of the architecture. This close relationship between house and garden, after all, is one of the central principles of good garden design. As one Alfred Austin (1835–1913), an English garden writer put it: "I am quite of the opinion that a garden should look as though it belonged to the house, and the house as though it were conscious of and approved the garden. In passing from one to the other, one should experience no sense of discord, but the sensations produced by the one should be continued, with a delicate difference, by the other."

In the design of one sitting area off the west-facing 24-foot-wide gable end of a brick house, I began with two freestanding walls (see figure 7.2). They would start off at either corner of the brick building and run west, thereby acting essentially as extensions of the two walls of the house. To determine how long they should be to stay in proportion with the end of the house, I measured from the foundation to the peak of the roof on the gable end, and that 22-foot measurement gave me the length of the two walls.

■ FIGURE 1.12 The stile is a way to go up, over and down the other side of a stone wall rather than through a gap in it. Dry stone waller Dan Snow dismantled a bit of an old wall and then set within it a stile of four long stones that jut out of both sides of the wall.

■ FIGURE 1.13 Stone solves many problems in this Hayward-designed entrance garden in rural New York State. A retaining wall separates the driveway from the house and creates a level entrance garden of birches underplanted with holly, myrtle and ferns. The primary stepping-stone path directs guests up broad stone steps to the front door while a narrower path provides sound footing between garage and mudroom. Lichen-covered boulders are set within the curves of a smaller stepping-stone path that invites people into the garden.

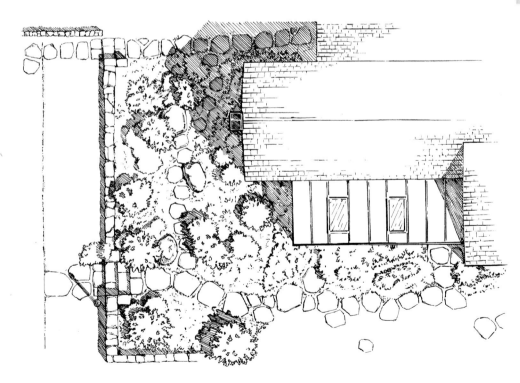

PLANTING IN THE FACES OF RETAINING WALLS

As you can see from these four images, retaining walls can give rise to a variety of flowering perennials that reduce the stony appearance of the wall and settle it into the garden.

Campanula formanekiana

Saxifraga fortunei 'Rubrifolia'

Phlox subulata in variety, *arabis* and *Cerastium tomentosum* among others

Roses along with lady's pin cushion

FIGURE 1.15 The garden designers at Shosein-in in Kyoto left the face of this ancient wall to stand alone as a testament to the artistry of its builders. We also need to know when not to plant in front of a wall.

Openings halfway along each wall provided access. A third wall, parallel with the gable end and 22 feet out from each corner of the wing, enabled me to connect the ends of the two walls to complete the 22-foot-long, 24-foot-wide stone wall enclosure. By determining the position and lengths of the walls in light of the adjacent building and its dimensions, I was certain that the stone walls and the space they enclosed were in proportion with the building. Having gathered flat fieldstone from the property, we paved the area within this enclosure to create an outdoor sitting area.

I then looked at the two east-west walls as backgrounds for a rich variety of perennials and annuals to provide color and fragrance for my clients as they sat in the stone-paved area. Finally I planted several terra-cotta pots with tender annuals and set them on either side of the entrances to the central sitting area to soften its otherwise stony appearance.

For walls at a distance from your house, you might still want to pay attention to the architectural lines of your home. If you want to build a stone wall out near the street or road, and your house is 50 to 75 feet away from the road, build the wall so that it is parallel with the front wall of the house, which may or may not be parallel with the street. In this way, the space between the wall

GARDEN
WALLS

and the house is geometric; gardens can then be designed along both the wall
and the house, and they will relate, contributing to a coherent garden.
In between the two will be a strong geometric panel of lawn to act as the
interloper between the garden along the house and the garden along the wall.

If you decide to build a freestanding wall 100 feet or more from the house,
or if the house isn't even visible from the wall, then architecture need no
longer play such an important role in the wall's design and siting. The lines
of these walls should derive from some other feature – the roll or sweep of the
land, boundary lines, the edges of existing or planned gardens, or even existing stone walls.

RETAINING WALLS

IF YOU LIVE IN A HILLY AREA, IT'S LIKELY THAT YOU HAVE SEEN examples of the many problems that retaining walls solve, in part because hilly ground and abundant stones generally go together geographically and geologically. Very often, land slopes because bedrock is underneath it. Consequently, the tradition runs deep for building stone retaining walls to create level spaces for roads, driveways, terraced gardens, outdoor sitting areas, or lookouts in hilly or mountainous areas of North America. The fundamental truth driving the construction of retaining walls is that people will readily walk or gather on level ground and, if possible, will avoid sloping ground. If the lawn and gardens around your home slope, no matter how steeply, toward or away from your home, then retaining walls may be just the thing you need to make your garden inviting and approachable.

FIGURE 1.17 If you are building a wall and you find you don't have the stone necessary to create steps that are knit into the two ends of the adjacent walls, change your style, as Dan Snow did in a garden in Vermont. He allowed the ends of the walls to dive down toward the ground to provide access through this retaining wall.

■ FIGURE 1.18 (*above, left*) **This wall curves gracefully around a simple stone seat. Ferns grow up while *Juniperus horizontalis* grows down to link wall to garden.**

■ FIGURE 1.19 (*above, right*) **Retaining walls can also run in straight lines as this one does through a linear vegetable garden.**

■ FIGURE 1.20 (*opposite*) **Tasha Tudor has used a 4-foot-high retaining wall to create a terrace above and a backdrop for a perennial border below.**

STONE

IN THE

GARDEN

If the land slopes away from one or several sides of your home, you have probably found it difficult to garden or even walk comfortably in those areas. By building a retaining wall anywhere from a few inches to 3 or 4 feet high, depending on the slope, you can create level terraced areas. In doing so, you will not only tie the house visually to the landscape by extending the floor plane of the house into outdoor spaces but also create more inviting spaces for you and your family to walk, gather, or garden. A retaining wall remains cooler than a freestanding one because its back side is set into the earth, so the exposed face of the wall can also become a place for vertical plantings. (You will find more information on this in Chapter 6.)

In many suburban communities, the area between the sidewalk and the front of the house slopes gently down to street level. Often there is little or no privacy and no chance for gardening at the front, and so you garden only in the backyard. This doesn't have to be the case. Building a retaining wall to create a level plane in the front can be the first step in making a place for a semiprivate or even totally private entrance garden (see figure 1.28).

■ FIGURE 1.21 Combining large stones with small ones adds a pleasing contrast within a wall. Here the base wall is the tallest and stoutest; as the builder ascended the slope, the walls became lower and lower, less and less linear, thereby fusing into the hillside more and more as they scale the slope.

Measure the height of the front wall of your house, and then build a retaining wall that same distance out from the foundation. This creates a level area, the dimensions of which are in direct proportion to the dimensions of your home. Plant low- to medium-size shrubs in the soil behind the top of the wall to partially or fully screen the resulting level area from traffic, thereby capturing a front garden space. Build a stone walkway with steps from the sidewalk up to and through the stone retaining wall and on to your front door, and you have created a welcoming entrance garden.

■ FIGURE 1.22 (*above*) **Knitting wall and step stones together is made especially clear in a retaining wall that Dan Snow built in southern Vermont. This set of steps runs alongside a retaining wall, so as he built the wall, he knitted the steps into it.**

■ FIGURE 1.23 (*left*) **Here a gray stone wall with gray mortar set well back into the shadow of each stone's overhang has a rugged, almost jagged appearance that lies in deep and pleasing contrast to the delicate pink camellia.**

GARDEN

WALLS

FIGURE 1.24 To tame a 6-foot slope in the land, Dan Snow created a series of low retaining walls up the slope rather than one tall monolithic wall at the base of the slope. Curving rather than straight steps invite visitors to explore the series of terraced gardens. (See figure 2.18 for a view of the topmost garden.)

Designing Retaining Walls

To help you see how to think about retaining walls near the house, here's an example of a design I developed for clients in New York State. Standing with them in the parking area, I saw nothing but lawn sloping up to the front door, not even a path from where I parked my car to lead my eye to the front door. There was certainly no feeling of arrival, and no separation between the kitchen windows and cars with their headlights coming down the driveway in the evening. A retaining wall helped us solve all of those problems.

First, I measured the height of the stone chimney on the west wall at the end of the house that faced the parking area and found it was 32 feet high (see figure 2.5). That gave me the distance the stone wall should be from the house. That same house wall also gave me the direction the retaining wall should run – parallel with it. How high should the wall be? High enough

FIGURE 1.25 Here a retaining wall levels the grade to create an entrance garden. The low stone wall is out from the house about as far as the wall of the house is high. Boulders mark entrances and create places for alpines. Finely crushed stone grouting knits everything together visually.

FIGURE 1.26 (*above, left*) Retaining walls can double as steps. This walkway/wall in a garden in South Africa has wooden ties as the risers while the backfill for the wall forms the step treads. This gravelly backfill supports many alpines that require scree or, at the very least, quickly draining gravelly soil.

FIGURE 1.27 (*above, right*) This set of steps fuses beautifully with a retaining wall. A cut stone path at the base of the wall draws people toward the steps.

STONE

IN THE

GARDEN

to create an apparently level 32-foot-wide garden that would still drain rainwater away from the house. The wall turned out to be 28 inches high. Now the question was, How long should the retaining wall be? I looked to the house for the answer. One end of the wall would enable me to build 3-foot-wide stone steps – the secondary entrance – that would lead family members from the garage door onto a stone walkway straight along the back wall of the house to the back kitchen door. The primary set of steps, 6 feet wide, would invite guests as well as family members to go up the steps and along the front of the house directly to the front door on 4-to-5-foot-wide stepping-stones.

The two stone paths would in turn provide the edges for an entrance garden between the retaining wall and the west wall of the house. A stepping-stone path through that garden would link the primary and secondary paths and invite people to walk through a level entrance garden of Heritage River birches, hollies, *Vinca minor* 'Bowles' and *Epimedium sulphureum*, punctuated by sitting boulders at three points along the path through the garden. I then had to decide which stone to use for the walls and had to look no farther than the chimney on the west end of the house to see that the wall material should echo that of the chimney. In the end, everything fit together – house, garden, chimney, wall, steps, and boulders (see illustration, page 23).

Florence Everts did much the same thing in her garden in the suburbs of Washington, D.C. By looking closely at figure 1.28, you can see that a roughly 2-foot-high stone retaining wall creates a small lawn and garden between the retaining wall and the front of her home. She is able to garden near the house, have some lawn, and then garden on the remaining sloping area between the base of the wall and the sidewalk. Take a close look at the left-hand side of the image, and you will also see a few stepping-stones leading through the garden along the side of the path to the front door. Those stepping-stones lead onto level lawn, which in turn leads to a pathway down a side garden to the back garden. But the key to this entire design is the retaining wall. Without it, people would not feel comfortable walking across an unenclosed garden on sloping lawn to a garden along the side of the house.

Many retaining walls close to the house, then, tie the building to the land; the space that assures that relationship is the level garden through which you walk. Foundation planting simply cannot form this link because it is too narrow, and the bed in which foundation plantings exist is utterly out of proportion with the height of the house. All you can do is walk past foundation planting; there is no participation between you and those plants.

FIGURE 1.28 In this image of a garden designed by Florence Everts near Washington, D.C., you can see that a 2-foot-high retaining wall enabled her to create a level lawn and garden area between the wall and the front of her home.

FIGURE 1.29 (*right*) Dan Snow built 5-to-6-foot-long stones into the heart of this retaining wall to create a stile. Half the length of each stone is within the wall.

FIGURE 1.30 (*below*) River rocks with a slightly reddish hue combine harmoniously with a sedum. Pay attention to colors shared between plants and rocks.

The gentle transition between the house and the rest of your garden is assured with the garden out front and a stone wall that establishes its outer edge; foundation planting essentially prevents that relationship between the house and the rest of your garden.

Most retaining walls 4 feet or higher lose human scale. Not only do people feel dwarfed when standing next to them, but they also don't feel safe walking on level ground near the top of such a high wall. When faced with the need to retain 4 feet or more of soil, design two walls, each 2 feet high, one set back from the other, to create two shallower terraces rather than one tall one.

Retaining walls, especially south-facing ones, gather heat during the day and release it at night. Use such walls to create wind-sheltering microclimates where you can grow plants not normally hardy in your area. Several years ago I transplanted clumps of snowdrops *(Galanthus nivalis)* along the base of our south-facing stone wall and then transplanted other clumps down in the woodland garden. The snowdrops along the base of the heat-collecting wall bloom as much as two weeks ahead of those planted in woodland.

GOOD WALLS VS. BAD: HOW TO TELL THE DIFFERENCE

When looking for a stonemason for a project, ask to see at least a few examples of his work. The following list will help you recognize the difference between good and bad walls.

Good walls have:

- stones that are laid one on two, two on one; all stones appear to be supported by others
- no running joints; that is, stones should be bonded as with brick-work, with a stone across each joint in the course below
- the largest stones at the bottom
- stones that all touch neighboring ones so that there is no room for movement
- a face that, when looked at from the end, is straight and true along its length, without waviness, bulges or overhangs
- an overall unified look in terms of color as well as structure
- an appropriate batter – the face leans back a bit from bottom to top for stability – and that batter remains uniform down the full length of the wall
- sound, well-drained foundations sunk into the ground
- a natural look that feels right for that region of the country and in harmony with old local stone walls
- been built of stone indigenous to the region
- cap stones that are level across the full width of the wall and touch the tops of the stones in faces of both sides
- a top that is uniform and level, and the stones don't move
- recessed mortar that is barely visible, hidden by the stones' shadow
- heavy, bulky stones at the corners for stability
- a height and width that is appropriate for their role in the garden
- steps that are integrated with the adjoining wall
- a distinctive pattern or quality that amounts to a mason's signature

Bad walls have:

- seams running top to bottom so that the stones are not knitted together
- a variety of stone types, lacking uniformity and cohesiveness
- bulges in their faces or sunken areas and protrusions along the top
- hearting stones or fill that is leaking out of the interior
- stones on the top or the face to which you can apply pressure with your fingers and they will move
- small stones at the corners, or stones that were simply stacked, not knitted together
- no batter, or even lean forward a bit and appear about to topple
- steps that are not knitted into the adjoining wall
- heavy-handed mortaring that is thick and obvious
- cracks running down the height of a mortared wall due to uneven settling
- little or no foundation; the wall appears to be sitting atop the ground
- a thrown-together, haphazard look, with no overarching idea informing construction
- gaps between stones that are 2 inches or greater
- a height that is inappropriate for its surroundings or role, or perhaps calls undue attention to itself

▓ FIGURE 1.31 In this informal garden in Vancouver, British Columbia, the designers used a relaxed style of wall making to bring many elements together.

WHEN TO USE WOOD, CONCRETE, HEDGING, OR STONE WALLS

Use pressure-treated wooden retaining walls, wooden trellising, or fencing if:

- you want to fence off or screen an area between 3½ and 8 feet high
- you want to retain soil inexpensively with pressure-treated landscape ties
- refined wooden fencing can be added atop a stone wall to extend the privacy screening upward in a less costly and lighter, more aesthetic fashion
- a precedent already exists in your garden for wooden fencing, trelliswork, or other aesthetic uses for the material
- landscape ties would fit in when retaining soil near wooden decking
- the lightness of picket fencing outside a cottagey home is called for, rather than the heavier, perhaps more formal

feeling of a stone wall
- you need to enclose the boundaries of a small urban garden
- budget precludes the use of stone

Use concrete retaining walls if:

- the aesthetic of the wall doesn't matter
- a wall is purely utilitarian and out of sight of all garden areas
- you have a concrete-stuccoed building
- you want to retain soil inexpensively and permanently
- you can cover this anonymous material with vines

Use plants and hedging if:

- you want a living hedge that will give you a deciduous or evergreen background
- the more translucent look of a deciduous hedge in the winter won't matter
- you are prepared to maintain the hedge annually

- the visual weight of a stone wall is not what you want
- you feel you have enough freestanding stone walls
- you want to create a pleasing contrast between existing stone walls and living hedges
- you want immediate and not inexpensive separation of space
- you know that deer or other wild animals will not decimate your hedge

Use stone walls if:

- you need to retain soil in a dignified, refined garden
- you want to enclose a garden in a formal manner
- you have other stone walls in the adjacent gardens that preclude turning to other materials
- you feel stone will tie your home to the existing landscape
- you are gardening around a historic home and the precedent is there for such walls
- permanence and a link with past traditions is important
- you can afford them

FIGURE 1.32 Small fieldstones set along the edge of a gravel path create a casual retaining wall that keeps the topsoil of the garden separate from the walkway.

HOW TO SOFTEN STONE WALLS

■ Place a 1-to-2-foot wide planting bed along the base of a wall so that plants can grow up along part of the face (or faces) of the wall.

■ In the case of a retaining wall, plant trailing plants that grow over the top of the wall and fall down over its face.

■ Use the wall as a backdrop for planted pots.

■ If you need to retain soil, do so with two or three lower walls set back one from the next, rather than build one high wall.

■ Break up the wall with a niche for a sculpture, or set a sculpture into the face of the wall as it is being built.

■ If you are building a mortared wall in a small garden, be certain to set hooks or nails for wires so that you can later train vines up the walls.

STONE

IN THE

GARDEN

█ FIGURE 1.33 (*left*) In this garden in
the American Southwest, the
designer uses river rock to create
a mulch that acts much like a wall.
The mulch retains soil and provides
pockets for native plants.

IN SUMMARY

ONE THING TO KEEP IN MIND IS THAT THERE ARE MANY LEVELS
of commitment regarding stone walls. You don't necessarily have
to sign up for a huge, expensive project. You could hire an expert
to build a retaining wall to create a terrace behind your home using stone
that you haul in from abandoned walls in the woods out back. You could
even construct your own 18-to-24-inch-high wall, whether freestanding or
retaining, and learn a great deal in the process.

But whether you build your own or hire an expert, a stone wall will link
you to an American tradition, one with remarkable depth and breadth.
According to an 1871 Department of Agriculture report, there were, in that
year, 20,505 miles of stone walls in Connecticut, 14,030 miles of walls in
Rhode Island, 32,960 miles in Massachusetts, and 95,364 miles in New York.
While many of those miles of wall have since been plundered for new walls
or bulldozed under to make way for highways or new construction, many are
still out there – along country roads, running through woodland that was
meadow 100 years ago, or perhaps even in your backyard.

█ FIGURE 1.34 (*above*) Dan Snow built
this stone artifact in a garden in
New Hampshire. By setting granite
cobble to outline the arrow slit of
a castle wall, he brought a feeling
of age to a modern structure. The
rectangular wall behind the turret
is meant to be the foundation of
an abandoned 200-year-old brewery;
antique vats and an old copper still
set nearby add verisimilitude.

GARDEN

WALLS

THE FACE OF A RETAINING WALL

IN HIS BOOK *Stonework,* John Jerome notes that every wall reflects the "personal signature" of the wall builder. These three images show how different walls can look, not only because of the builder, but also because of the stone and the demands it makes on the builder. But in all three cases, the waller's dictum "two stones on one; one stone on two" holds true.

■ FIGURE 1.35 At Dumbarton Oaks, in Washington, D.C., the late designer Beatrix Farrand used this mortared wall as a dramatic end to the planting of figs.

GARDEN
WALLS

43

CHAPTER TWO

STONE UNDERFOOT

F ANY SIGN SHOWS THAT GARDENING HAS TRULY GOTTEN UNDER your skin, it's when you put down your first stone path. Lay a 4-foot-wide walkway from the parking area to the front door, a stepping-stone path through a bit of woodland, or even a stone patio, and you are making a long-term commitment to your home and its garden. I can't tell you how satisfying it is to get to that point in gardening, for it undercuts all that restlessness, all that "But what if we move and…?" When it comes to laying stone underfoot, it's important to do it right so that re-laying all that stone doesn't become necessary. This chapter is about designing it right; Chapter 7 is about doing it right.

When first starting to plan a stone pathway, landing or terrace, think big, even if you intend to put only one path in at the time. By "thinking big," I mean two things. First, make roomy surfaces: a 5-foot-wide walkway to the front door, not a niggly 2-to-3-foot-wide path; an 18-by-24-foot stone patio out back, rather than a little stone surface for two chairs and a table. Second, see the first stone paving project in light of future stone paving projects throughout the whole garden, even if it's the 20-year plan. In that way, all the parts will relate to an eventual whole.

When you start thinking about how to design and where to install stone paved patios and paths, begin by assessing the style, materials, dimensions, and proportions of your home. Measure the width of your doors and trim, or measure the width of the portico by the front door, for those measurements will provide clues as to the width of paths leading from them. Measure the height of the back wall of the house, and that will suggest how far from the foundation the back patio should go. And look carefully at your house for clues as to the style of paved areas. A refined formal home in the suburbs calls for a fine, tightly fitting cut-stone patio; a simple rural home calls for a loosely fitted fieldstone patio with thyme in the gaps between the stones.

Pay attention to your own style as well. If you like everything in its place, then a tightly fitting patio or walkway will feel right for you, no matter what

Stones are the

bones of heaven

and earth.

– Chinese philosopher

■ FIGURE 2.1 Here 2-by-2-foot pieces of bluestone form a broad welcoming landing to the front door of a gracious home in Connecticut. The formality of geometric bluestone is softened by the brick surrounds, which also visually tie the landing to the house.

FIGURE 2.2 (*right*) Irregular blue-stone creates an informal feeling in this New England garden. The designer used larger pieces of bluestone, surrounded by ground-hugging perennials, as stepping stones through the entrance garden. Purple lobelia and roses create a welcoming, relaxed feeling.

FIGURE 2.3 (*below*) At Shokokuji in Kyoto, Japan, the strong geometric use of stone in its various forms contrasts with the free-form shapes of boulders, shrubs, and moss.

style your home is, but if you're more casual, your stonework should be casual.

The path from the driveway to the front door is a good place to start laying a stone path. This is also one of the few areas where there might already be paving, so it's a sensible place to begin assessing, or reassessing, your first project. Is the existing path wide enough? Is there a generous landing by the front door? Could you add stone paving along the sides of the existing path, no matter what its material, to make it wider? And keep in mind as you develop the design that the paving for this path should be made of stone laid to create a reliable, easily maintained, uniform surface. After all, this is a path to get people simply and safely from point A to point B.

A broad stone landing by the front door is also important for it can be a hub for paths going right and left along the front of the house, leading to similarly paved paths (and gardens) along the sides of the house. When those paths get to the back, they link up with a stone paved patio or terrace to form a unified garden plan that surrounds your home. Stepping-stone paths can in turn lead through a small woodland garden, through an herb garden or from the garage to the kitchen door.

And why stone? Because once it is set firmly and correctly in place, stone stays. As attractive as gravel paths are, gravel tends to migrate into adjacent gardens, and grit tracks into the house on the soles of your shoes; lawn paths get soggy and squelchy and need a weekly mowing and monthly edging; over time, even pressure-treated lumber rots. But properly laid stone paths are low

■ FIGURE 2.4 The curve in this
sandstone path is made logical
by the placement of a strikingly
simple black stone sculpture. This
sleek work of art creates a pleasing contrast to the relaxed garden
of evergreens and cut-leaf maples,
of which the sculpture forms the
center. Notice that the designer
has paved a sitting area and
edged the adjacent beds across
the crushed gravel walkway with
the same sandstone to ensure
unity.

FIGURE 2.5 (*below, left*) I used a retaining wall to bring a formerly sloping lawn up into a flat plane on which the house sits more comfortably. The choice of stone for the wall was determined by the color and scale of the stones used for the existing chimney. Mica schist steps and stepping-stones lead from the parking area, through the entrance garden to the front door.

FIGURE 2.6 (*below, right*) In the Hall garden on the coast of Maine, rectangular cut-granite stepping-stones match the material of the large broad steps and lead people up to the gardens along one end of the house. Stepping-stones are set in a field of contrasting colored crushed gravel and on line with the trunk of a tree espaliered against the house.

maintenance and stay right where you put them. Stone controls erosion, holds down dust and provides a durable surface on which to walk. Lawn paths wear with use and thin out as trees overhead spread their limbs, shedding more and more shade. Stone stays. Moles heave up soil across a lawn path time and again; stone repels them. Place furniture or garden ornaments and planted pots on grass, and they need to be shifted around every week to make room for the lawn mower; place them on stone panels, and you'll rarely have to move them. Put planted pots on wood, and circular stains form; place them on stone, and no problems arise. But set any of these objects on stone, and they can stay right where they are. And no matter how much rain falls, if you laid the stone with just the slightest slope away from the house to assure good drainage, you can walk virtually dryshod over any stone, anytime.

The first step in knowing how to use stone underfoot properly is to understand that all the various stones useful for terraces or paths fit within a hierarchy from formal to informal. By acknowledging this when deciding what stone to lay, and where and how to lay it, you avoid some of the pitfalls of using stone in inappropriate ways: choosing bits or red and gray slate to form a muddle; laying too narrow a path to a very important door; choosing too many different stones with too many different textures and colors to create an incoherent, busy look. I have found that this hierarchy is especially useful when it comes to choosing appropriate materials and styles for paths: the closer to the house, the more formal; the farther away, the less formal.

◼ Paving Stones – Formal to Informal

Bluestone, sandstone, limestone, granite, and marble that have been shaped into rectangles or squares are the most formal. Use this geometric form of tightly fitted cut stone in straight-edged, formal areas of your landscape – the straight path from the parking area to the front door, the broad, geometric landing by the front door, or a rectangular paved terrace off the back of the house. In Japanese design parlance, this path is *shin,* the most formal of all types of paths.

Some people are interested in creating a curving path with geometric cut stones. Rather than cut each stone to form that curve, the best way to do this is to offset each straight-edged stone in a series by leaving a thin, elongated triangle of lawn between each pair to allow for the curve. In that way you'll be able to create a long, broad curve that will also respect the geometry of the individual stones.

◼ FIGURE 2.7 Stepping-stones can help you create an informal entrance to your home. In this New Mexico garden, the designer has chosen large indigenous Arizona flagstone. When designing curves in paths, be sure there is a reason for the curve, as with the small tree in this garden.

STONE
UNDERFOOT

FIGURE 2.8 (*above*) **Cut York stone in a garden in Warwickshire, England, forms the surround for square gardened areas and a pool.**

FIGURE 2.9 (*opposite*) **In this entrance garden in Tangiers, the same fieldstone is used in a stone carpet through an informal entrance garden, a set of mortared steps and a mortared wall.**

STONE

IN THE

GARDEN

Irregular pieces of limestone, bluestone, sandstone, or quartzite are next on the hierarchy. Like cut stone, they are generally 1 to 2 inches thick but are irregularly shaped in that they have come directly from the quarry without having been cut into geometric shapes. Use this type of stone for less formal straight or curved paths, such as between two perennial beds, for terraces, or for paths that lead to the front door of an informal rural home. The informality comes from the irregular shapes and the gaps between the individual stones when laid in the pathway or terrace. Because these gaps need to be filled with some type of grouting, you can further manipulate the look of the paved surface: wide gaps backfilled with sandy loam in which you can plant ground-hugging perennials will be the most informal; concrete grouting in very narrow gaps between the stones will be more formal.

Even less formal are fieldstones – whether quartzite, mica schist, unpolished granite, or any number of other stones – which are collected from fields and abandoned stone walls or blasted from a quarry. They generally

50

■ FIGURE 2.10 At Rodmarton House in Gloucestershire, England, a straight-edged Cotswold stone carpet of randomly shaped fieldstones lines up with the door to the stone summerhouse, linking architecture and garden. The lawn edging, yew hedge and stone wall in the background all support the strong linearity of this design.

have a rougher surface than the bluestone, sandstone, or limestone and are available in random shapes, sizes, and thicknesses. Use fieldstones to create less formal stone terraces, patios, or walkways in which you fit together all the separate stones into a jigsaw kind of surface. The more tightly you fit the individual stones, and the straighter the outer edge, the more formal the surface appears. The more the path curves in and out of adjacent beds, and the larger the gaps between the individual stones, the more informal the surface becomes. The most informal use of fieldstones is to set them separately as stepping-stones down the length of a path, whether through perennial gardens, shrub plantings, or woodland. In Japan, these stepping-stone paths are known as *tobi-ishi,* the most ancient form of stone path anywhere.

At the bottom of the hierarchy are rounded river rocks 2 to 6 inches in diameter embedded in crushed gravel or concrete. Use embedded stones to form irregular or patterned walkways and large freeform paved surfaces; they could even have a playful look about them, especially if you also set terra-cotta tiles or other materials within them.

While this sequence of paving materials, from most to least formal, is certainly helpful, breaking out of these rules can add interest. By mixing materials, you create all kinds of appealing new stone features underfoot. Surround each large cut stone in a path with embedded river rocks. Place fieldstone panels within a cut-stone path to produce a contrast of shape and texture, or use cut-granite cobbles or brick to surround each large piece of cut bluestone in a front-door landing. Scribe a fine cut-stone terrace up to the base of a boulder in a fieldstone retaining wall to create an attractive meeting of contrasting materials. Just be careful not to mix too many colors and textures together, or you'll end up with a mishmash.

▪ Prioritizing Paths

To determine how wide paths should be, and whether straight or curved, it's useful to see paths in terms of priority, from the most to the least important: primary, secondary, tertiary. View the path from the driveway to the front door, or from the back terraces out into the gardens, for example, as straight, primary paths that are 4 to 6 feet wide and are made of tightly fitting cut stones. Secondary paths, which might be 3 to 4 feet wide, lead from the primary paths, that is, from the landing by the main door and across the front of the house to paths leading down either or both sides of the house. Still narrower and less formal tertiary paths of 18-inch-wide stepping-stones could meander from secondary paths out into woodland, to the compost area, or to other practical working areas of the garden (see figure 1.5). Once you

▪ FIGURE 2.11 Perhaps the least formal use for stone edging is to set small rounded stones along the edges of perennial beds. But beware. Small stones will not keep the lawn out of the bed. Take up the lawn and topsoil between the beds, replace the organic matter you removed with finely crushed gravel, set the small stones along the edge and then top-dress the gravel path with an inch of 3/8-inch peastone.

STONE

UNDERFOOT

■ FIGURE 2.12 (*above, left*) Large river rocks are set here and there in this gray, white, pink and blue garden. White and sand-colored river rocks contrast with the flat pink stepping-stones.

■ FIGURE 2.13 (*above, right*) In her garden designer Florence Everts laid a straight yet informal carpet of small fieldstones surrounded by river stones. The plantings of tulips, grape hyacinths, pansies and dicentras add up to a garden that has a definite though unselfconscious structure provided by the path.

combine your understanding of the hierarchy of materials with your knowledge of path priority, you then have a good sense of how to design the dimensions and direction of the path, as well as what paving materials to use.

■ Planting Paths

Having chosen the material as well as the design for your path, you can begin to consider what to plant along it; and what's really interesting is that plants fall into all the same categories as stones and paths. Boxwood is formal; daphne is less formal. A tree is a primary plant, a shrub is a secondary plant, and perennials are tertiary plants. So what good are these hierarchies? Well, I believe they're very useful indeed.

Stone paths provide structure and establish mood; plants adjacent to paths need to support that mood. For example, a broad, straight cut-stone path to the front door establishes a formal tone. Support that formality with an elegant boxwood or peony hedge along one or both sides of the path, and plant a pair of stately trees to frame the entrance to it. Underpin the familiar, sunny mood of an informal fieldstone path to the front door with a cottage garden of daylilies, fragrant dianthus, peonies, poppies, hardy geraniums,

■ FIGURE 2.14 The path through this perennial garden in California is made of cut stones. Perennials are allowed to flop down onto the tightly laid pinkish sandstone, providing a perfect visual foil.

STONE
UNDERFOOT

55

FIGURE 2.15 The structure of this English garden is generated by a combination of flat cut-stone paths and hedges that follow the edges of the paths. The broad central area of tightly fitting York stone, marked by a terracotta urn, gives rise to subordinate paths that lead out from the center. The formality of the layout is underpinned by a restrained planting pallette.

catmint, columbine, and a profusion of roses. Let a simple stepping-stone path through a bit of woodland suggest its own plantings: moss between the stones, boulders with ferns planted near them at curves in the path, may-apple and periwinkle, bloodroot and woodland phlox.

Choose plants not only in light of the mood but also the color of the stone paving. Cherry petals falling onto a bluestone path look gorgeous (see frontispiece), as do the gray-green leaves and lavender flowers of catmint, the chartreuse flowers of lady's-mantle, or the burgundy-red leaves of the new heucheras flooding into garden centers at the moment. Plant scarlet red peonies and hardy blue-flowering geraniums along a white marble path for stunning contrast. Or take a cue from such a grand garden as that of Prince Charles: set gray fieldstones 3 to 4 inches apart in a broad 6-foot-wide path straight out from the back stone patio, and plant a collection of many types of thymes between the stones to create what he calls his thyme walk.

PAVED PATHS AND LANDINGS

■ The Primary Path

The entrance garden is often the most crucial part of a garden design because it is the first thing guests see when they arrive and it leads to the most important door of your home. It should therefore welcome people by inviting them from the semiprivate driveway and on through gardens to the privacy of the front door.

For example, several years ago, clients asked me to redesign the entrance to their home. They (as well as the UPS deliveryman) were able to pull their vehicles to within 10 feet of the front door; but there was no feeling of arrival, no sensation of entering a private home.

To create an inviting entrance garden, I turned first to stone and second

■ FIGURE 2.16 In the Cotswold Hills in England, geometric stone edging keeps the lawn from encroaching into the perennial beds and provides a surface onto which perennials can flop and not be damaged by a lawn mower. The stone also reinforces the linear quality of the design.

STONE
UNDERFOOT

57

FIGURE 2.17 (*above, left*) In our garden in southern Vermont, we took advantage of a slight rise in the lay of the land to create an enclosed and paved garden room with steps leading up into it. Whenever appropriate, use steps to define grade changes.

FIGURE 2.18 (*above, right*) Dry stone waller Dan Snow made this broad expanse of stone on which our clients could display artifacts they enjoy collecting. I planted *Rudbeckia* 'Goldsturm' and *Miscanthus sinensis* 'Gracillimus' to soften the stone feature.

to plants for my solution (see figure 1.5). I moved the driveway away from the front door 60 feet or so. Then halfway between the new driveway end and the front door, I designed a 2-foot-high stone wall to divide the new 60-foot-long entrance area into two 30-foot level lawn areas with a gap in the wall 6 feet wide for access for people and the lawn mower between these two areas. Next I designed a tightly laid 6-foot-wide fieldstone path that leads from the driveway and through a gap in the stone wall to then curve broadly to the front door. Two maple trees on either side of the beginning of the path help provide a feeling of entrance and frame the path. A 3-foot-wide perennial and shrub border along the inner side of the wall further separates the inner garden from the driveway while introducing color, scent, and texture with the hollies, the fragrant-leaved *Geranium macrorrhizum, Vinca minor* 'Bowles', sun-tolerant chartreuse-leaved hostas, and fragrant viburnums. Before this redesign, no one ever gathered around the front door. Now the children play on the lawn and in the safety of the area enclosed by house and stone wall. Their mother sits on the ends of the walls, and someone is often relaxing on the bench later put on a stone landing near the front door. And being in New England, where stone walls abound, the entrance garden now fits within the broader local tradition.

The primary path from the driveway to the front door is often the widest in everyone's landscape. By widening either end of this principal path, you further enhance the feeling of welcome. The beginning, out by the driveway or sidewalk, could fan out over the last 6 or 8 feet of the path's length as an invitation for guests. This wider stone-paved area is also an appropriate place to gather all kinds of planted pots, perhaps a lamppost, a pair of granite fenceposts, or other design elements, all of which will combine to say, "Welcome. This is the way to my front door."

At the other end of the path, near the front door, widen the primary path into a broad, generous landing so that people can gather there before entering or leaving your home. If the dimensions and proportions of the landing are at least the same or slightly larger than the width of the steps into the house, for example, or the width of the portico or front door and its trim, then house, steps, landing, and path are all tied together. Just be certain that those steps into your front door are generous; if they are too pinched, the path gets pinched, and the feeling of welcome disappears.

One result of this expansive path and landing by the front door is that the house seems linked to the ground. One of the basic elements of good garden design is that a house should appear to be resting on a level plane. Oftentimes this is not the case, so you should look at your front entrance with this principle in mind. One of the problems with the front of many homes is that this primary path to the front door gently slopes up from the sidewalk or driveway. It is preferable to create level steps and landings, because they extend the planes of the floors of the house while at the same time satisfying the need for people to walk on level surfaces.

Retaining walls can help solve this problem of the gradual slope. By combining a low retaining wall with a set of steps up through that wall, you are able to set the house onto that all-important flat plane. Then the path as well as the steps up through the retaining wall will provide your guests with a series of level landings and steps to take them all the way from their car to your front door. (Look back to the section in Chapter 1 on retaining walls for more information on the major role retaining walls can play in the entrance garden.)

▣ Secondary Paths

Secondary paths lead from primary ones. For example, about 15 feet from the beginning of the 40-foot-long, 6-foot-wide path I mentioned above, I designed a 4-foot-wide path of shaped fieldstones that veers off to the right, directing people through a long, narrow garden bounded by a stone wall running parallel with the north side of the house. But for those who continue on toward the front door, another – 3 feet wide and paved with shaped fieldstones – secondary path directs people to the left up a set of steps through a retaining wall and shows them the way along the other side of the house to the swimming pool.

DESIGN PRINCIPLES

▣ Create more than one center of activity to increase the feeling of size in the garden, and pave those areas with stone if furniture will be part of the area.

▣ Limit paving materials to one or two to ensure coherence.

▣ Take advantage of slopes to build low retaining walls with a step or two running through to create level changes.

▣ Use simple patterns in the paving material.

▣ Use garden ornaments or potted plants to mark entrances.

▣ Keep the forms and shapes simple, elegant, and geometric. Don't build fussy curves.

▣ Consider where you will sit and how you will move within your small garden. You may end up paving areas most difficult to plant.

▣ Stone paths create unity and itinerary, even in the smallest of gardens.

FIGURE 2.19 (*below*) Here mortar has been used only to hold the small edging stones and step risers reliably vertical. All other stones are laid in sandy loam that supports grass grouting between them. The green grass contrasts sufficiently with the stone to clarify pattern and to soften what could have been a severe garden image.

FIGURE 2.20 (*opposite*) You can also make steps out of stepping-stones. By combining such a natural-looking stones set quietly into existing soil, you create steps that nearly disappear into the landscape yet remain serviceable.

STONE

IN THE

GARDEN

Secondary paths can also lead from back terraces or patios out to areas you have developed at a distance from the house but never linked to it. For example, if you have a cut-stone or tightly fitting fieldstone terrace at the back of your house and a perennial garden or shady sitting area across the lawn, consider linking the two with a stone path. Once you get people out to the far reaches of your garden, you can then invite them to walk even farther along narrower tertiary paths of pine needles or bark mulch that lead into woodland or shrub plantings.

Path leads to path. By making this articulate itinerary from primary to secondary to tertiary, you send clear messages to visitors as to how you want them to move through your garden. Once you get that movement right, then all kinds of ideas begin to develop for the placement of plants. The junction of primary and secondary paths, for example, is a good place for a tree, a boulder, or a large shrub to lend logic as to why the path splits just there. Likewise, the beginning of a primary path might suggest a place on either side for a pair of trees, or, less formally, a tree on one side, a large shrub on the other. Paths can also become the spine of gardens that run down one or both sides of the path, thereby turning the path into a walk through a richly planted garden.

Tertiary Stepping-Stone Paths

The stepping-stone path is the lowest on the hierarchy of stone paths. Stepping-stone paths meander through woodland gardens or through perennial beds or vegetable gardens. Because you can plant thyme, lady's-mantle, sedums, mosses, ajuga, chamomile, or any of a vast number of low-growing perennials between stepping-stones, you can seamlessly integrate the path with adjacent gardens. Or you can set stepping-stone paths in beige or gray gravel, depending on the color of the stones.

Make a stepping-stone path by choosing individual stones based on the beauty of their shape, color, texture, and size. In a 40-by-12-foot perennial garden I designed in New Hampshire, for example, the individual mica schist stones were about 18 inches in diameter and set 4 to 6 inches apart in the ground so that the concave of one answered the convex of the next, relating the shape of one stone to that of its neighbor. (See Chapter 7 for more specifics.)

Stepping-stone paths curve and wind around trees and shrubs, beds and boulders, and are always meant for people walking singly or in single file; straight stepping-stone paths are too staccato, too rigid, for such a flexible paving material. And these paths, in their own quiet, unassuming way, are

FIGURE 2.21 At Bourton House Garden in Gloucestershire, England, cut York stone has been laid tightly to form the basis for the path leading along a boxwood-edged garden. The York stone is edged on both sides with pebbles set carefully into mortar to add variety. The pebble portion of the walkway is in turn edged with steel. To add further interest, a section of the pebble strip was filled not with pebble but with sandy loam to provide a place for a groundcover to bring green onto gray.

insistent. You have to place your feet exactly where the stones show you to place them, and at a very specific pace. Place 16-inch-wide stepping-stones 2 inches apart, and visitors tiptoe through the garden; set those same stones 12 inches apart, and people will rocket through your garden.

When designing a stepping-stone path, I set stones close together when the path passes through detailed or highly refined plantings. I place them much farther apart when people simply need to get from point A to point B. If you don't want them to go down a path for whatever reason, you might try this. In Japan, one 6-to-8-inch-diameter rounded river stone — the *yogoseki* — is bound with braiding and knotted material following exacting and ancient patterns and then placed at the beginning of a stepping-stone path to act as a subtle stop sign.

Finally, individual stepping-stones are useful in helping to make transitions from one material to another. For example, to make the transition from a bark mulch path to a lawn path in our garden, I placed one 24-inch-diameter flat stone so that 12 inches of it sits within the lawn path and the other 12 inches in the mulched path. I've done the same to make the transition from a lawn path that leads to a gravel walkway through our herb garden. Stepping-stones are also useful where grass could be worn down by concentrated traffic in one spot: at the bottom or top of steps; in gateways; in entrances or gaps in stone walls. When choosing stones to make such transitions, make sure they match nearby existing stone in the garden. We have an acre and a half of garden, and every irregularly shaped stone on the ground is mica schist; every piece of cut stone is Pennsylvania bluestone. That's it. Visual coherence is one result of staying within such narrow limits.

MIXED MATERIAL PATHS

IN THE HIGHLY PROSCRIBED VERNACULAR OF JAPANESE GARDEN design, the *nobedan* is a stone carpet made up of an artful combination of two types of contrasting stone to form one walkway. For example, many Japanese garden designers combine water-rounded stones with contrasting cut-granite slabs to create paths 5 to 6 feet wide on which two people can walk side by side, or they incorporate natural fieldstones in a matrix of cobble or large pieces of rectangular cut granite. These are formal pavementlike walkways designed to get people through a garden, celebrating at the same time the art of the pathmaker. In general, the *nobedan* requires little attention on the part of the walker; you don't need to look down to

■ FIGURE 2.22 In this garden in
Gloucestershire, England, brick is
combined with pebble embedded
in finely crushed gravel to provide
a surface under a circular rose
arbor. Brick is set in radiating lines
(as well as around the perimeter
of the circle) to draw your eye to
a fine terra-cotta pot marking
the center of the space.

see where to set your foot next, as you do with a stepping-stone path.

If the idea of a *nobedan* path appeals, consider combining slabs of cut sandstone, bluestone, or limestone with panels of river rocks of a similar color embedded in crushed gravel. In this way, you juxtapose these two different materials – large, flat geometric stones surrounded by much smaller, rounded stones – to create an appealing pattern and texture to the path.

To add even more interest, set a massive boulder in the inside curve of a path and then bring a section of embedded river rock right up to or even around the boulder to draw it into a relationship with the path. That boulder might even anchor a small pool surrounded by rounded river rocks. The late James Rose, one of the preeminent landscape architects in America,

STONE
UNDERFOOT

63

often surrounded each 3-to-5-foot-long irregularly shaped New York bluestone in his paths with rounded river rocks set flush with the surface of the bluestone. This style of pathmaking meant that the edges of the paths were fluid – that is, river rocks could reach out to surround the trunk of a tree or the mass of a boulder, thereby integrating tree and garden and path and boulder into a unified whole.

You can also combine materials to enhance the contrast between two different materials. Lay square or rectangular cut stones in a path, and surround each with a narrow band of rounded river rocks or rectangular granite cobbles. The result is a pleasing interplay of color and texture and shape.

RIVER-ROCK AND PEBBLE PATHS

ROUNDED RIVER ROCKS AND PEBBLES BETWEEN 2 AND 8 INCHES across embedded in finely crushed gravel or set in mortar can be combined to make a wide range of whimsical paths. Because this type of decorative element is highly detailed, it is best used within an intimate setting or as a patterned panel at the junction of two or more paths to show it off.

The Chinese have been making this kind of embedded path, and panels within them, called *luan shi pu di,* or pebble flooring, for hundreds of years. Some have geometric patterns outlined by pebbles of differing sizes and colors. Others have swirling patterns of white and gray pebbles within a black square pebble or brick surround. Still others are representational – a cyclist, a bird, a boy flying a kite – drawn with contrasting colors and sizes of pebbles.

Spanish gardeners took up this idea centuries ago and continue to create *los pavimentoes decorativos.* Travel through Spanish gardens today, and you will see a wide variety of new and old embedded paths and panels: a square pattern at the center of a four-quadrant herb garden; a rectangular panel at the junction of two cut-stone paths or at a place where a bench sits along a path; a circular decorative panel in the midst of a cut-stone terrace. They are all meant to draw the eye, to stop progress through the garden, and to celebrate the craftsmanship of the artist who embeds river rocks to create pleasing patterns on the ground.

But not all river-rock paths are patterned. In the Southwest, where rounded stones are so plentiful, you can embed 5-to-8-inch river rocks in the

FIGURE 2.23 By limiting yourself
to two colors of uniformly sized
pebbles, you can clarify curving
patterns within rectangular areas.
Swirls and curves add a playful
tone to any walkway, even when
set into mortar.

existing sandy soil to create meandering and serviceable paths 3 to 5 feet wide leading to side doors to your house, to doorways through adobe walls, or out into the desert. (Such paths at the far edges of your garden can often double as paved drainage ditches.) These same river-rock paths can segue out to form secondary paths or a rock mulch under nearby trees and large shrubs. Set rounded 4-to-5-foot-diameter boulders or 1-to-3-foot river rocks along such paths to justify curves in the path or to mark entrances or ends of walkways.

STONE STEPS

S TONE STEPS CAN ADD NECESSARY MASS, FORM, AND LINE TO A garden. Steps are inviting; they beckon you up or down into different areas and levels of the garden. Take advantage of slopes in your ground to create steps that will define grade changes, for with each grade change comes a unique vantage point, a new level from which to look at your garden. When choosing a location for steps, pay attention to what doors of the

FIGURE 2.24 (*above*) In this path at the Komine Shrine in Tochigi, Japan, uniformly sized and colored stones set into mortar draw a long curving shape through the mossy floor of the garden. Partway along the path, a secondary stepping-stone path insinuates itself into the *nobedan*, or stone carpet path. The designer broke what could have become a monotonous path by setting three slightly mounding stepping-stones into it.

FIGURE 2.25 (*right*) By varying the size and color of the stones, a vast range of patterns, sweeps and curves opens up as you design embedded-pebble paths.

house you might align them with; and because people often stop at the top of steps to look out before proceeding down, consider the view you will be emphasizing.

This design principle – that the view from that top step needs to be a good one – dates back nearly two thousand years. In Italian gardens that go back even to Roman times, the position of stone terraces and the alignment of walkways or the tops of stairways that lead from those terraces would be designed to frame views of distant hills or mountains or views of a lake or the sea. Furthermore, the ends of paths would more often than not dovetail with the distant views of the natural world: hills, the sea, a lake. The result is to underpin the relationship between manmade and naturally occurring beauty in the Italian landscape.

The degree of formality of steps is largely determined by the nature of the stones you choose and the way they are held in place. Cut-stone treads set atop cut-stone risers, all of which are mortared together, result in the most formal of steps. To tone this formality down, use rounded fieldstones for the risers that hold the cut-stone steps level. You can create even less for-

▓ FIGURE 2.26 (*below, left*) When blocky ashlar stone is used for adjacent stone retaining walls, long blocky stone of the same type can be used in an informal set of steps. By planting between the steps, you integrate garden, steps and walls.

▓ FIGURE 2.27 (*below, right*) Here a set of informal stone steps in the Hayward garden has been constructed without mortar. Thymes and oxalis creep among these rugged steps for a wild look that is consistent with the informal sloped garden either side of the steps.

FIGURE 2.28 (*right*) In this side garden, 2-inch sheets of slate are set so as to follow an elongated S-curve up through a garden of azaleas and evergreens to the upper lawn. There the same slate set in the lawn is used as stepping-stones to direct people to the side door of the house. Having such low 2-inch risers slows people down and invites them to look around at nearby gardens.

FIGURE 2.29 (*opposite*) One of the primary goals of good landscape design is to relate the house and garden in as many ways as possible. Stone can help. The color of the stucco walls and terra-cotta tile roof of this home in the American Southwest closely relates to the color of the iron oxide in the steps. The gray in the stone echoes the gray of the trim around the arched windows. The repetition of one material to create all the stone elements of this garden image creates a pleasing unity.

mal steps by building both riser and tread out of fieldstone, as I have done for many clients; the size of the gaps between the stones can further determine the degree of formality. Fit the stones tightly to one another, and the steps become more formal; set them an inch or two apart and plant drought-tolerant ground-hugging plants such as *Alchemilla alpina*, *Thymus pseudolanuginosus*, sempervivums, or *Sedum spurium* in the gaps and you relax the look.

Steps made out of stone need to be both attractive and safe. Here is a simple rule if you are not going to use mortar (and you know my opinion on that score): Use large, heavy stones 5 to 7 inches thick to build steps. If the steps are near the house, choose the stone in light of the color of your house or existing walls, stone that already exists in your garden, or stone that is indigenous to your area. Steps well out in the garden can have quite different moods and textures than those nearer the house because they are not so closely dominated by its architectural demands. Often such steps can be combined with small retaining walls to define even the smallest of grade changes.

▦ FIGURE 2.30 If you have a sloping area between two relatively flat areas in your garden, you might find inspiration in these steps. Notice that they are very wide at the bottom and then narrow as they curve to the right.

PAVED TERRACES
AND PATIOS

WHEN CREATING TERRACES AND PATIOS, ESPECIALLY NEAR the house, design the stone-paved area so that it is in proportion to the nearby architecture. Too often, we build stone terraces off the back of the house that are too small, too pinched. Only when we first begin to entertain or have dinner guests on a terrace, with all the furniture in place and with people moving about, do we realize that we should have paved a larger space.

What I often do to ensure that a stone terrace off a house is in proportion with the architecture is to first measure the height and width of the wall of the house adjacent to which the terrace will be installed. I then determine the dimensions and alignment of the terrace with regard to those measurements. For example, while designing a terrace in Massachusetts overlooking the Connecticut River, I found that the east wall of the house was 36 feet long and the measurement from the peak of the roof to the foundation was 18 feet. I started my design thinking with those dimensions: 36 feet wide and 18 feet out from the foundation of the house.

Seeing how it looked on paper, and learning from my clients that they rarely entertained groups larger than six to eight guests, I lopped off 2 feet of stone terrace between the house foundation and planted perennials, thereby creating a finished terrace dimension of 16 feet by 36 feet. A low perennial garden, which did not block views of the river, also ran around the other three sides of the terrace. Stone steps provided access into the house as well as out through the perennial beds and onto adjacent lawn.

Having determined the dimensions of the terrace or patio, I then decide whether to pave the terrace with cut stone, fieldstone, or some other material. To help me make that decision, I look to the house for clues as to the appropriate mood and color the patio should have. In the above case, I took one other thing into consideration: maintenance. Because my clients were just starting new businesses and didn't want to be spending time looking after new plantings in the gaps of their fieldstone terrace, I turned to tightly fitting cut bluestone for a low-maintenance patio. Had their house been rural, simple, and unassuming, and if they had had the inclination to garden, then I would have made the terrace of fieldstone. To better understand these two types of stone most often used for terraces and patios, I want to look at them more closely so that you can clearly see how they can be used.

▪ Cut Stone

The most elegant terrace or patio off the back doors of a house is geometric and made of tightly laid cut bluestone, limestone, or sandstone. Such a stone-paved terrace not only provides a beautiful, firm, and safe surface on which to walk as well as set furniture and planted pots but also displays the beauty inherent in the grain of the stone itself. One of the most stunning stones for this purpose is Tennessee Crab Orchard stone, which looks something like cut petrified wood, with remarkable striations of beige, brown, and even purple; when wet, it is even more beautiful.

Lay 2-, 3-, or 4-foot squares of cut stone to create a geometric pattern, or lay rectangles of various sizes for a more random look. Ryan Gainey designed a bluestone terrace for a client in the Buckhead district outside Atlanta; the whole patio was made of 2-foot squares. In another in Atlanta, the designer surrounded the perimeter of a patio with 4-by-4-foot squares, infilling it with 2-foot squares. Because each pattern has its own mood and tone, draw different patterns on graph paper to help you visualize your options.

Once you have chosen a pattern, decide whether or not you want to make it less formal by planting in the gaps between the individual stones. For example, you can set all the stones 1 inch apart and allow moss or some other groundcover appropriate for your region of the country to grow between the stones. Or you can lay the majority of the stones very tightly and then leave out 12-inch-square areas here and there which you could backfill with sandy loam and plant with perennials that will accept foot traffic. (See Chapter 7 on constructing stone paths for such a list.) The tighter the stones are laid, the more formal the terrace; the larger the gaps and the more plants in them, the less formal the terrace becomes.

▪ Fieldstone

If you want a less formal terrace, choose randomly shaped fieldstones for a level and livable surface. Again, the nature of the gaps between the stones allows you to manipulate the degree of formality that you desire. You can also control mood with fieldstone: terrace edges that are perfectly straight are more formal; curving or irregular edges are less so.

If you want to create a tightly fitted look and you want a straight edge on all four sides of the terrace, you need to choose an easily shaped stone. Mica schists, limestones, and sandstones can easily be shaped with a mason's scribe and a hammer and chisel; quartzite, on the other hand, is nearly impossible to shape. Then again, if you don't want a tight look, don't shape the stones. Leave irregular gaps of 2 to 4 inches here and there in the surface of the terrace. Backfill these gaps with sandy loam, and plant. (See the plant list at the end of Chapter 7 for suggestions.)

Mixed-Material Terraces and Patios

By reviewing this entire chapter with a creative mind, you will see the limitless possibilities for combining different types of stone to create fabulous stone terraces. Just be careful that you don't choose too many colors and textures and sizes, or the design for your terraces will collapse into chaos. Limit the color of the stones to one or, at the very most, two, and even then, try to keep those two colors compatible: beige and brown; gray and gray-blue; pink sandstone with pinkish rounded river rocks. Keep in mind, too, that you need to have a dominant stone and a subordinate stone and that the mixed-material patio or terrace requires a strong visual center so that the design is anchored. Here are several examples of how to appropriately mix materials so that the design for the surface holds together visually.

■ Pave the perimeter of the terrace with long rectangular cut stones, and then infill with tightly fitted fieldstone of a similar color.

■ Create a cut-stone terrace, but leave a large square in the middle for river rocks set into the same base that you used for setting the cut stones.

■ Lay 3-to-5-foot-long pieces of irregular bluestone, limestone, or sandstone to form an irregularly edged terrace, surrounding each stone with 2-to-3-inch river rocks.

■ Make a terrace out of 3- or 4-foot squares of cut stone, each surrounded by granite cobble, and then edge the whole terrace with the same cobble.

■ Make a loosely laid fieldstone terrace, and at three places within the terrace, set at least 3-to-4-foot-long boulders that are at least 24 inches above the terrace grade for sitting.

■ Create a randomly shaped fieldstone terrace, and then have two or three stepping-stone paths spin off from the terrace out into other parts of the garden; set a large boulder where the terrace meets the first stones of the paths.

■ Create a terrace solely out of tightly fitted 2-foot-square pieces of cut stone set on a perfect grid; surround this with pieces of 1-by-4-foot pieces of the same stone.

■ FIGURE 2.32 Use cut and shaped stone to create pattern and form on the ground. Here the garden designer used the pattern of the compass rose. Notice that the gravel surround makes the pattern stand out. The center of the pattern is a good place on which to display a planted pot of a contrasting color.

STONE

UNDERFOOT

73

ROOTS UNDER STONES

With her husband Harold Nicolson, Vita Sackville-West created the renowned modern gardens around her home at Sissinghurst Castle in Kent, in southeast England. It is now in the hands of the National Trust and has become the most visited garden in the world. From 1947 to 1961, one year before her death, she wrote a popular gardening column that appeared weekly in the Observer *newspaper. The following is from one of her articles:*

I HAVE COME TO THE CONCLUSION, after many years of sometimes sad experience, that you cannot come to any conclusion at all. But one simple thing I have discovered in gardening; a simple thing one never sees mentioned in gardening books. It is the fact that many plants do better if they can get their roots under stone.

I am not thinking specially of Alpines whose natural habit it is, but of casual strays, often self-sown, sometimes bulbous plants, sometimes merely annuals or biennials, which by a successful accident have pointed the way to this method of gardening. The narrowest crack in a path or paved terrace will surprisingly send up the finest seedling; I have known even such large unwanted subjects as delphiniums and hollyhocks to make the attempt. The reason, obviously, is that they never suffer from either excessive moisture or excessive drought; the stone preserves such moisture as is in the soil, but prevents the soggy puddling consequent on a heavy rainfall; furthermore, it protects from the scorching sun and consequent wilting which demands the watering can. . . .

I should then fill up the cracks with good soil or compost, and sow quite recklessly. I should not mind

how ordinary my candidates were, forget-me-nots, pansies, wallflowers, Indian pinks, alyssum, because I should pull up 95 per cent later on, leaving only single specimens here and there. It is not, after all, a flowerbed that we are trying to create. If, however, you think it is a waste of opportunity to sow such ordinary things, there are plenty of low-growing plants of a choicer kind, especially those which dislike excessive damp at the root throughout the winter: this covering of stone would protect them from that. The old-fashioned pinks would make charming tufts. *Dianthus allwoodii*, for example, with their suggestion of chintz and of patchwork quilts, should succeed under such conditions; I confess to repeated failures with them in open borders, but their neatness and variety encourage perseverance.

(From *A Joy of Gardening* by Vita Sackville-West, published by her son, Nigel Nicolson in 1968.)

◼ FIGURE 2.33 Stones and plants go together. Heucheras, sedums, sempervivums and other low-flowering perennials gather around these stepping-stones to integrate stone steps into a garden seamlessly.

IN SUMMARY

WHEN MAKING OUR GARDEN HERE IN SOUTHERN VERMONT, I discovered we had a section in a long and wide perennial border that rose about 12 inches or so above the rest of the garden. Rather than remove the soil to level that area, I turned to stone and its many uses to create a small garden room that would invite us to sit on a paved area within the 14-foot-wide perennial bed and look down the length of the garden from that slightly higher vantage point (see figure 2.17). I used 12-to-14-inch-thick rounded fieldstones to retain an oval area 25 feet long and 14 feet wide. Then I set two shallow steps into that low retaining wall, using 3-by-3-foot pieces of mica schist paving stones for both the risers and the tread. In doing so, I created a raised sitting area bounded on one side of the oval by *Chamaecyparis pisifera* 'Filifera' and three shorn hedge maples *(Acer campestre).* Having created steps and wall, I then paved the resulting flat area with bluestone, each piece of which was surrounded by brick to emphasize pattern and to create a long and broad area for a bench, two chairs and a table. Now we can sit within the perennial bed, close to fragrant and flowering perennials and annuals. Stone was the key to the whole idea.

HOW STONE HELPED DESIGN A GARDEN

WHILE MARY AND I LIVE and garden in Vermont, we recently purchased a small cottage in the North Cotswolds of England, where Mary is from originally. Along the north side of our cottage (US Zone 7) is a garden approximately 15 feet by 35 feet in full view of large sitting-room windows. A pair of French doors open from that sitting room onto an outdoor stone patio in the shape of a quarter circle set into the ell of the cottage. The exterior entrance to the garden leads from the parking area, through a gate in the stone wall, and onto a cut-stone path that runs down along the north side of the house to the patio.

When we bought Courtyard House, the garden consisted of a small free-form central lawn planted around the edges with a mixture of shrubs as well as many familiar varieties of perennials we grow here in Vermont. From the bench on the quarter-circle stone area, we looked into the garden surrounded by stone walls on three sides (one being the side of the house) with a shrub border on the fourth, but the plant choice and design didn't inspire; all we could do with the space was look at it.

We started the redesign by thinking through how we wanted to use the space. We found we had three primary uses: to have meals outside while sitting at a table for at least four; to have a place where eight or ten family members and friends could sit together outside; to surround these two sitting areas with wonderful plants and to get rid of the lawn all together.

We knew the existing quarter-circle York stone patio would hold as many as eight chairs, so that would be our main gathering space. We decided to pave a dining area under the branches of the Robinia with stone for a dining table and chairs and then grow perennials in the sunny center of the garden.

But how to increase the feeling of separation from the parking area? The 4-foot-high stone wall helped, but it wasn't enough. We ended up designing 2-foot-high trelliswork that would run along the top of the stone wall and then arch up and over the existing gateway to be attached to the house. By installing this trelliswork and by defining the space more clearly, we also made the garden feel bigger.

Next we needed to design the stone-paved dining area. Knowing that too many paving materials in a small garden can create incoherence, we decided to repeat the York stone that already made up the surface of the quarter-circle sitting area. That sitting area also suggested the shape for the paving in the new dining area: a full circle, thereby further relating the two paved areas.

Because we wanted to set the circle under at least some of the branches of the Robinia, we had to solve a small problem: how to create a flat surface in what was slightly sloping ground under the tree. We designed an 18-inch-high omega-shaped stone retaining wall that would define the outer edge of the 9-foot circle, though we would leave a 3-foot wide gap to provide access into the dining area. It was clear that the stone used in the existing walls was the material we would use in the new wall. We sought a source of old mossy wall stone and found it at a reclamation yard. We also removed two mock orange shrubs to expose 20 feet of beautiful old Cotswold stone wall

over which we could then see the back of our neighbor's mature garden.

During the winter of 1998, we traveled to England to build the stone wall, install the stone paving, and pre-

pare the soil for planting. It took us most of the week, with two helpers.

Designing a small garden is all about restraint. We selected plants in light of the color of the Robinia; we limited ourselves to the one wall and paving material already in the garden: Cotswold stone. We used the stone

circle and the quarter circle to help us create a unified ground plan, and we opted for teak as the only wood to use for garden furniture because it would age to the same color as the

old stone. By restraining ourselves regarding materials and layout, we provided a structure in which a wide variety of plants could flourish within a coherent design. We also provided ourselves with a richly planted new garden where we could entertain friends or read quietly at the table.

CHAPTER THREE

BOULDERS AND BEDROCK

I am drawn

to the stone

itself.

Andy Goldsworthy,
sculptor

BOULDERS AND BEDROCK, THE ANCHORS OF NATURAL GARDENS, have come down through the eons, bringing with them a deep sense of time that can lend an impression of age to even the newest garden. If you are fortunate enough to have either in your garden, or if you are prepared to purchase and install boulders with heavy equipment, then you have the beginnings of an extraordinary naturalistic garden. By thoughtfully exposing existing bedrock and planting at its perimeter, or in its crevices, or by gardening around boulders, whether indigenous or brought in from elsewhere, you draw a pleasing contrast between timeless, still stone and ephemeral, ever-changing plants.

The key to planting around large stones is to acknowledge that they are an essential element of the natural landscape and that any gardening you do in relation to them should be inspired by trees, shrubs, and perennials native to your area. While fine perennials and shrubs introduced from across the world can certainly be interplanted among native plants or hybrids derived from them, indigenous plants should predominate. For example, imagine how beautiful a grouping of balsam firs would look among a gathering of boulders or clustered along the face of bedrock. Once the trees were in, imagine underplanting them with variegated Solomon's seal, Christmas ferns, and *Tiarella cordifolia* 'Slickrock' (a hybrid derived from a native) out there at the edge of your woodland or as an entire entrance garden to your home in the mountains where balsam firs grow naturally. Or if you live in the Southwest, imagine setting boulders in a garden at the edge of the Sonoran desert out behind the house and then setting out a group of palo verde trees interplanted with Mexican evening primroses, red yucca, purple lantana, bush dalea, and blackfoot daisies, all knitted together with a uniform drought-tolerant groundcover.

Years ago I saw a stunning garden designed by landscape architect James Wheat around a home overlooking Phoenix, Arizona. It was built among red sandstone boulders 4 to 24 feet high, and atop bedrock, one part of which

■ FIGURE 3.1 At the edge of this woodland garden, two boulders anchor
the scene and provide it with a visual center to which all trees,
shrubs, and perennials relate.

79

formed a section of the living room floor. That same bedrock then ran under a broad window and on out to form a shelf of rock overlooking the city below. Boulders acted as diving platforms overhanging the edge of the swimming pool; water flowed over rocks and gathered in a small pool below. Boulders framed the sandstone path to the front door, and all plantings were indigenous to Arizona. It was an extraordinary sight that showed how beautiful and dramatic a natural garden among great boulders and bedrock can be.

The very best boulders for a garden have been above ground in fields or woodland or prairie for decades or centuries or have been in a supply yard long enough to seem old and settled. Patches of moss and lichen grow on them; a patina of age is intact. They're not scratched or gouged by a backhoe, and they may have dirt attached to the bottom third of their bulk.

When you do place boulders or expose bedrock in your garden, think big. Big boulders and broad shoulders of bedrock have a presence; little rocks and bits of bedrock do not. Think in terms of feet, not inches. And if you're going to clear off the bedrock to make it part of your garden, treat it with kid gloves. It's been there for a very long time, so use your shovel, hoe, and other hand tools with care so that you don't scratch it, thereby giving away the fact that you've recently exposed its surface.

BOULDERS

GOOD GARDEN DESIGN SETS A HOUSE INTO RATHER THAN ON the landscape. Boulders are just one element often used to make this connection between the house, its new garden, and the old natural landscape in the distance. When it comes to selecting boulders, which are, in fact, abundant here in the Northeast, I invariably choose large, weathered 3- to 4-footers and, using a backhoe, carefully transport them, protected with blankets and boards, from the client's woodland or fields into their gardens. Whenever possible, position groups of boulders of varying sizes and shapes (just as you would find them in nature) so that when you see the group, you also see others like them in nearby gardens as well as in the distant landscape, and the whole scene looks natural. Boulders then become a strong form that gets repeated in the foreground, the middle ground, and the background, thereby linking all three into a comfortable relationship.

Drive up through a mountain pass to a high Montana home or to a mountain home in Utah or even into the suburbs of Wilton or Stonington, Connecticut, and you will pass naturally occurring boulders everywhere. Arrive at that home, and find those same boulders used in the garden in natural, unself-conscious ways, and you will see how boulders tie your garden to the larger landscape. But where to position those boulders? That is always the question.

▪ How to Position Boulders

I look to the stone path as one very practical way to find the right places for boulders. For example, when clients here in Vermont asked for help in developing an entrance garden to their new three-story home set high in a meadow, I knew trees would have to be central to the design because of the height of the house. Given that birches were growing in the woods 100 feet away, birches that were often growing right near big boulders, they were the obvious choice for a tree that would link the new gardens to the existing landscape.

▪ FIGURE 3.3 At the Japanese Garden in Portland, Oregon, natural boulders in the foreground and background create a place for a carved-stone Japanese lantern. Moss covers the ground around both, visually linking them. Such a pairing of a natural boulder and carved artifact of the same stone reflects the yin-yang resolved opposites of Eastern philosophy.

BOULDERS
AND BEDROCK

FIGURE 3.4 In the Hall garden in Maine, boulders, ferns, native evergreens, moss, and cleared paths through indigenous woodland give rise to a serene, Japanese-inspired garden. The standing stones at the end of the pathway provide a visual center around which the woodland gathers.

I started the design by developing a plan for a primary 6-foot-wide fieldstone path that would run the 18 feet from the driveway to the front door. I then ran a secondary stepping-stone path parallel with the driveway (and perpendicular to the main entrance path) through the 70-foot length of the entrance garden. Partway along that path, it split to direct people either to a stone terrace to the right or along a short path to the left that would invite them to walk across the driveway and onto a mown path through meadow and on through a gap in an old stone wall and onto a woodland path.

Once paths were established, I placed the major elements of the design: trees and boulders. Just to the right as people stepped onto the main path from the driveway to the front door, I placed a broad-backed dark, mossy boulder 5 feet long, 3 feet wide, 24 inches thick to act as an entrance to the walkway. The placement of the boulder in turn provided the placement of the first birch, in part because it so beautifully contrasted the horizontal mound of the boulder with the verticality of the birch. Across the path, but asymmetrically, I placed two similarly shaped boulders – one slightly larger than the other – and in the gap between the two, I planted another birch, again to create a kind of marriage between vertical tree and mounding boulder.

Where the primary and secondary paths met, another mossy boulder added logic to the junction; I then planted several summer blooming azaleas just near it. Partway along, the secondary stepping-stone path curved to avoid monotony. To give the curve logic, two boulders (both mounding, but one big, one small) went into the inside of the curve of the path, and then we planted a birch between the boulders. By burying at least one-third of the bulk of all of these mossy boulders in the ground, it turned out, as my client said, that they looked like sleeping animals.

Paths, then, give rise to good ideas for boulder placement: at junctions, at entrances, in the curves of paths, and then well within adjacent beds. Boulders help find good places for trees and major shrubs, and those, in turn, give rise to logical places for herbaceous perennials and groundcovers. It's a logical progression, and it all starts with the stone path.

Once we had installed these gardens, I went across the driveway and into the meadow's edge, where there was an old stone wall with countless old boulders just like the ones we had placed in the entrance garden. We cleared brush and debris away from the base of the old wall to expose the old mossy boulders to view from the entrance garden. Those boulders, placed there 200 years ago by farmers clearing woodland to make hayfields, echoed ones set

■ FIGURE 3.5 In this Japanese-inspired pool garden, boulders and river rocks are combined with shaped wooden panels, pines, cut-leaf maples, ferns, and shorn boxwood to create a serene garden image.

■ FIGURE 3.6 For this small garden, landscape architect Patrick Chassé used tightly fitted fieldstone to bring people along the side of the garage into the formal garden set into the ell of a two-story house. He also used fieldstone paving to bring the family from the kitchen (lower right) into the garden. Chassé blasted existing bedrock (upper right), and moved pieces of it to the far side of the formal area to create faux bedrock, adding drama and a naturalistic background. Fieldstone retaining walls and granite setts outline different parts of the space.

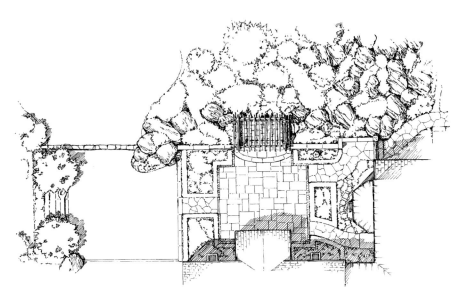

BOULDERS
AND BEDROCK

FIGURE 3.7 AND 3.8   Michael Schultz, a designer in the Northwest, carefully cleared around naturally occurring boulders in the woodland near a home and then planted Solomon's seal, maidenhair ferns, and other natives.

At another property, he placed boulders right near the house and surrounded them with flowering herbaceous perennials to create a dramatic interplay between huge boulders and delicate perennials.

within the entrance garden. In this way, we established a firm visual relationship between the old woodland edge and the brand-new gardens – and the linchpins were the birches and the boulders, and, later, the ostrich ferns. While your plants and your site may well be very different, all the same principles pertain.

Respect Their Shapes

When setting boulders in the garden, respect their individual shapes and forms and "grain" – that is, the flow of striations, the lines or layers of sedimentation – so that you place the boulder in the garden in a way that reflects its innate qualities. For example, if a stone has a mounding shape, it does not want to be set on end but in a fashion that reflects its mounding nature. If you have a sloping boulder, set that slope to direct your eye to some important element of the garden or to direct movement down a path. Boulders simply plunked onto the earth, with no reference to their form, add little to your garden.

If you have several boulders that clearly have a distinctive grain, set them all in the garden, no matter how far apart, so that the grain of each stone runs in the same direction. That way, they look as though they had been placed by the glacier rather than by your hand.

BEDROCK

I COME FROM THE SCHOOL OF THOUGHT THAT SAYS YOU NEED TO make the best out of what you have, and bedrock is something you might well have. Rather than call it bad names, rather than wish it weren't there right at the edge of your garden, it is far better to see the elemental, fundamental beauty within it.

▥ Defining the Beauty of Bedrock

I have found that a good question to ask of each area is "What can I do here that I can't do anywhere else in my garden?" If a part of your property is dominated by bedrock, then you need to think how you can garden it in a way that defines the beauty and mass of the rock and creates a garden that is in keeping with it.

If you are fortunate enough to have existing bedrock in your garden, and chunks of it have fallen off or could be carefully pried off, then you might consider using the resulting boulders to create a link between garden and bedrock. While acknowledging the grain of the bedrock, lay them out so that individual pieces look as though they had fallen off the bedrock and come to rest naturally. To help you place these chunks of bedrock in your garden, drive around your area and see how nature has scattered similar pieces at the base of bedrock.

One thing I've found is that rocks of varying sizes often gather together at the base of bedrock or cliffs in descending order. Large rocks fall, and their weight propels them away. Middle-size rocks don't travel quite so far, while gravel and tiny bits gather at the base. Consult nature. See how she does it.

▥ FIGURE 3.9 This spare, Japanese-inspired use of bedrock, ferns, birches, hemlocks, and native groundcovers gives rise to a peaceful garden. The owners respected these woods and bedrock rather than trying to make them over in their image.

■ FIGURE 3.10 Crevices, cracks, and spaces between mossy boulders make perfect places for herbaceous perennials. By burying at least a third of the boulder in the ground, moisture is wicked up, giving rise to mosses and lichens that turn the boulders themselves into miniature gardens.

■ Gardening On and Around Bedrock

These boulders at the base of bedrock and placed as nature would set them can become the structure of a wild garden. As I mentioned in the introduction of this chapter, turn to plants indigenous to your area or to hybrids that have been developed from them to develop such a garden. It might comprise native herbaceous perennials, woody shrubs, and trees. Again, drive around your area, and you may discover that certain native plants seem to like being near rocky outcroppings and stony sites.

Walk into the Sierra Nevadas or other mountain ranges near your home, and you'll find evergreens growing in the spare soil near bedrock. Ground-hugging spruces, windswept pines, or native junipers might be growing in the crevices; these natural "gardens" offer inspiring clues as to how to garden around your own bedrock.

Bedrock is massive, so plant in masses. Certainly a tall specimen fern might be placed here and there in crevices of the rocks or where a great rock splits at ground level, but then you need to consider big masses of ground-covers that are either indigenous or are similar to regional natives. If your bedrock is shaded by overhanging trees, consider great swaths of ferns, mayapple, European ginger, or *Phlox stolonifera*. Punctuate these groundcovers with patches of more vertical herbaceous perennials or woody plants that look right in a woodland garden: azaleas, *Fothergilla major*, witch hazel, or, in wet woodland, rodgersias, ligularias or *Ilex verticillata* (winterberry).

In sunny dry areas, plant groundcovers, such as *Pachistima canbyi*, *Juniperus horizontalis* hybrids, or creeping spruces punctuated with vertical or mounding plants, such as dwarf conifers, or ornamental grasses. If many crevices in the bedrock can be backfilled with sandy loam, trailing herbaceous and woody plants will look like they belong as they flow with the lines of the crevices.

And finally, consider creating sophisticated gardens around naturally occurring bedrock. The photo of the late Jane Platt's garden in Oregon shows a refined combination of plants that produces a garden of trees, shrubs, herbaceous perennials, bulbs, and groundcovers. This is a gardenesque treatment of bedrock, a treatment that is certainly an alternative to the natural look.

▪ Not Gardening Around Bedrock

Having written at length about gardening in relation to bedrock, I think it's important to make another point: old, weathered, lichen-covered bedrock is beautiful all on its own. When working with two artists in their garden here in the village, both of whom were keenly conscious of visual coherence, we used stone to establish a visual link between their home, the lawn and gardens, and the bedrock and native woodland at the edge of the lawn. Bedrock was, to a point, already a unifying element: the back of the house was built

▪ FIGURE 3.11 In this garden in the American Southwest, most of the boulders have been gathered to suggest that water has been running down a shallow swale over the years, washing soil away from the larger stones to expose their mass. This idea lends logic to this use of stone in the garden, one that mimics naturally occurring drainage swales in the surrounding mountains. In turn, the boulders and river rocks provide places for drought-tolerant perennials, shrubs, and trees. Notice that the boulders share the same color as the adobe walls of the house.

FIGURE 3.12 At Naumkeag in Stockbridge, Massachusetts, landscape architect Fletcher Steele wanted bedrock to protrude from this corner of Mabel Choate's garden to form a promontory with a view of the valley and the setting sun. Bedrock did not naturally exist, so he went into the nearby Berkshire Hills to find the massive stone you see in the photo. He had it carefully split and the pieces numbered and then trucked to the site and put back together.

on it; it existed 20 feet back from the east edge of the lawn as well as deep into the woods.

I started by designing a stepping-stone path and marked its beginning with a rough piece of bedrock we had brought up from the woods with a front loader. The boulder came from behind a 70-to-80-foot-long mass of weedy, sapling-covered bedrock just across the lawn and set well into the woods. A year later we completed another stepping-stone path that led from the same lawn and through plantings of azaleas, hostas, ferns, birches, and ajuga to a secret stone-paved sitting area. We used several chunks of stone from behind the same bedrock to mark the entrance to this path too.

Weeks later I went to see how the garden was doing, and in the meantime, my clients had cleared the entire 70-foot length of bedrock on the east side of the lawn. They had uprooted saplings and small trees that had a tenuous hold on the bedrock anyway. They had carefully raked the bedrock with plastic rakes to keep from scratching its surface and had cleared the area between the lawn and the base of the bedrock, sown seed, and had grass growing where unsightly undergrowth previously grew. Lawn now came right up to the bedrock base, thereby co-opting the face of the great 70-foot-long and 12-foot-high bedrock into a relationship with the lawn and, thereby, the rest of the garden. As the years have passed, hay-scented ferns have crept along the crevices in the bedrock, lichen and moss have spread, and the bedrock forms a beautiful, natural edge to their garden, behind which grow mature maples and birches interspersed with hemlocks. As artists, they saw the beauty inherent in the bedrock itself, beauty that needed no human intervention other than a gentle cleanup.

IN SUMMARY

NATURE HAS RECENTLY BECOME ONE OF THE PRIMARY SOURCES of inspiration for garden making in North America. Harvard-trained landscape architect Patrick Chassé, for example, designed a garden on an island off the coast of Maine that utterly respects the natural bedrock, boulders, and indigenous spruce forest of the island and the larger region. Within an acre of spruce forest near the house, Chassé cleared lichen-covered granite bedrock of saplings and debris and covered the exposed earth around the bedrock with thousands of plugs of haircap moss, highlighting the intrinsic beauty of both bedrock and moss. At the Fuller House near Phoenix, Arizona, Gage Davis Associates brought boulders into the adoquin stone terrace to visually link naturally occurring boulders in the nearby desert to the manmade terrace. In the Pacific Northwest, designer Michael Schultz planted woodland perennials among existing boulders and trees and then brought boulders of a similar scale and color right up next to the house, where he interplanted them with sun-loving perennials. With the new eye you have as a result of reading this chapter, you could do the same.

FIGURE 3.13 At Rocky Dale Gardens in Bristol, Vermont, Bill Pollard and Holly Weir judiciously cleared bedrock of unwanted shrubs and trees and then used the massive rock as backdrop for their display garden.

FIGURE 3.14 Bedrock in the hands of a fine garden designer such as the late Jane Platt in Portland, Oregon, can become the basis for a sophisticated garden. Here Mrs. Platt combined upright, mounding, and trailing evergreens (especially the *Picea pungens* 'Glauca Procumbens') with sedums, mosses, ferns, and flowering perennials to create a rock garden.

WATER AND STONE

WATER AND STONE COMBINED IN A GARDEN HAVE THE rare capacity to introduce an aura of tranquility into your garden. Whether in the form of water in a basin, a formal or naturalistic pool, or in a simple stream and waterfall, both moving and still water have the capacity to focus our attention and thereby calm us down. Water and stone are absolutely central to the successful garden.

However, many gardeners don't introduce water, which has a mind of its own, into their gardens out of fear of expense and maintenance. While professionally designed and installed streams, formal pools, rills, and waterfalls are certainly costly – but perhaps not as costly as you might think – you can bring water into your garden in many practical, affordable ways. Chapter 10 provides all the how-to information you need to site water basins or to construct your own naturalistic pools and small fountains with confidence. This chapter presents a broader range of ways you can introduce water and stone into your garden. If you do choose to work with a professional designer or installer, you will have the knowledge necessary to be an informed and integral part of the design and installation process.

Children's safety is another reason many people don't bring water into their gardens. If you have young children, either wait to design and install a pool until they are old enough to understand the dangers of water or fence the area around the pool in an attractive way so that you don't have to worry.

Part of the appeal of stone and water is how gracefully these very different elements interact. Stone is solid, immobile, opaque, and of an unchanging color; water is liquid and crystal clear, and its colors and highlights are everchanging, depending on what is being reflected on its surface. I particularly enjoy the sound of plashing water in the little pool just outside as I sit here in my office with the windows open. At the flip of a switch, a single jet of water from a simple submerged pump rushes up about 1 foot through the hole in a 5-foot-diameter 150-year-old marble well-cap and then

■ FIGURE 4.1 In the Hall garden, bedrock was hollowed out and the seams sealed with hydraulic cement tinted to match the color of the rock to form this naturalistic pool. Periodically it has to be refilled with a garden hose.

FIGURE 4.2 (*above, left*) In this concrete-lined seasonal drainage rill in a public garden in South Africa, river rocks are used to backfill the rill. Stepping-stones of a similar color set into the small river rocks turn the rill into a pathway. Boulders along either edge cover the concrete and add solidity to the drainage system that is both practical and aesthetic.

FIGURE 4.3 (*above, right*) In the Volum Garden in the Pacific Northwest, the designer made a section of driveway out of flat black stones set a few inches apart in concrete to allow water to flow from one side of the drive to the other. (See figure 2.4 to see the entrance garden just around the corner.)

plashes back down onto the white stony surface to flow back into the shallow pool.

Water needs to be introduced into your garden in natural ways that will lack obvious artifice. Water in a small stone basin on which floats a pink peony bloom is deeply alluring in its simplicity and honesty; a costly waterfall plonked out back in the middle of flat lawn is so unnatural, it has little appeal. If you want flowing water to bring peace and tranquility into the garden, you must respect its simple nature: to fall from naturally occurring higher places; to gather and lie still in lower places and to be associated with hard rounded river rocks and, more often than not, the shade of overhanging tree branches.

Nature as Inspiration

Water and rock go together well in a garden because they are so closely related by the forces of nature. As a stream moves along, it first washes away topsoil, gravel, and sand to expose the larger rocks underneath. As time passes and the stream or river builds, especially every spring, even small stones and eventually larger and larger stones are washed away.

As a result of this action, hard rounded cobble and boulders of all sizes are left behind to make up the bottom of the stream. Rocks near water are usually harder because softer stones have already been broken up and carried away; they're rounded and smooth because of the relentless flow of water and sand suspended in it over their surfaces or by being tumbled along the streambed and thrown against harder rocks.

More than with any other use for stone in your garden, you should learn firsthand from nature the many facets of this symbiotic relationship between stone and water. Go out into one of the national parks, a wilderness area, or simply a nearby stream. If you pay attention, you will see water in virtually every natural form that you could consider for your garden. Stop at the bend in a stream, and you'll see how sand and fine particles gather on the calm side. However, as the water picks up speed and force as it gets closer and closer to the opposite bank, the stone particles get bigger and bigger so that on the far side of a bend, erosion has exposed the faces of large rocks and perhaps even boulders. If you intend to build a simple lined stream, that gradation from sand to pebbles to stones to boulders will be a good model for you as you build a bend in your stream.

Or sit next to several waterfalls, large and small. Notice what makes one waterfall with a deep echo chamber under it sound quite loud, yet water sheeting down the face of a boulder makes virtually no sound at all. Notice also how small pools of water gather in relation to sand, gravel, rocks, and boulders at the edge and within the water. Notice how plants have insinuated themselves among the rocks and boulders and perhaps even into the sand and soil in the streambed. And notice the very simplest way that water can be introduced into your garden: in naturally occurring basins in stone and boulders. If you want water to honestly bring tranquility and peace into your garden, nature is the most important source of inspiration when it comes to combining water and rock in your garden.

But if you can't get to streams easily, study *Reflecting Nature: Garden Designs from Wild Landscapes* by Jerome and Seth Malitz. It is rich with photographs taken across North America of indigenous plants and rocks in relation to naturally occurring waterfalls, streams, and pools. The photographs will give you an armchair vantage point from which to see many inspiring examples of what you could do to create naturalistic water features in your garden.

WATER BASINS AND BIRDBATHS

On your way to that stream, you'll see a model for the easiest possible way to bring water into your garden – a hollow in a stone in which water has pooled. The stone basin, whether carved or naturally occurring, has always been important to the Japanese garden. Along the path to the secluded tea garden of 2,000 years ago, for instance, the garden master would set a stone basin, or *chozubachi,* into which pure running water was directed for the ritual cleaning of the hands and mouth before the tea ceremony. Such a stone can hold water that reflects the sky and your surrounding garden. It couldn't be simpler.

■ FIGURE 4.4

Does the bowl

In the garden

Mock nature

When night after night

Green frogs gather

To prove it's a pool?

— *From Han Yu,
an 11th-century
Chinese poet*

WATER

AND STONE

But equally simple are more modern small cast- or carved-stone basins. I placed a pair of 16-inch-diameter cast-stone urns just by the entrance to our outdoor dining area on a stepping-stone path. Each holds 3 gallons of water. Before guests come for lunch or dinner, I fill one of the basins to the brim and then float flowers in it, usually choosing blooms that will lie flat in the water, such as peonies, heleniums, or composites like shasta daisies. Depending on the stoutness of the flower, many will look quite good for several days before we have to change them and the water.

Across the pathway is the other urn; its stem is pierced from the base up into the urn with a ¾-inch-diameter hole through which pumped water can pass (see figure 4.4). I took advantage of that hole to create a simple fountain. Having dug a hole in the ground, I buried a water basin with a simple pump and various other materials outlined in detail in Chapter 10. The result was a small fountain that introduced the sight and sound of dripping water into our outdoor dining area. You could do the same with any vessel with a hole in its bottom through which the water tubing could pass. It's easy to make and maintain.

Elegant cast- or carved-stone birdbaths (as opposed to many rather maudlin concrete or plastic ones) are another classic way to bring still water into the garden. However, for them to have impact, you have to put them in the right place, where they have a context: at the end of a path; in the center of a four-quadrant garden; at the side of an entrance garden, just next to a boulder, or in the corner of a stone wall. Just don't put them out in the middle of the front lawn where they have no context, no relationship to the larger garden. Look for fine old stone birdbaths in antique fairs, as they add considerably to the feeling of age and elegance in your garden.

We have a 70-year-old cast-stone birdbath that was in my grandmother's

■ FIGURE 4.5 The basin and the arched wall behind it in this garden in the Cotswold Hills of England are extensions of the stone wall into which they have been set. The designer used cut stone for the basin coping and a stone bridge. Water flows under that stone pad and through a planting of moisture-loving plants to a pool under two apple trees some 50 feet away. From that pool, the water is pumped back to the beginning where it flows out of the dragon's mouth again.

garden in Oyster Bay, New York, until she passed away many years ago. It now resides here in our garden in Vermont. It is about 52 inches high and contains 4 gallons of water in a 3-inch-deep bowl 30 inches in diameter; seven ceramic birds stand on its dry perimeter. The reflection on the surface of this circle of water is a constant source of simple beauty in the garden, a beauty I sometimes enhance with floating flowers. Several years ago the bird-bath sat at the end of a path into my herb garden, and it looked fine there, framed by a gateway. But other garden ornaments were also in the area, and the garden was starting to look a bit busy; I also realized that this large cast-stone object was out of scale with the small herb garden. More recently I found a much better place for it; now the birdbath provides a focus in another garden that lacked a center around which to gather plants.

At the far end of our garden is a corner in a stone wall; 15 feet out from the corner is a broadly curving lawn path that roughly follows the same lines as the wall and its corner. In the 15 feet between the lawn path and the stone wall, I planted about 25 *Hosta plantaginea* to anchor the corner, but as it turned out, the plants alone were not strong enough to accomplish the task. The stone wall had too much mass. The minute I set that large cast-stone

FIGURE 4.6 There is no simpler way to bring still water into the garden than with a bowl-shaped boulder, large rock, or cast-stone bowl. Even such a small pool captures reflections of the sky and gives you water on which to float flowers such as peonies, roses or daisies.

birdbath into the center of the hosta planting, the corner garden felt anchored. The birdbath provided the white-blooming hosta bed with a center so that it looked at rest. Floating brick-red helenium blooms from the perennial border across the lawn path completed the picture.

And needless to say, maintenance of a birdbath or basin is simple indeed. Every week the water needs changing and topping up from a hose. Each spring a bit of scrubbing with a stout brush keeps the bowl of the basin clean. The most time-consuming task, however, has to do with those ceramic birds I perch on the edge of the birdbath. Every day our three cats knock at least two or three birds off the edge.

FORMAL STONE-EDGED POOLS

POOLS, BOTH FORMAL AND INFORMAL, ARE ANOTHER WAY TO bring still, contained water into your garden. While the earliest pools were in naturalistic gardens in China and later in Japan, designers of subsequent European gardens, principally those in Italy and France, created

■ FIGURE 4.7 At Chevre d'Or in France, the designer used carved stone as a formal pool surround and pebble-embedded concrete as the pool liner. The elegance of this pool and its stonework is mirrored in the simple planting style of the surrounding garden. Notice that the pool is placed at the end of a long formal path.

geometrically shaped pools that were, and still are, edged with dressed stone. European garden designers often used flamboyant stone statuary at the end of geometric stone water rills (water channels) or within fountains to decorate their water features and gardens.

Freestanding formal pools are geometric: square, circular, rectangular, elliptical. These architectonic and usually shallow pools need to be set in open, sunny, flat spaces, such as in panels of crushed gravel or lawn, and edged in stone. Formal pools often have fountains in their centers or at their corners to show off the movement and sparkling nature of water. Formal pools can also be still, thereby defining water's ability to reflect light and images – trees and sky – near and far. The most fitting place for such a pool is near your home, set in relation to stairs, doorways, windows, or terraces. By setting the pool just outside east- or west-facing windows of your home, you might well enjoy the morning or afternoon light reflected off the shimmering surface of the pool and onto the nearby ceilings inside your home.

In one formal pool I designed in New Hampshire (see figure 4.9), the proportions, placement, and choice of coping material for the pool were

WATER

AND STONE

based on a nearby bluestone terrace off the south end of a Colonial home. Having centered the 6-foot-wide, 18-foot-long pool (a 1-to-3 proportion), aligning it with the middle of a set of 4-foot-wide bluestone steps down from the terrace, I edged it in 1-by-4-foot-long pieces of the same material. For animation, a central jet shoots water 4 feet above the surface, while angled jets at the four corners arc water toward it.

To keep the whole picture in proportion, lawn panels that are the same width as the pool surround it. The depth of the gardens on all four sides of the lawn were different, but that fact didn't unbalance the design, because the strong shape and form of the centrally located pool and its lawn surround dominated the picture. Gardens became background and were simply planted with hostas, ferns, *Anemone vitifolia* 'Robustissima', *Vinca minor* 'Bowles', and hollies, and low boxwood-edged surrounds for four lead urns in the corners. While the dimensions of this pool determine the lawn surround, you can set up many other proportional relationships. By using a scaled drawing ahead of time, you can play with all kinds of alternatives: making the lawn surround half the width of the pool or twice the width of the pool; extending the lawn at either end of the pool the full length of the pool to create a long, narrow garden.

Then comes the stone for the pool coping. By repeating bluestone in various ways, I satisfied one of the primary principles of good design: theme and variation. Bluestone was the theme. The various ways in which it was used within the one garden were the variations: for terrace and steps; for a landing at the bottom of the steps; for the pool coping; and for the bases on which sat the cast-stone pedestals for the lead urns.

If you're interested in installing a small formal pool, consider aligning the

FIGURE 4.8 (*opposite*) In our garden in Vermont, I covered an 18-inch-deep 18-foot-diameter concrete bowl – an old barn silo base – with 2 inches of sand and then laid down a rubber liner that also covered soil about 12 inches out from the rim of the pool. I then set stones that edge the pool and hide the liner. Having covered the rubber liner with pebbles, I set a 150-year-old marble well-head on four 6-inch-high stones in the center of the pool. Under the central hole I set a small pump to create a plashing fountain.

FIGURE 4.9 The bluestone patio and arbor at the south end of this New Hampshire home existed when the owner asked me to design a formal pool garden in what was featureless lawn. Bluestone was my unifier; as coping for the reflecting pool; as the base for the two benches; as the base for four large terra-cotta pots planted with boxwood; and as the base for the cast stone sculpture to the right. The width of the existing bluestone terrace determined the width of the lawn. The steps down from the terrace determined the axis for the pool and sculpture.

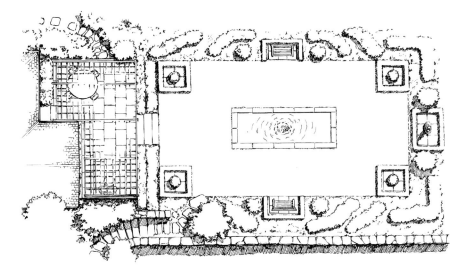

WATER
AND STONE

length of a rectangular pool with the center of steps that come down from a terrace. Set a circular pool at the junction of four paths in a formal herb garden or at the center of a minimalist boxwood-hedged garden on line with the dining room window. Set a square pool in the central lawn of a square enclosed garden off one wing of the house. By lining up formal pools with the lines of your nearby house, you establish a clear relationship between the two. But always be certain that the pool dimensions (the positive space) are in proportion with the dimensions of the lawn or gravel surrounding it (the negative space). To help determine the size of a formal pool near your house, consult the proportions of a door, window, or wall of the house with which a formal pool is associated for clues as to what might work well.

To design and install a fine formal pool is not a simple matter and is best left to professionals, and regular maintenance is crucial. In general, formal pools are made of concrete or mortared stone, and these materials have to be installed simultaneously with electrical lines, water lines, valves, pumps, and lighting. Because the water has to stay clear all the time or the effect is lost, a filtering and skimming system is necessary to keep the surface clean. But once up and running, nothing is quite so elegant as a formal stone-edged pool, with a single jet coming from its center, surrounded by a well-maintained panel of lawn.

Your gardening style around a formal pool should reflect the formal nature of the pool and its fine lawn or gravel surround. Symmetrically placed hedges, garden ornaments, benches and chairs, perhaps a small gazebo at the far end of the pool with a pair of trees either side would all support the formal shape and mood of the pool.

NATURALISTIC POOLS

N ATURALISTIC POOLS ARE A COMPLETELY DIFFERENT MATTER. Whereas formal pools are geometric, elegant, and European in inspiration, informal pools are free-form, in natural settings at a distance from the house, and were originally inspired by gardens of the Far East. The Chinese have been using stone and water in their garden pools and ponds for 5,000 years; in fact, they constructed their very word for landscape – *sanshui* – out of two characters, one for mountains, the other for water. For the past 2,000 years, Japanese garden masters have been combining these two fundamental elements of nature into their naturalistic and symbolic gardens, with rocks representing the male *yang*, water representing the female *yin*.

FIGURE 4.10 Small pools surrounded by large boulders feel permanent. The arching stems of the abelia and fountain grass link garden to pool. By repeating boulders near and at a distance from the pool, the designer establishes a sound relationship between garden and pool. To give a pool visual depth, place stones and even boulders below water level.

The other major difference is that informal lined pools are considerably less complex. You can build one yourself, and Chapter 10 will give you all the information you need. Informal pools are often set within a shady nook or corner in the garden, and they don't require such a high degree of maintenance. Nor do they demand water lines and filtering systems as do formal pools. A bit of algae in them won't ruin the effect, and if the water level drops, all you need to do is fill it back up with a hose.

Whereas stone around a formal pool is invariably geometric and flat to mirror the flat surface of the water, stones can be cast in many roles in and around an informal pool. On a practical level, rounded as well as flat natural stones hide the lining around the pool's edge and hold soil in place; on an aesthetic level, they set the pool into the landscape and give it a presence of natural simplicity, age, and solidity.

WATER

AND STONE

WATER-TOLERANT PLANTS NEAR SMALL POOLS

Plants both in or around water are a world unto themselves. Broadly, perennials are broken down into the four categories listed below. Within each of those are plants that will flourish in varying water depths and in different types of soils and growing mediums. It is not possible to fully address such a complex world in this book. While the lists below represent some of the most beautiful plants appropriate for small ponds, you will want to research further.

Zone information is included to tell you which plants will overwinter in your area. All of these plants and myriad others, however, could be grown in submerged pots as annuals anywhere in the country. You can begin that research by turning to Appendix E of this book for sources of information on pool construction and plants.

Perennials for boggy soil:
Chelone lyonii – pink turtlehead
  Zones 4-8
Darmera peltata – umbrella plant
  Zones 5-8
Lobelia cardinalis – cardinal flower
  Zones 2-9
Onoclea sensibilis – sensitive fern
  Zones 4-9

Perennials for the edge of the pool, where the crowns of the plants would be submerged:
Caltha palustris – the marsh
  marigold – Zones 4-9
Hymenocallis liriosme – spider lily
  Zones 8-10
Iris kaempferi – Japanese iris
  Zones 2-8
Iris pseudacorus – yellow flag iris
  Zones 4-9
Lysichiton americanus – skunk
  cabbage – Zones 4-6

Nymphoides cristata – white
  snowflake – Zones 8-11
Pontederia cordata – pickerel weed
  Zones 3-10
Sagittaria latifolia – arrowhead
  Zones 5-10

Perennials wholly submerged but with floating leaves:
Aponogeton distachyuos – water
  hawthorn – Zones 3-10
Marsilea drummondii – water clover
  Zones 6-10
Nymphaea – the water lilies
  Zones 3-10

Aquatic perennials for oxygenating:
Egeria densa – Elodea – Zones 8-10
Hottonia palustris – water violet
  Zones 6-8
Hydrocharis morsus-ranae – frog's-bit
  Zones 4-7
Ranunculus aquatilis – water crowfoot
  Zones 5-8
Stratiotes aloides – water soldier
  Zones 5-8

■ Siting the Naturalistic Pool

Siting a naturalistic pool is, in many ways, much more subtle than siting a geometric pool. Whereas the formal pool is frankly designed, architectonic, and a major focus of attention from the house, the naturalistic pool settles into the existing natural world. It should be a surprise you come upon. It must look convincing and right in its site, or no amount of planting and boulders will make it settle in.

Water has certain intrinsic properties that you have to respect in the design and siting for a naturalistic pool (and associated waterfalls). First and foremost, water runs downhill and naturally collects in depressions and low

■ FIGURE 4.11 (*opposite*) When using large stones, choose a variety of shapes, and lay them in a variety of ways: flat, sloping, mounding. Some of the boulders slope right into the depth of the pool.

spots. Second, any pool needs to be in proportion to the place where it is sited. Place a small pool out in the midst of a big lawn, and it will look insignificant and trite. Place it in the corner or curve of a stone wall, as part of an already-existing intimate, natural garden, or near the base of a rock outcropping or gathering of boulders, and you will create a harmonious relationship between the pool and its surroundings. A naturalistic pool needs a natural context so that it feels settled and right for that particular site. The overhanging branches of trees or shrubs, combined with boulders and smaller rocks, can provide that context. But if you want to set a naturalistic pool in full sun, boulders, perhaps bedrock, and other stony anchors can help create context and the right placement.

If you set a pool in a shady spot, you simply have to treat it differently from one in sun. It is a bit harder to maintain, primarily because of falling leaves and debris. Our 18-foot-diameter boulder-rimmed pool (see figure 4.8) is situated under the branches of a young cork tree *(Phellodendron amurense),* so every autumn I have to spend a good deal of time getting leaves out of the water and from between the rocks. To discourage algae buildup in a shady pool, I turn on a small pump in the center of the pool three or four times a week for several hours to oxygenate the water and keep it clear. Even so, in hot July and early August, long strings of algae form but can simply be raked out, usually twice during that six-week period. Shade does have its advantages, though. The water stays cooler, discouraging the buildup of algae, and evaporation is slowed. Depending on the season, I run a hose to the pool to bring its surface up to the right level only five or six times from April until October; if you live in a hotter climate, the frequency of hauling out the hose will clearly be greater.

Another clue as to where you might site a natural pool – either in sun or shade – is the stone on your property. Snuggling a small natural pool into the curve or corner of bedrock or next to, or even within, a group of existing or planted boulders would both look right. Set a pool at the base of, or even in the terrace just behind, a retaining wall, or within the curve of a stepping-stone or stone-carpet path, or among widely spaced trees at the edge of (or within a clearing in) woodland.

One of the most important things to keep in mind when positioning stones around a pool is that a few large stones and boulders look far more satisfying and right than do hundreds of smaller stones. So many home pool builders use stone so poorly: mismatched bits of stone here and there; some moss; a bit of slate next to a granite rock – and all of it disjointed and unsatisfying. Rocks should appear in groups of varying sizes around a pool, just as they would in nature. And one large stone should form the visual core of the stone layout. This is where the insight you gained while studying nature at the side of a stream becomes so important.

▦ Grouping Rocks at a Pool's Edge

To make a coherent grouping of rocks around and within a pool that feels right for your area, choose one type and color of indigenous rounded river rock and boulder and stick with it – introduce too many types and colors of stones, and the overall design collapses into busyness. Once you've selected a single type, choose the main position from which the pools and rocks will be seen: a bench, a sitting boulder set at the edge of the path, a gazebo. Make your aesthetic decisions regarding the layout of rocks with this key vantage point in mind. If you are able to walk all around the pool, keep other views and vantage points in mind as well, but hold on to that main one to help you organize your thoughts. Make your practical decisions based on the need to cover all the black rubber liner, especially at the water's edge.

In nature, rounded river rocks on the side of a small pool would normally be found scattered in groups of varying sizes, smaller ones resting atop larger ones, some submerged completely, others partway, and still others fully out of the water.

▦ FIGURE 4.13 Small rounded river rocks combined with flatter and larger stones create a pleasing contrast for the surround of this concrete pool. The massed planting of liriope produces a tranquil atmosphere. The bedrock in the background further enhances this feeling of calm.

WATER

AND STONE

On the other hand, if you want to create the illusion that the rocks around your pool are part of bedrock or outcroppings, then choose only large rocks that give the impression of bedrock. Set them so that the grain of each runs parallel to one another, and set them deeply into soil; you'll see the grain on the surface of the rocks in the form of parallel lines. Always bury at least one-third of the bulk of stones that go into making faux bedrock in the soil. The result, quite contrary to your expectations, is that they will appear larger than they might actually be because, since you cannot tell what the full dimensions of the rock are, your imagination goes to work.

Here is an alternative to the naturalistic pool – one that I designed with no water in it, so it could well be a model for those of you who have young children. Clients in the Berkshires in western Massachusetts asked me to design a naturalistic pool and boulder grouping that would have no water in it but would look as if it did; they didn't want the maintenance headaches in their weekend home. It was going to be set in the island in their driveway. With two helpers and a man named Steve – who operated a massive excavator with such finesse that he could have served us lunch on a platter with it – we set boulders to create a faux pool. First we set two 9-foot-long, 3-foot-wide boulders 3 feet into the ground and on end to form the focus of the roughly 18-foot-diameter garden. I then placed a mounding boulder next to the two uprights by way of contrast, and then a 12-foot-long, 28-inch-square rock set horizontally as a picnic rock for the grandchildren. We then set three more mounding and long boulders to create an approximately 10-foot-wide absolutely flat area within these boulders. We backfilled the entire area with topsoil, including the area between the two upright boulders. I then planted 45 *Sedum spurium* 'John Creech', a 2-inch-high groundcover, to mimic water flowing out between the two upright boulders and then flowing down to gather in the flat area among the boulders. I planted other mounding areas of topsoil with deciduous azaleas, mountain laurel, maidenhair fern transplants, and European ginger. My clients then set two 48-inch-high metal sculptures of standing birds – actually cranes —within the faux pool.

To set this dramatic and sculptural set of boulders and plants into the larger landscape, we then placed upright and mounding stones at the entrance of the path to the front door. We also positioned a grouping within a mass of *Pieris japonica* 'Mountain Fire' under a hemlock tree, at the entrance to the driveway, next to a river birch on the corner of the driveway, and 100 yards farther along the drive under an oak to create a theme of boulders along its entire length. The result was to pull the entire garden together through boulders and to create a faux pool in the process. The project took us eight hours, and the result was simple and serene. But it was also safe. This approach to creating a faux pool might be a way for you to build the framework for a later actual pool, once your children are older.

▦ Planting a Naturalistic Pool

When thinking about the overall look and feel of a small pool with rocks and plants in and around it, keep in mind that one of the characteristics of water is its perfect horizontality. Contrast that horizontal surface with vertical plants: irises, rushes, tall ferns, ornamental grasses, rodgersias, and ligularias, and many other verticals that naturally grow in moist soil. Another classic way to plant a pool's edge is to use arching plants, the stems of which rise and then arch back down toward the water, such as *Chasmanthium latifolia* and pennisetum grasses.

Plant in natural-looking masses and drifts of at least three to five or even more. But don't plant one of this and one of that, here and there and everywhere around a pool, because the result is a busy planting, one that will run contrary to the peaceful nature of still water. Keep it simple, just as nature does. And, with water, big is beautiful: large water surfaces reflect more light; you have increased planting opportunities inside and around the pool; large pools react more slowly to temperature fluctuation; and they cope better with decaying leaves and detritus.

Privacy and a sense of being in a separate part of the garden is also important around a naturalistic pool. To screen our little pool from the driveway and nearby dirt road, and to provide a backdrop for the pool, we planted a hedge of seven Miss Kim lilacs on one side of the pool and an arbor vitae hedge (*Thuja occidentalits* 'Smaragd') along a second side. We created a context for the pool by setting it in the corner of the two hedges and under the branches of the cork tree. We also surrounded the pool with mossy rocks and one-man boulders.

I then massed *Hosta* 'Betcher Blue' between the dark green arbor vitae hedge and the pool for its contrasting silver-blue foliage, and then, in turn, contrasted it with massed crimson-red *Astilbe* 'Fanal' and 'Professor Van der Weilen'. A groundcover of *Phlox stolonifera* 'Blue Ridge' encircles the base of both the large standing stone near the pool and several *Fothergilla gardenii*. As a vertical accent near the pool, I planted single divisions of the arching *Chasmanthium latifolium* among the rocks that edge the pool. I then set out 25 divisions of European ginger, with its shiny green leaves among the gray and mossy rocks. These simple, unself-conscious plants set out in naturalistic ways, help settle the pool into the natural landscape.

▦ FIGURE 4.15 If you have a drainage problem in your lawn, this decorative solution might be a good model. A liner was set into a trench in the lawn, edged with wood, and then river rocks were placed within the trench to carry off excess seasonal water.

WATER

AND STONE

■ FIGURE 4.16 A rubber liner was laid down with its outer edges coming up at least a foot above the bottom of the stream. Rounded river rocks were then used to form the base as well as the sides of this stream. *Lavandula angustifolia, Helictotrichon sempervirens* and *Oenothera speciosa,* among other woody and herbaceous plants, were then set out between the rocks to knit garden and stream together.

STREAMS

Formal Channels and Rills

Streams, which emphasize the flowing nature of water, can also be formal or informal. The oldest formal streams were in ancient Persian gardens. The typical Islamic garden was walled and divided by four straight stone-lined water channels to produce a *chakar bagh,* a four-quadrant garden, with a circular or square pool at the confluence of the four channels. This form of garden is mentioned in the Koran, where paradise is likened to a garden symbolically divided by the four Rivers of Life. Such straight rills are very much a part of formal garden design today. Marble or granite-lined rills direct water to pools and fountains, all of which are clearly associated with doors or windows leading into the house.

In one particularly beautiful example I saw, designed by landscape architect Dan Kiley, a water rill 12 inches wide and lined with white cut stone ran parallel to a 6-foot-wide white marble path that was essentially an extension of the long central corridor of a home overlooking Los Angeles. Kiley designed the marble path and rill to run side by side some 90 feet out from the house until the rill swooped in an arc at the far end to form a semicircular pool with a 6 foot radius at the end of the path. Nearby stone walls ran parallel to the path and rill, but were set back to allow for gardens. A bronze female nude stood within the center of the semicircular pool and was the focus and destination of both the path and the stone-lined rill.

As with any formal pool, this entire setup was professionally designed and installed. Pumps switched on just inside the sitting room keep the water flowing down the rill to the pool and back again through hidden pipes; another pump keeps the fountain alive behind the sculpture; filters keep the water clean. Periodic maintenance keeps the rill clean and white; float valves keep the water level right. This is no simple project, but what a look!

Informal Streams

When thinking about working with a professional to design a formal rill or an informal natural stream, look again to nature for inspiration. Natural boulder-edged streams introduce the movement of water, which draws people to the water's edge, helping you to find places for paths along the stream. As water moves, it catches light, and therefore your eye, in all kinds of ways. Moving water also produces sound, and when disappearing from sight around a corner or under a stone bridge, it introduces mystery.

■ FIGURE 4.17 Rough volcanic rock is used in this garden in the Pacific Northwest to retain the edges of the stream and the edges of steps, as well as hold the bank in the upper part of the garden. Once the stream was in place and working well, the designer planted sedums, a cut-leaf maple, cotoneaster, and *Selaginella kraussiana* (the mosslike groundcover) within the gaps in the rocks to complete this pleasing garden that can be seen from up near the house and from down below.

■ Stepping-Stones Through Streams

Too often on properties where streams already exist, water becomes a barrier. I have seen so many beautiful gardens planted along both banks of streams, but I couldn't get to or over the water. Stepping-stones set into a shallow stream or a stone bridge over deeper running water invite you to walk across a stream or to dangle your toes or run your fingers through it.

Stepping-stones through a shallow stream can even have a formal touch. The designers of a bridge at Sezincote, a spectacular 18th-century garden in the Cotswold Hills in England, set eight 18-inch-square limestone blocks at regular intervals just above the water's surface and under the bridge, allowing visitors to walk from one side of the stream and under the bridge to the gardens on the stream's far side. You could do the same under any bridge that has sufficient headroom.

Or in a small stream through woodland, perhaps, at the back of your house, simply set large stones or even rearrange existing boulders firmly into the streambed to allow people to walk safely, and perhaps even sit, on stones as they make their way across the water. Setting pairs of boulders and just a few stepping-stones between them to mark both entrances to this path to, through, and beyond the stream will send a clear signal that there is more to see on the other side of the stream. One place to site such a set of stepping-stones is just downriver from a waterfall, from which your guests would be able to look straight into falling water.

■ FIGURE 4.18 In this Japanese-style garden, heavy stepping stones, which could withstand strong spring runoffs, have been set down through a sloping garden and across a shallow stream, enabling visitors to walk over running water. Note that the steps wind down and between a boulder and a tree trunk before leading over stones set in water. Every stone element of a garden needs a context.

FIGURE 4.19 At the Highberg
Garden in Vermont, the designer
lined a hillside with a 45-mil rubber
liner, allowing her to lay large
boulders and rocks, as well as
crushed stone, down a slope to
create a series of waterfalls that
end in a pool.

Waterfalls

The character of a waterfall is determined by the edge over which it spills.
Water flowing over a wide stone will produce a fine, broad sheet of water.
The more that wide stone juts out from its base, the more effectively the area
under the stone acts as a sound chamber, amplifying the sound of the water
as it falls into the pool below. By contrast, water flowing over a flat stone set
in a narrow passage between two stones will create a dense column of water
that will create a deeper, more robust sound than if it were falling in a thin

■ FIGURE 4.20 Water flowing over rocks can get lost among the spaces between the rocks. By creating a series of waterfalls, so that the water falls from one specific rock to another, the sight and sound of the water is featured.

WATER
AND STONE

113

■ FIGURE 4.21 At The Japanese Garden in Portland, Oregon, you can understand the logic of placing boulders and large rocks along a waterfall or stream. Over time, the action of the water would wash away soil, sand, gravel, and even smaller rocks, leaving behind only the large, immovable rocks. To make a series of waterfalls convincing, then, they need to fall between or on boulders and large stones.

STONE

IN THE

GARDEN

sheet. The longer the drop from the lip of the fall to the pool below, the louder the sound. The more rocks you place at the bottom of the waterfall – whether you mound up several river rocks or lay out one big flat stone – the more splashy the sound will be.

If you have a stream on your property, you can easily create your own waterfall by taking advantage of the way water moves over and around stone. Align a few stones across your streambed to create a dam a foot or so high, thereby increasing the volume of sound the stream makes. To channel water more tightly toward the center of the stream, use higher stones at the two ends of your dam and chink them with smaller stones. As you move toward the center, set medium-size stones slightly lower in the water and then, in the middle, place many smaller stones with two long flat stones on top for the water to rush over.

If you don't have a stream but you do have a sloping area, you might consider consulting with a garden designer regarding how you might take advantage of that slope to create a stream and waterfall. By having water flow from the top of the slope and over a waterfall and then pool at the bottom of the slope, you create a water feature that is set into a context. By planting trees and placing boulders and stone around the perimeter of the pool, you set the whole picture into a context. But as I mentioned above, hire a professional to help you develop the concept and see it through to completion.

IN SUMMARY

WATER HAS A MIND OF ITS OWN, BUT THAT NEED NOT deter you from creating a water feature in your own garden. You just have to find your own level of comfort as you combine stone and water in your garden. Start simple, with water in a basin or a small fountain, and as you gain confidence, graduate to a small pond, the construction of which is wholly feasible if you follow the sequence in Chapter 10. Water is the soul of the garden; find a way to bring it and stone together in the garden, and you will introduce an entirely new dimension to your garden.

■ FIGURE 4.22 (*above*) In the Asticou Azalea Garden in Northeast Harbor, Maine, a great slab of granite acts as a bridge across a small stream. Boulders large and small set this bridge into the landscape. Boulders also tie the bridge to the water, and the garden to the bridge.

■ FIGURE 4.23 (*left*) Wood is a classic bridge material, but it can appear light and without substance if not accompanied at either end by boulders. In this garden, the narrow cedar boards used to make the bridge look elegant and refined, yet in concert with the massive boulders assure you that the span will support your weight.

WATER
AND STONE

115

CHAPTER FIVE

STANDING STONES AND BENCHES

Somewhere in every

garden there must

be at least one spot,

a quiet garden seat,

in which a person –

or two people –

can reach inside

themselves and be in

touch with nothing

else but nature.

Christopher Alexander
The Pattern Language (1977)

AS YOU EXPLORE THE MANY TYPES OF STONES AVAILABLE IN stone yards today, you'll eventually come upon dramatic 4-to-6-foot-long stones (or even longer) that are broad, narrow, or columnar. These impressive stones can be used either vertically in the garden as standing stones or horizontally for benches.

For millennia, man has been setting long stones on end to mark spiritual places or burial sites of great importance to ancient peoples, and they were often associated with the supernatural, with folk legends, or, as modern research is suggesting, with astronomy. The stele, for example, is an ancient upright stone slab or pillar, oftentimes engraved, inscribed, or painted, that was religious in nature; they have been found in such diverse ruins as those of Greek, Chinese, and Mexican civilizations.

The first use of carved, representational standing stones in gardens likely took place in ancient Greece in the form of the herm. Named for Hermes, the messenger of the gods and protector of boundaries and entrances, the herm is a human-scaled statue composed of a head and shoulders, often those of Hermes himself, atop a quadrangular pillar that represents the stylized torso and legs. Sometimes, the toes protrude from the base of the pillar. It was first placed at the doors of houses or tombs and later in gardens.

Standing stones are anthropomorphic. They have a power all their own, one that needs to be acknowledged in the garden or setting in which they are placed: in woodland, desert, prairie, rocky mountains, or other strong natural sites. Imposing standing stones need to rise up out of simple horizontal surfaces so that their verticality predominates. Big upright stones benefit from big vertical surroundings. The landscape architect Beatrix Farrand acknowledged this when she set an 8-foot-high standing stone at the end of a 200-foot-long gravel path through a spruce forest in her garden for the late

■ FIGURE 5.1 Two thick stones can form a simple bench: one horizontal
stone atop another, paved in front with a stone of a similar color,
backed by garden plants.

Abby Aldrich Rockefeller near the coast of Maine. Farrand set the black upright stone at the edge of a steep slope in a mature woodland, trees that reflected the stone's verticality. From that stone rising up out of a level area of moss and gravel, one looks out over miles of hilly woodland; the stone epitomizes the spirituality of the site while at the same time establishing a destination for the path and a visual center there in the wilderness.

In many ways, stone sculptures act like standing stones because, whether figurative or abstract, they stand alone, upright, commanding the atmosphere of the garden in which they stand. Stone sculptures are a powerful presence in the garden, but because they take on a limitless range of shapes and sizes, forms and purposes, they can introduce a wide range of emotions into the garden.

Whereas native and mossy standing stones produce awe and mystery, stone sculpture can take a garden in all kinds of directions. Some can be humorous and lighthearted; others can be somber and dark, elegant or wild, familiar or challenging. Hannah Peschar is a gallery owner who displays the work of European sculptors in her landscape architect husband Anthony Paul's garden in Ockley, Surrey, south of London. She set a perfectly executed 5-foot-high pyramid made up of hundreds and hundreds of tightly fitted thin vertical black slates on a 15-foot-long peninsula in a pond so that the black pyramid could be seen against the backdrop of the silvery water. It was an impressive, mysterious presence there in the woods, at the edge of the pond. On the other hand, if you have visited Rosemary Verey's garden in Gloucestershire, you have seen 4-foot-high male and female carved-stone figures on either side of the gateway that leads from the main ornamental garden to the potager across a farm track. These Simon Verity sculptures are of a young man and woman, each holding a basket of flowers; Verity set the heads of these two figures at such odd and unexpected angles that they dispel all sentimental associations and become fresh, compelling images.

At the other end of the spectrum of standing stones are more familiar antique and frankly practical granite fenceposts that were once used for tethering horses, outlining a village common, or, with attached swags of rusty chain, forming the edges of an entrance garden to the front door of a Colonial home. These standing stones are useful in marking entrances; a 4-foot-high pair frames the beginning of a path through our *Viburnum prunifolium* hedge and on into the herb garden. I have also set them every 8 feet down the center of a 50-foot-long perennial garden or to mark the beginning of a path to the front door of clients' homes.

Long stones can also be used for benches. Sometimes the bench is polished granite; other times it is carved marble. Sometimes a bench is simple

SACRED STONES

CHINESE GARDENS OF THE SECOND
century B.C. were very much an
extension of landscape painting and, as
such, were designed as stylized interpre-
tations of the natural landscape. Most
important within the very early – as
well as contemporary – gardens are the
upright and eroded limestone rocks.
In Sun Yat Sen, a recently constructed
Chinese garden in British Columbia,
upright boulders are set in a traditional
way, dramatically on end, and not
obscured in any way by plants. The nearby garden pavilion provides shelter and
sitting places from which to contemplate
the mysteries of these stones and the
spiritual power and mystique of the
mountains they symbolize. The water-
eroded stones that emporer Hui Tsung
(1100-1125) had installed in his gardens
were excavated from the bottom of Lake
Tai Hu near what is now the city of
Suzhou. They look very much like the
stones used here in this Vancouver
garden. The Chinese believe these rocks,
often displayed against white stucco
walls, hold a sacred energy within the
hollows and perforations of the rocks.
The ribs and striations of the stones acted
as the conduits to bring that energy into
the garden and thus to the owners.

SYMBOLIC STONES

DESIGNERS OF THE EARLIEST Japanese gardens in seventh century A.D. took their initial cue from Chinese gardens wherein limestone boulders were set on end as the focal point of their gardens. But after only a few centuries the Japanese began to develop their own style, one embodied in this image from the Portland, Oregon Japanese Garden. Here the moss-covered standing stone, combined with smooth granite and gneiss boulders singly or in small groups in other parts of the garden, is used to underpin a controlled but natural look to the garden, one that was meant to relate to naturally occurring landscapes nearby. Stones visually tie all elements of a Japanese garden together, but they are above all symbols within a landscape: in a classic Japanese boulder triad, for example, horizontal stones symbolize earth, uprights symbolize heaven (as is the case here), and diagonals represent man.

The ways that stones inhabit Japanese gardens are myriad, and proscribed. Over the centuries, Japanese designers have been creating stylized and symbolic landscapes within ever more widely accepted principles of design, all of which are deeply rooted in the animist Shinto religion (and later in Buddhism) wherein all things on earth are possessed of a spirit. Stones are dramatically displayed in Chinese gardens; stones *inhabit* Japanese gardens.

slab limestone with no armrests, and other times the armrests are carved-limestone winged griffins. Landscape architect Patrick Chassé set a perfectly round cut-stone bench 12 feet in diameter with two gaps for access in a pine needle-mulched clearing in a garden at the tip of Soames Sound on the coast of Maine. One looks down on this perfect stone circle from the house and deck one story above it to marvel at the pure perfect geometry set within the wild Maine woods.

Like the standing stone, that bench and all stone benches will last for centuries, and therein lies part of their appeal. They may not be meant as a place to sit for a leisurely read – after 10 minutes, a stone bench feels pretty hard – but they add immeasurably to the lasting beauty in a garden.

STANDING STONES

▪ Large-scale Stones

To help you understand how standing stones can be used in modern North American gardens, I want to show you how I used one such stone in my garden, for the use of this one stone illustrates many of the principles that you need to learn before setting one in your garden.

Wanting to create a garden that would enhance a feeling of peace and introspection, I laid a stepping-stone path from the beginning of the area, right by an 18-foot-diameter pool set just slightly above ground level. The stepping-stone path wound through a shady garden and came out some 30 feet later onto the lawn. What was lacking was a feeling of entrance into this garden; neither end of the path was visible from a distance, so there was no obvious invitation to explore this part of the garden. It wasn't until André Bernier, a stonemason and friend, told me he had a long hefty stone for me that I realized a standing stone would be perfect for marking the entrance to this particular garden.

With the help of a backhoe and nylon straps, I set the 9-foot-long, roughly 18-inch-square stone on end 3 feet deep into the ground at the beginning of a stepping-stone path, which happened to coincide with one end of the 2-foot-high stone wall (see figure 4.8). Now when guests come to that part of the garden, they see this impressive deep brown upright stone and are drawn toward it. Once they arrive next to it, they see the beginning of the path as well as the stone-edged pond, in the center of which is a 4-foot-diameter marble wellhead. Water bubbles up out of a central hole in the stone and flows along its level surface to fall back into the pool.

▪ FIGURE 5.2 The sleeping lion in the gardens at Jenkyn Place in Hampshire, England, is a stone composite cast from the original in St. Mark's Square in Venice. Here the designer set the sculpture near the end of and between a pair of long yew hedges that are closed off just past the lion's pedestal. This refined, gentle sculpture is powerful, yet there is a vulnerability and peace about the lion's expression.

FIGURE 5.3 American garden designers have borrowed from Japanese traditions. In the Hall Garden in Maine, the designer has set a magnificent pair of standing stones in a spruce and birch wood and at the end of the woodland path. He then encouraged moss to grow throughout the surrounding forest floor, enhancing the calm feeling of this section of the garden.

The context we created for the standing stone in this garden picture has to do with pleasing contrast. A 6-foot vertical contrasts beautifully with the 2-foot-high horizontal stone wall, the horizontal stepping-stone path, the 12-inch-high mossy stone surround of the circular pool, and, of course, the absolutely horizontal water.

The dark brown pumicy look and feel of the upright stone also stands in pleasing contrast with the weathered white marble wellhead at the center of the pool. The small fountain of water that mounds up out of the wellhead adds the plashing sound of water, underpinning the introspective mood we wanted to create in the area. The cast-stone Buddha sitting on a flat mossy stone at the edge of the pool completes the picture of calm.

The designers of the Hall garden in Maine used a pair of stones to draw people into their garden as well. In their case, they set a pair of lichen-covered upright stones into native woodland and at the end of a straight cleared path. The stones, then, just as in our case, draw people toward the garden. The pair of upright stones, like ancient Greek steles, act as a destination for the path. The stones also infuse the woods with mystery. Even if you had only a small bit of woodland, this use for a standing stone or two might well add an entirely new dimension to your woodland garden.

■ Smaller Standing Stones

While large standing stones add drama and a profound mysterious presence in the garden, a wide variety of smaller standing stones can play strong visual and practical roles in the garden. These roles have immediate precedents in our American past: granite fenceposts as standing stones, as boundary markers, or as gateposts.

When first developing our garden here in Vermont, I was faced with the daunting task of clearing 1½ acres of disused farmyard before beginning our garden making. One of the benefits of that process was finding twelve 6-to-7-foot long granite fenceposts that had once been part of the farming operation as far back as the late 1700s. At the south end of our garden was a row of mature cherry, black locust, and maple trees that ran east-west along an old stone wall separating the garden from our 10-acre meadow. When I first planted this dry shade garden with ground-hugging perennials like *Phlox stolonifera*, *Phlox divaricata* and *Tiarella cordifolia* 'Slickrock', I found that the garden lacked structure. The stepping-stone path through it helped, but once the perennials were up and blooming, the path disappeared from view. The garden needed verticals.

That's when I got the idea to set our nine granite fenceposts irregularly

HOW THE BREWER BOYS' GRANDMOTHER MADE GRANITE FENCEPOSTS

Dᴀᴠɪᴅ Bʀᴇᴡᴇʀ's ꜰᴀᴍɪʟʏ has lived in Mendon, Massachusetts, on a 300-acre farm ever since the third trip of the Mayflower, and they still do. About 20 years ago, David moved to Putney, Vermont, and one day, when he was in our garden, he saw some of the 150-year-old granite fenceposts we had set upright in the woodland garden.

Whenever he and his father (and his grandfather before him) had the time down at their farm, they would load up the stoneboat with 6-to-7-foot-long blocky granite boulders left on the surface of their fields by retreating glaciers. With horses or a tractor, they would draw the stoneboat up to the shed near the house and unload the stone.

Throughout the year, Brewer's grandmother, Clarisse Southwick, would go out to the shed whenever she had the time and tap-tap away with a 3-pound sledgehammer and a small star-shaped drill. She was fashioning a line of 3-inch-deep holes 6 to 8 inches apart and about 6 inches in from the end of the granite to form a 6-foot-long, 6-inch-square fencepost. Each hole would take her about half an hour to make.

During the summer, she would fit metal feathers and wedges into all the holes and then tap each wedge equally down the line until the stone snapped straight. During the late fall, winter, and early spring, she would take an easier route to snapping the section off by filling each hole with water. At night, the water would freeze and expand and snap a long, narrow piece of granite off the boulder.

She would then repeat the process three more times to make the other three sides. Over the decades she made a lot of fenceposts. In 1990, she died at the age of 93.

■ FIGURE 5.4 The world of farming provides inspiration. Here granite fence posts combined with rusty chain swags provide structure along the length of this garden. The finely shaped uprights contrast beautifully with the indigenous granite stone wall in the background.

through the length of the 100-foot-long-by-30-foot-wide woodland garden. I set two on either side of the beginning of the stepping-stone path to mark its entrance, burying the 6-foot-long stones 2 feet deep; I set another near the far end of the path, where it led out onto a lawn path between perennial beds. I then set upright stones approximately 20 feet apart, at various points along the stepping-stone path. The result was that the upright stones created a spine, a lietmotif, a repeated form that helped hold the garden together visually. The two uprights on either side of the path entrance also sent a clear invitation to walk into, rather than past, the woodland garden; those two uprights became an important part of our overall garden itinerary.

▪ Stone Sculpture in the Garden

Representational carved-stone statues of people and animals, as well as carved-stone urns, all of which we place in our gardens today, can be traced back to the early Greeks. It wasn't until the 18th century, when the sons of the wealthy families of England were sent abroad, particularly in Italy, on the Grand Tour to study did fine Italian stone carvings begin to appear in the great English gardens of the day. While classic statuary should be limited to classic, formal gardens, we can find appropriate places for modern stone sculptures in our own modern gardens.

▪ Siting Stone Sculptures and Artifacts

Sculptures or stone artifacts should be integrated into their surroundings, not preside over them. Keep in mind where you will be when you first see the sculpture and what it will be like to come up to it. Background for sculptures is key to successful siting. A sculpture needs to contrast pleasingly with a uniform backdrop so that people see its lines and forms set against a dark green yew or arbor vitae hedge. People also should be able to walk around a sculpture to admire it for all 360 degrees.

When choosing a site for a sculpture, look throughout your garden for hedges, or for alcoves in which you could create hedges. Look for shrubby corners that have a uniform background. Place sculptures in a curve in or at the end of paths, or create simple backgrounds, as Anthony Paul did, by mulching with peastone under an elegant cutleaf Japanese maple and then set a sculpture under the tree and atop the peastone. View stone sculptures as magnets along your itinerary, using them to draw guests into the garden. Having arrived at your first sculpture, they will perhaps see a second or a gazebo or an entrance to a pathway, thereby drawing them yet farther.

STONE

IN THE

GARDEN

Also pay attention to how sunlight illuminates the sculpture at different
times of the day. For example, if you often visit a certain area of your garden
in the late afternoon or evening, set the sculpture so that it faces the setting
sun. Place a sculpture at the edge of woodland so that it is backlit by the setting (or rising) sun, or try various places in sun and shade to see how light
changes its nature. Take notice of the difference between front, back, and
side lighting. Front light tends to flatten depth, whereas back and side lighting create the illusion of greater depth.

If your sculpture is a figure, consider what the person is doing, and that
action will help you find the place where he or she belongs. For example, a
winged figure might be elevated on a slope above a path to be seen against
the sky. Place a figure of a woman holding a basket of flowers within the corner of a perennial border and in front of a massed planting of one particular
shrub or herbaceous perennial. A sculpture of a rustic person could appear

coming to the woodland edge, or a classical figure could mark the center or axis of a formal garden.

The piece itself will dictate where it wants to be. Having tried to set a serene, introspective black bust of a woman titled "Hero" by Patricia Volk in many places throughout our garden, we finally settled on a calm, shady place atop a stone wall. There she could underpin the calm nature of the spot, and placing her just a few inches above most people's eye level, we acknowledged the aloofness of her demeanor.

Gardens change with time. Trees and shrubs grow, and sculptures and artifacts can fall out of scale with the surrounding garden. As time passes, you may find it necessary to raise stone sculptures up onto pedestals or plinths or to move them into other sites in your garden where they will be in scale with their new surroundings.

Fine stone sculptures can act as the center, as a point around which all else revolves. They can also define mood and tone. If a stone sculpture has enough presence, it can override the mood of the garden within which it is found and thereby establish tone, just as our Patricia Volk sculpture does.

Perhaps the most subtle use to which I have seen stone sculpture put was in a woodland garden designed by Patrick Chassé on an island off the coast of Maine. The wooden home, for which Chassé had played a design role, was Japanese in style, with views through the spruces to the Gulf of Maine, a low horizontal profile, and wide overhanging roofs that covered a wraparound deck. From this deck, I stepped down onto a large stone block and then onto the first of perhaps 50 stepping-stones that wound me through existing spruces and introduced white birches. The ground was completely covered with hair-cap moss that Chassé had planted.

As I got farther and farther along the stepping-stone path, the steps got farther and farther apart. Sometimes a stone was missing, and the next step was onto a section of bedrock. Soon I was searching for the next stepping-stone and, it wasn't there. Now I was within an indigenous spruce forest punctuated by mossy outcroppings of bedrock. The stepping-stone path no longer existed and was replaced by an edgeless spruce-needle path. I felt absorbed by the forest. And then there, to my right, and set into a corner of a mossy granite outcropping, was a 200-year-old 24-inch-high granite Korean tomb figure. The same moss that was growing in great patches on the granite outcropping was also beginning to grow on the base of this tomb figure. The two were one.

FOUND STONE OBJECTS

ANTIQUE SHOPS, REGIONAL antique fairs, tag sales, and junk and secondhand shops are good places to find stone artifacts to decorate or build in a sense of humor in the garden. You might run into three or four old circular sharpening stones that you could use as stepping-stones through a narrow garden, or an old stone pedestal or birdbath that could be set into the corner of a garden or beginning of a path. Old stone plaques that you could attach to a wall of the garden shed are sometimes for sale too.

The key to this idea, though, is a creative eye. And don't worry about exactly what you will do with this old bit of stone. Just buy it. You'll always find a place for it somewhere in the garden.

STONE BENCHES

GARDEN BENCHES INVITE SITTING, CONTEMPLATION, AND relaxation while at the same time underpinning or establishing the tone of a garden in much the same way that standing stones and sculptures do. Stone benches draw you to them; they encourage sitting, reflecting, looking out onto a view highlighted by the position and angle and the bench. Two- or three-person benches can also form the focus of a garden. Place one under an arbor that looks out into the garden or in a niche in a hedge off the central axis of the garden or looking down the length of a lawn path between two perennial borders, and the bench becomes the main vantage point from which to appreciate that section of your garden.

◼ When Wood? When Stone?

Stone benches need to be used differently from more frequently used wooden ones. Stone is much harder than wood, and rarely are stone benches shaped, as wooden ones often are, to fit our bodies. While you can certainly provide

◼ FIGURE 5.6 A stone bench need be nothing more than two vertical chunks of granite supporting a third larger piece set across them. This simple one-person bench fits the simplicity as well as the scale of the garden in which it sits. It feels right being set between two trees with a perennial garden and hemlock hedge at its back. There is no stone base, only lawn, another mark of the informality of this bench.

cushions for stone benches, it is generally not appropriate to provide a stone bench for your guests in a place where they might enjoy sitting for long periods of time. Choose stone benches for those spots where you want people to alight for a few moments, especially when that spot is related to other existing stone features: a stone wall, boulders or bedrock, a stone sculpture.

In a small, simple garden, a stone bench for one or two people adds considerably to the charm and approachable quality of a garden. On the other hand, a fine carved- or cast-stone bench underpins elegance and formality in a refined parterre garden.

The other quality that stone has that wood does not possess to the same degree is visual as well as physical weight. There are times when you want to make a strong statement with a bench in a visually strong area of your garden: at the end of a long, straight, and broad lawn path between perennial borders; under mature trees from which you look out onto a grand view. Think of antique stone benches you may have sat on in England, France, or Italy that are set in similar sites. These benches make formal, strong, impressive statements that wood could simply not manage. Even simple polished granite benches have a feeling of visual and physical weight that wood could never match. So when considering whether to buy wood or stone, consider its aesthetic as well as practical role in the garden, and then choose the material and style accordingly.

◼ Roles and Sites for Garden Benches

Visitors to our 1½-acre garden often see benches in the garden and ask whether we ever have time to sit and enjoy a quiet moment. We often respond by saying that we sit down, see something that needs doing, and get up. That's partially true. We do sit, especially when guests come. But even if we rarely sat on a bench, that is no reason not to put one in. Benches suggest respite. They are calming and restful to the eye and body. We Americans oftentimes do not have enough places to sit in our gardens, so the idea of a stone bench is one that is particularly relevant to us.

One design element is true of all benches, no matter what their style, material, or size: people don't like to sit on a bench without some protection from the back. When you set a stone bench in the garden, place it against an existing stone wall or fence or just out from shrubs that will grow at least 5 to 6 feet high. Create a feeling of enclosure and protection from behind, and guests will frequent those benches far more than they will ones that stand separate and alone, out on the lawn, for example.

◼ FIGURE 5.7 A simple stone bench in a meadow invites people to walk through an area they might not otherwise explore. A small tree planted at the back of this bench would make its placement feel cozier.

FIGURE 5.8 The context for benches is always important. Here the curving stone bench at Broughton Castle in Oxfordshire, England, is an extension of the adjoining stone wall. The bench is made of the same material as the wall, and the opening in the wall provides the cue as to the placement for the center of the bench.

Benches also direct your view. First, they attract people to those important areas of your garden where special views exist. Second, when they do sit down on a well-placed bench, their view is directed out into the distance or to some particular quality of the garden that deserves highlighting or that guests might otherwise overlook. Benches provide an opportunity to show people something important about your garden. I was helping a client on the eastern shore of Maryland with her garden, and one day we spent nearly 20 minutes looking for just the right place for a new bench she had purchased. We finally found the spot under the overarching branches of a pine tree, with the back of the bench close to its 24-inch-diameter trunk. We aligned the bench so that anyone sitting on it would look over a low woodland garden through high-pruned trunks of trees and across the surface of a beautifully planted pond to the stone terrace at the back of a house set among mature willow oaks. In 20 minutes of looking, we simply did not find a view to match it. In turn, when sitting on her stone terrace, she and her guests now see the bench set at the base of that pine some 150 feet away, and it acts as an invitation to that part of the garden.

In this way, too, benches define depth. If you see that stone bench 150 feet away, you roughly know its dimensions because you know how big most benches are. You therefore can perceive how far away that part of the garden is. The result is a clearer understanding of the garden and its dimensions.

I'll give you another, specific example. When people drive into our driveway and park, they can see across a section of lawn, over a low mounding rock garden, and between a pair of high-pruned maple trees to our 10-acre meadow. Having planted three pin oaks in the meadow some 400 feet from where guests park their cars, I mowed a path that leads from the garden through a gap in a stone wall and across the flat meadow to the shady circle of mown grass under the pin oaks.

I then set a two-person bench under those three oaks, with the back of the bench near the trunk of one of the trees. Instantly I could see from the driveway, as well as from an infinite number of places in the garden, how far away that sitting area was. Before the bench went in, the only clue as to distance was the size of the oak trees or the length of the path. Neither was sufficient, because neither was of a recognizable scale. The bench was.

That same bench accomplishes a second and even more important goal; it invites people to walk from the garden out into the meadow. Even though a mown path was there before, few people would want to walk out into the meadow, regard the view for a few seconds, and then walk back into the garden. The bench offered respite, a shady place under the oaks to sit, and a comfortable spot from which to contemplate the beauty of a Vermont meadow and the distant hills.

▒ FIGURE 5.9 This curving bench is integrated into a section of curving stone wall so that its back is the retaining wall. The designer used the same type of stone to create the low retaining walls either side of the walkway as well as the back and sitting surface of the bench. This varied use of one material results in a quiet, unified image that does not draw undue attention to itself.

FIGURE 5.10 You can use stone as I did here to simplify the shape of gardens along the sometimes complex shapes of a house façade. Existing freestanding walls enclosing the rectangular entrance garden to the right gave me the idea for the larger stone-wall-enclosed garden on the left. The panel of lawn, with the retaining wall between it and the five-sided sunroom, provides a simple rectangle of green against which to look at the flowering perennials and shrubs at its perimeter. A set of steps and a fieldstone path under existing and planted birches and groundcovers provide access to and through the central shade garden. A fieldstone side path leads to a chair under birches. The bluestone coping around the pool with its central fountain, placed on line with the fieldstone path, is the center of attention. The semicircular mortared stone pad by the front door, as well as the two stone paths leading to it, sends a clear message as to the location of the main door into the house.

A stone bench looks especially well-placed when set near other stone elements in the garden. Place it near bedrock, boulders, in front of stone walls, or along paved walkways, and the stone bench is visually linked to other stone elements in the garden. Coherence results.

Finally, consider where to site the bench in light of its degree of formality. A beautifully carved stone bench or a fine cut-stone bench needs to be at the end of a formal path or at the side of a formal pattern garden so that it creates the destination and vantage point from which to view a garden. A small, informal bench should be set in a small informal setting: the corner of an informal perennial or shrub garden; under an apple tree out at the edge of the garden; at one end of a path through a vegetable garden.

Stone Pads

One thing to consider with stone benches is whether or not you also want to lay stone on the ground in front of the bench so that when you do sit on it, your feet can rest on stone slabs, not lawn or mulch. Small benches need small landings; big benches need big landings so that the whole picture stays in scale.

If you have a large cut- or polished-stone bench and you want it to be visible from a considerable distance, or if you want to place it in a formal setting, you can accomplish either of these goals with the choice of bench and the pad on which you set it. To increase the formality of a bench and its pad, set a refined cut-stone bench atop a panel of cut-stone rectangles and squares that are set tightly, one to the next, and then surrounded on three sides by garden. By choosing cut stone for bench and pad, you increase the visual weight of the bench and its landing, thereby increasing its power and its visibility from a distance. Once you have the pad and bench in place, be sure to plant along the back and sides of the bench and pad to settle the bench in the garden.

You can control the degree of formality of the stone pad on which any bench sits by the type of stone you use and the size of the gaps you leave between them. If you have an informal, roughly cut stone bench, set it on a pad of loosely laid fieldstones interplanted with moss. If you have one of either polished cut stone or ornate cast stone, create the pad out of tightly fitting cut stones, the most formal of paving materials. The nature of the bench and its degree of formality determine the type of pad you will set under it. In turn, the nature of the garden in which you set the bench will determine what bench style and material will help you underpin the mood and tone of that area of your garden.

IN SUMMARY

STANDING STONES AND BENCHES CAN HAVE A POWERFUL, ordering effect on gardens. They can form the destination of a path, the center of a garden, or they can mark the heart of a woodland. As I was writing this chapter, I found myself thinking often about a poem by Wallace Stevens (1879–1955), a poet and insurance executive in Hartford, Connecticut. One of his central themes was perception. This poem, one of the most influential for me as a garden designer, is about how a man-made object (a jar) placed in a previously unordered and wild landscape (a field in Tennessee) provides a visual center to which all parts of the visible world relate (no longer wild). See the jar as a standing stone in your garden, in your woodland, or in your field in Tennessee.

ANECDOTE OF THE JAR
by Wallace Stevens

I placed a jar in Tennessee,

And round it was, upon a hill.

It made the slovenly wilderness

Surround that hill.

The wilderness rose up to it,

And sprawled around,

   no longer wild,

The jar was round upon

   the ground

And tall and of a port in air.

It took dominion everywhere.

The jar was gray and bare.

It did not give of bird or bush,

Like nothing else in Tennessee.

PART TWO

WORKING

WITH STONE

IN THE

GARDEN

CHAPTER SIX

DRY-LAID WALLS

BUILDING A STONE WALL NEED NOT BE THE INTIMIDATING challenge that it could well appear to be. With an understanding of the information I've included in this chapter, you will be able to create a wall yourself; or if you choose to hire a professional, you will more fully understand his work. Before getting too far into planning, however, check local building codes; they may require you to get a permit for wall construction above a certain height.

In order to write this chapter, I turned to dry stone waller Dan Snow from southern Vermont. With several years of study in design at Pratt Institute in New York City, he went on to apprentice in Mexico, Italy, and Scotland, each of these apprenticeships being separated by several years of professional wall building in southern Vermont and New Hampshire. He has been practicing his craft for 23 years and is one of about five stone wall builders in America holding a certification from the Dry Stone Wallers Association of Great Britain. Following is the step-by-step sequence that Dan Snow and dry stone wallers like him follow when building either a free-standing or a retaining wall. It's a good sequence to follow.

DAN SNOW'S SEQUENCE

BEGIN BY LOOKING OVER YOUR WHOLE PROPERTY TO SEE WHETHER any stonework already exists on it, for one of the keys to good wall building is to make new walls look as though they have been there for a long time, thus creating a more coherent property. Then clarify in your own mind what roles those old walls play in your landscape (boundary marker, privacy, or separation or enclosure of spaces) and what purpose the news walls will have. Will you garden the level area behind the retaining wall, or will you use it as a play area for children? What shape will it be: straight or broadly curving? Will it have steps or a gateway in it? By answering these and other questions, you gain a broader understanding of the dimensions of the wall, its style, position, and shape.

My garden sweet

enclosed with

walles strong

The arbores and

ayles so pleasant

and so dulce.

At Snowshill Manor,
Gloucestershire, England

■ FIGURE 6.1 Homes need to be set on level ground so that they feel settled. Tasha Tudor had this retaining wall built to level the land that once sloped away from her home, thereby providing her with gardening space close at hand. The wall itself is a beautiful backdrop for perennial beds.

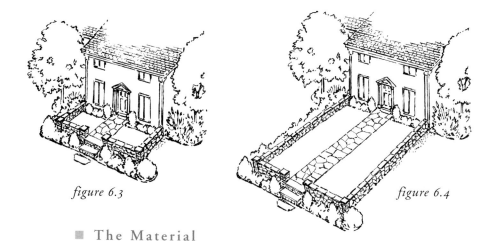

figure 6.2   figure 6.3   figure 6.4

■ FIGURES 6.2, 3, 4 The freestanding walls in these three illustrations come off the two corners of the house, so wall, garden and house relate. The question is how far out from the house should the garden and wall go. Figure 6.2 shows a garden that is as long as the front wall of the house is high, so the two share a common dimension. Figures 6.3 and 6.4 show poorly proportioned gardens.

■ FIGURE 6.5 If you measure the height of a house wall and then flop that dimension down onto the ground to determine the length of stone walls, you ensure a handsome proportion between garden and house.

figure 6.5

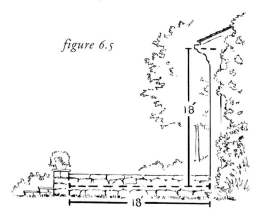

■ The Material

The next major question is where you will get the stone. Does it exist on your property, or will it have to be trucked in? If there is a source on your property, then consider what kind of wall you would build in light of those stones. For example, small jagged stones that come from decomposed ledge will enable you to create an adequate though rough wall, but it may lack the deep solidity or formality that would come from using much larger, blocky stones purchased from a supplier. Rounded smooth stones might be available from a nearby source but would clash with existing geometric fieldstone walls. Perhaps all existing walls on your place are made of flat stones, but there don't seem to be any left for new walls. Might there be a close match in a supplier's yard? Explore all the possibilities for stone choice with regard to walls already built on your land. If you don't have walls on your property or in the area, your choices are much wider.

■ The Design

Once you know where the wall will go, decide how tall and long it should be and what clues the house or other buildings nearby provide to answer that question. You also need to take into account large trees, underground utilities, septic systems, buried cable, or wet and poorly draining soil, for acknowledging each of these obstacles will help you zero in on the specifics of your wall. The better you understand your property, the clearer your understanding of the nature of your wall becomes and the more local the style can be. As Dan pointed out about a stone wall, "The more local its qualities, the more universal it becomes."

Once you understand the range of the wall-building styles and materials appropriate for your wall, go out into the space where you will build the wall and walk around the area, seeing it from a variety of angles. To help you visualize what the wall will look like, put stakes in the ground to show the beginning, corners, steps, and ends of the wall. Tie brightly colored twine or tape that can be seen from a distance from stake to stake to suggest height and width. If you're building a wall near your house, take the lines and proportions of the house into account.

Then step back and take in the bigger picture, from far and near, from inside and outside the house, to see if this new wall fits into the existing or planned landscape. How does your planned wall relate to the lines and proportions of existing stone walls, to the walls of your house and outbuildings, to the edges of existing or planned garden beds, and to distant horizon lines? By relating the lines between buildings, walls, and gardens, a coherent and settled landscape results. Reviewing Chapter 1 of this book will help with this process.

The Wall Base

Once you have designed the wall, you are ready to determine the nature and dimensions of the base for the wall. To do this, you need some background information. The weight of a wall is always trying to squeeze its foundation material out from under it. If the foundation can shift and move, it will. If a wall is built on water-absorptive material such as topsoil, for example, the soil will either freeze and thaw in cold climates or soak up water and then dry out in hotter climates, thereby expanding and shrinking constantly. Furthermore, when soil is wet, it becomes slippery and the wall has a much easier time squeezing out the soil below it. As soil under a wall shifts, so does the wall. That's nature.

■ FIGURE 6.6 Blocky stones set in an 18-inch-deep trench that is twice as wide as the top of the completed freestanding wall forms one of the most solid bases you could produce.

■ FIGURE 6.7 Rounded stones can also be set and chinked at the bottom of a 24-inch trench.

■ FIGURE 6.8 Excavate a 14-to-16-inch deep trench about 6 inches wider than the top of the completed wall. Backfill to within 6 inches of ground level with 1 1/2 inches crushed stone and then lay your large base stones atop the crushed stone.

■ FIGURE 6.9 If you are building on wet soil, set a 4- or 6-inch perforated PVC pipe in the crushed stones, with the holes down. Be certain the pipe is exposed at the end so the water can drain out and down a slope or low spot on your property.

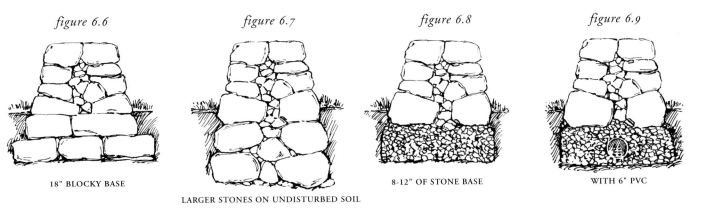

figure 6.6 *figure 6.7* *figure 6.8* *figure 6.9*

18" BLOCKY BASE   8-12" OF STONE BASE   WITH 6" PVC

LARGER STONES ON UNDISTURBED SOIL

There is a good deal of controversy among wall builders as to the appropriate base for a wall and how deep that base should be dug into the ground. Cautious wall builders in the colder regions of North America will come in with a backhoe and dig down 4 feet, then backfill the resulting trench with

DRY-LAID

WALLS

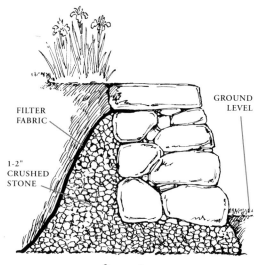

FILTER
FABRIC

GROUND
LEVEL

1-2"
CRUSHED
STONE

figure 6.10

1½-inch crushed stone. Others will pour a 6-inch concrete pad 1 foot below grade and build atop that. Others will dig from a 6-inch to a 24-inch-deep trench, backfill with some rubble or crushed stone, and lay stone atop that.

Dan Snow would argue that the soil you are building the wall on determines the depth to which the base should be laid, and it's a good commonsense attitude. Here's what he suggests: Take shovel in hand to see what kind of soil you'll be building a wall on, and you will find one of three types of soil. If your shovel turns up gravelly, well-draining soil or even the surface of a ledge or bedrock, just shovel away any organic matter on the surface and you're ready to start building your wall. If your shovel turns up quickly draining sandy soil, don't bother trenching and installing a crushed-stone base unless there is a danger of surface water running down a slope and along either side of the wall, thereby eroding sand and undermining the wall.

If your shovel turns up topsoil that has a lot of organic matter or clay in it, you are going to have to excavate down 12 to 18 inches to organically starved subsoil or gravel. When you put a crushed-stone base in clay soil, water will be attracted to the voids between those crushed stones, so, in a sense, you're making a drainage ditch under your wall. Given this fact, be certain that water has a place to run to. Extend the crushed-stone base of the wall either at the ends or somewhere along its length so that you send water away from the wall and downhill. You can also put a perforated PVC drainage pipe within the base and run that downhill through the existing topsoil to daylight.

If you require a crushed-stone base for your wall and you know how deep it has to be, you then need to determine its width. Here's a good rule of thumb: for every 1 foot of height, extend the base 1 inch beyond both the front and back of the wall. For example, if a wall is 2 feet high, extend the base 2 inches beyond both the front and back of the wall; if the wall is 3 feet high, extend the base 3 inches beyond front and back.

If you are going to build a new retaining wall, the banking must be cut back to a distance at least equal to half the height of the finished wall. If the material behind the wall is loose or liable to slumping, cut back farther and/or slope the face of the bank away from the wall.

■ Choosing Stone

If you have old walls, you might have a ready supply of the very best and most appropriate stone at hand. But keep two things in mind before breaking down old to build up new. First, in most parts of the country, it is against the law to remove a boundary wall between two adjacent properties.

Second, take your time to assess the merits and demerits of pulling apart an old wall. You'll be dismantling part of the history of your place; but then, that history may have deteriorated to nothing more than a pile of old stone just waiting to be used in a new wall.

If you don't have a supply at hand, go to a stone supplier or quarry. Before you do, refer to two other sections of this book for help. First, take a look at Chapter 11, The Geography of Stone. It has many close-up photographs of various types of stone as well as a series of questions to ask of the stone supplier. Second, look at Appendix A – "Sources of Stone in North America" – where you will find many names, addresses, phone numbers, and web sites of suppliers. Try your best to get as close a match as possible to indigenous stone.

■ Estimating Amount of Stone

Stone is sold by the cubic yard or ton. Because the amount of stone you'll need is determined by volume, not weight, you'll want to ask your stone supplier how many cubic yards (or cubic feet) of stone are in a ton of a specific stone. To determine the cubic yardage of the wall you intend to build, and therefore the amount of stone to order, multiply its length times its width times its height. For example, if you have a 20-foot wall that is 2 feet wide by 2 feet high, the cubic footage would be 20 x 2 x 2 = 80 cubic feet. Add 20 percent of that for waste and for the wider wall at the base, and you get a total of 96 cubic feet. To convert cubic feet to cubic yards, divide the total cubic footage by 27; in this case, you would need 3 cubic yards of stone to produce the 20-by-2-by-2 wall.

■ Dry-Laid or Wet-Laid?

There are pros and cons to both ways of constructing a wall. If you choose to create a wet-laid wall, hire a professional. Working with mortar is a world unto itself, filled with its own myriad variables. Most masons today who do make mortared stone walls construct them to look dry-laid. That is, they set the mortar back into the shadow of an overhanging stone to hide the mortar. The amount of mortar a mason places between and among the wall stones determines the look of the wall and the amount of time required to create the wall. (See Chapter 11 for photographs that illustrate this point clearly.) The less mortar he uses between stones – typically an inch or less – the more time he has to take to find just the right fit and the more refined the wall looks when completed. The more mortar he uses to fill large gaps, the less time spent looking for close-fitting stone and the more cemented the final walls looks.

■ FIGURE 6.11 In building a wet-laid wall in which concrete holds the core of the wall together, you can use two styles. As shown on the left, you can keep all the concrete within the wall, out of sight, or, as on the right, you can expose some of the concrete. The style on the left is called "wet-laid to look dry-laid."

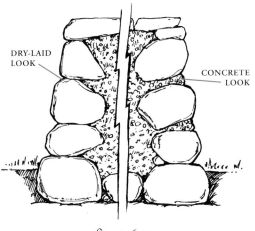

DRY-LAID LOOK

CONCRETE LOOK

figure 6.11

DRY-LAID

WALLS

The wet-laid wall is much more vulnerable to the effects of weather in general and water in particular, and herein lies the relatively temporary nature of a mortared wall. Its longevity depends on mortar, not on stone. Wind-driven rain can be wicked into and deeply saturate mortar. With a dry-laid wall, wind passes through the wall, constantly drying its interior.

Dry- and wet-laid walls alike settle as time passes, and both do so at different rates along their length, depending on the base material, drainage, and any number of variables. As a wet-laid wall settles, stones separate from mortar and gaps result. Water then gets into the gaps and accelerates the breakdown of the wall.

However, sections of dry-laid walls settle independent of one another without separating and, in doing so, do not rend the fabric of the wall except under the most disrupting of shifts in the soil under a wall.

▦ Gravity: the Waller's Greatest Ally

Before laying the wall, it is helpful to know about two elements that form the basis for wall work: gravity and the action of water. Let's look at gravity first.

It's the weight of the wall that causes one stone to grip another and therefore stay in place. Gravity is the most important and free tool the wall builder has, and it can reduce the amount of energy he has to expend. Take advantage of it however you can. For example, ask the stone deliveryman to dump the load of wall stone above your work if he feels that is possible so that you can bring the individual stones downhill to the wall. Rather than lift a stone, leave it on the ground and flip it end over end, directing the topple to where you need it when the stone is on end. Rolling, flipping, and spinning are all preferable to lifting. And with the help of gravity, sliding can be facilitated with metal or heavy PVC pipe or wooden rollers set on boards or plywood.

▦ Water: the Waller's Greatest Enemy

Once you set wall stones, you don't want them to go anywhere, but moving water can erode soil under stones and cause them to drop or shift. Water can also pull soil particles into a wall and then deposit them in a fine silt layer that fills in all the tiny voids between stones. When that silt gets wet and freezes, it expands, causing stones to shift ever so slightly. When water in the silt thaws, stones slide on the resulting slurry. To protect the integrity of your wall for many years, then, you need to be certain that undue amounts of water will not run through or along the base of your wall. You also need to be certain that the water collecting in the crushed-stone base has a way to drain out.

BEGINNING WORK

NOW THAT YOU HAVE MADE ALL THE NECESSARY DECISIONS regarding the design, you've made the base and chosen the type of stone, it's time to gather the stone. Be sure that if it is going to be delivered, you have it dumped and spread out as close to the work as possible. (Consult the first few paragraphs on Chapter 11 regarding preparing for a delivery of stone. We're talking about weight, lots of it, so plan ahead.)

Once the stone has arrived, your next decision is to have a plan for where you will *finish* the job. Think about building a wall the way you would think about painting your way out of a room. Knowing where you want to end up will help you know where to start. Begin at corners. It's easier to work away from a finished corner than toward one. And as you take stone from the stockpile, keep in mind that later on, you will need long flat stones for steps, heavy stones with right angles for corners, and broad, thick stones for the cap of the wall. Set them aside as you build the body of the wall.

Start by laying the largest stones in the base. You want to do this for three reasons. First, they're the heaviest stones you have, and it's easiest to simply roll them into the trench. Second, they form the soundest foundation for the

figure 6.12

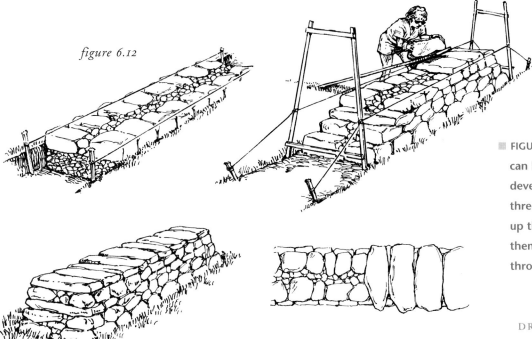

FIGURE 6.12 Strings and frames can help you keep the line as you develop your wall following the three steps: lay the base; build up the two wall faces, stabilizing them as you go with chinking and throughstones; lay the capstones.

DRY-LAID
WALLS

143

DAN SNOW ON THE BODY

My body is the most important tool I have. I need to stay aware of it throughout the day, especially near the end of the workday, when I'm getting tired. When I'm working with another person, one of my main jobs is to keep the other person safe. I focus on what the stone is doing in light of where the other person's hands and feet are. Accidents happen fast. Be vigilant and be ready to move quickly. As a professional, I want to be able to go to work the next day, so my guiding principle has been, "What do I have to do today to be able to come back to work tomorrow?"

■ **Hands and Gloves** It's a matter of choice. I wear out two pairs of leather gloves a week when I wear them. Although working with stone builds up calluses, it also wears those calluses away, leaving the skin of the palms thick but smooth. Wear gloves if you can find some that fit really well, but don't expect gloves to help you grip wet stones.

■ **Back** It is especially important not to twist when lifting a stone. When I twist while holding a weight, I weaken the structure of my spine by loading it unevenly. The goal, then, is to position my body so that the stone is right in front of me, and not to my side. If I have to lift and turn to the side, I lift the stone onto my upper thighs in a semi-squat, and then I pivot on the balls of my feet. There is an old French saying that I often recall when I'm not paying attention and make a mistake in lifting: "Pain is the craft entering the apprentice."

■ **The eyes** I wear safety glasses all day. They deflect flying stone chips and reduce the amount of dust that blows into my eyes.

▨ FIGURE 6.13 Two stout boards with 2-to-4-inch dowels as rollers can help you get a heavy stone up and onto the top of a wall, where it can then be flipped across the top of the completed wall and into its final position. This requires two people: one to push the stone, the other to move the last roller into the first position as the stone advances up the board ramp.

▨ FIGURE 6.14 An alternative to rollers is a 2-by-12-inch board used as a ramp up which one or two people can flip heavy stones to the top of the wall and then into place.

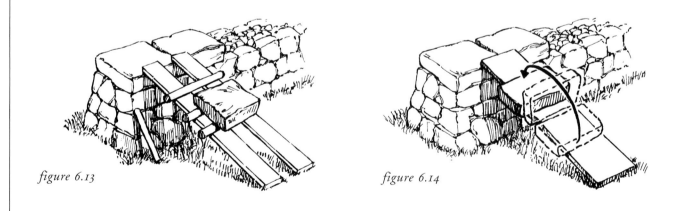

figure 6.13

figure 6.14

LEVEL	STEPPED	SLOPED

figure 6.15

subsequent courses. Third, the biggest stones low to the ground lend a look of stability to the wall, especially when burying at least 6 inches below ground level.

Once you have the base laid, bring both the front and back faces of the wall up at the same pace, filling in the center as you go. Start with the largest hearting pieces possible, placing them so as to fill in between the face stones. Use smaller pieces to pack the heart tightly. The back of a retaining wall is one exception; because it will be out of sight, it can be more roughly textured than the exposed face.

Dan Snow also stresses how important it is to continually develop a good surface on which to build the next course. That means that you are constantly hearting and building up level planes for the next stones. If you create that level base on which to set the next stones, rather than having all kinds of voids and big moundy stones and flat ones to build upon, wall building becomes an inviting process rather than a seemingly endless series of difficulties.

Have a large surface of wall under construction at any one time so that you can choose a stone and increase the likelihood that you will find an appropriate place for it. Oftentimes, beginning wall builders look only at one void and search and search for a stone for only that one space, thereby using up a lot of time. Pick stone for spaces, but at the same time, pick spaces for stone. Keep both options open simultaneously. And never use the laying surface as a storage shelf for unset stones. They will keep the eye from seeing all the possibilities.

Finally, take advantage of individual shapes of the stones and minimize the trimming and shaping you will have to do with hammers, which takes time and energy. As Dan Snow pointed out, "The job is not hitting stone; it's choosing stone." If you find amorphic and ungainly shaped stones, use them in the base or at the back of a retaining wall, where they won't be seen. Conversely, don't waste flat-faced or geometric stones at the back of the wall or as hearting. Use them right up front where they will be seen. Place a stone firmly on the wall, let go of it, and don't touch it again, period.

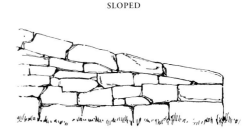

FIGURE 6.15 Freestanding and retaining walls can end in one of three ways: level, stepped, sloped.

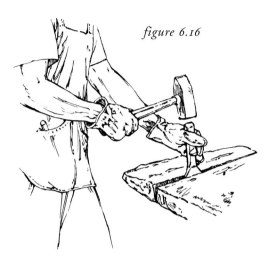

figure 6.16

If a large stone needs to be shaped and you know what it should look like to fit on the wall properly, it is smarter to trim the stone roughly in advance to reduce its weight; then, when the stone is close to its final position, do the fine shaping. An edge can be nibbled away in small pieces to create the desired finished edge, or you could trace the line by making small blows with the hammer along the desired break line, flipping the stone over, and doing the same on the opposite side. Continue this process back and forth until the surface tension has been weakened along the desired line. Then if that line is set up on another stone, a heavy blow can break off the waste.

Bedding is the process of setting the stones into place. The one rule that Dan Snow and other dry wallers insist upon is to set the stone's length into the wall, rather than parallel to its length. The best-looking end of the stone is oriented out to create the wall face. Set its tail, the end of the stone that will be buried in the wall, pointing toward the center. By setting the length of the stone into the wall, with its most level surface facing up, you knit interior and exterior, back and front, to create an interrelated whole, and you help form a flat base for the next course. Steady any rocking stones by trimming or shimming before moving on to the next choice.

Joints Most important is a homogenized construction, so that the face of the wall over its entire length acts and appears as a whole. And one rule that wallers always keep in mind is this: one stone need lie atop two; two stones need lie atop one. This rule is meant to assure the waller that all face stones are bonded together, with no weak seams created by long vertical joints. This is also true within the interior of the wall. The tail of stones coming from the A side need to lie atop the tail of stones coming from the B side; in that way, the interior of the wall is knit together. Finally, place the largest surface area of each stone within the wall: the more area, the more friction, and that means stronger gripping of one rock to another.

Batter is the angle or taper of the exterior face of the wall as it leans back ever so gradually toward the center of the wall as its height increases. This taper can be created by tilting the stones down toward the center of the wall, or each course can be set back just a bit so that over 4 feet of height, for example, the face of the wall recedes about 4 inches. This ensures that the balance of the wall is inward, and the weight of the wall is centralized. There's a lot of weight at the top of the wall, and if you get it leaning forward or even plumb vertical, it will collapse over time.

DAN SNOW ON TOOLS

TOO MANY TOOLS ARE A disadvantage. They get underfoot or get lost, and they distract from the subject, which is stone. By having a few carefully chosen tools at hand and using them creatively, I keep the job simple. I generally use two sizes of pry bars: a 3-foot pinch bar and a 16-inch pry bar that looks a bit like a large screwdriver. I think it's important to make lots of small pries, rather than one large movement that forces my body into vulnerable positions. I don't need longer pry bars, because I move large stones with heavy equipment. There is no need to make grand gestures when you only need to use a lot of 1-inch lifts with a pinch bar and a properly placed fulcrum.

The other tools I always have with me are two different sizes of mash hammers that look a bit like wood-splitting mauls, each with a squared end and a wedge-shaped end. The 3-pound mash hammer is good for trimming, breaking up, or splitting stones in the 10-to-50-pound range. For stones heavier than 50 pounds, I use an 8-pound mash hammer. I use the square end for trimming edges or breaking stones into smaller pieces. I use the wedge-shaped end for roughly splitting stones along their fissures or bed layers and for tracing a fracture line across a surface before snapping a break. I set the pointed end of the 3-pound hammer in a fault line on the edge of the stone and then strike the blunt end of the hammer with the blunt end of my 8-pound hammer.

I also take along a brick hammer. I use this for fine-tuning the surfaces or edges of smaller stones. Also, in the interest of simplicity, I substitute it for a chisel by setting the flat end of the brick hammer in a weakness or fault line on the edge of the stone and then strike its square end with my 3-pound hammer.

Finally, I take three other tools I couldn't be without: a 4-foot-long aluminum spirit level to keep my walls level and to check their batter; a spool of braided mason's line that I set up to establish the tops and sides of my walls; and a 25-foot tape measure.

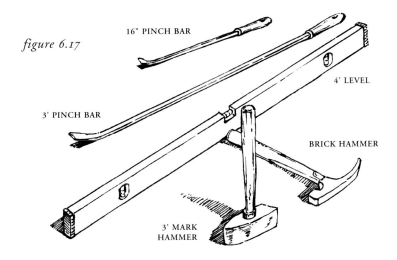

figure 6.17

16" PINCH BAR

3' PINCH BAR

4' LEVEL

BRICK HAMMER

3' MARK HAMMER

▦ FIGURE 6.17 Experienced dry stone wallers like Dan Snow see these as the only essential tools. The pinch bars give them leverage over stones; the level helps them keep each stone level in relation to the next; hammers let them shape the stones for a good fit, one to the next.

PLANTING THE FACE
OF A RETAINING WALL

To plant in the face of a retaining wall to soften the stony look, you must build a dry-laid wall; mortar precludes planting. If you live in the cooler northern half of America, the face of the retaining wall should look south or west so that plants benefit from the sunlight and warmth that the stones gather through the day and release at night. If you live in the southern half of the country, retaining walls should face north or east, where the cooler morning sun or the shade of the north-facing wall keeps the wall cooler. Also, given these caveats, try to avoid building the face of the wall into a prevailing wind. Plants will need all the moisture they can get when growing in a quickly draining and heat-absorbing wall. Plant the wall as you build it, but keep one thing in mind. Because you will need to backfill the wall with soil rather than the usual amount of crushed or small stones, choose particularly large, hefty rocks for your wall construction so that they will stay in place over time. Once the wall is 8 to 10 inches above grade, lay two stones 4 or 5 inches

apart and then backfill that gap with soil appropriate for the types of perennials you'll be planting. Alpines need quickly draining, gravelly soil; erigerons will grow in standard topsoil; dianthus or arabis appreciate sandy loam. Splay the roots of the plant out atop the soil mix, and work the roots into the soil. To keep the soil in place as you water, stuff hay or mats of sphagnum moss around the place where the foliage and stems meet the root system. Then lay a rock so that it spans the gap and holds the moss in place.

When placing plants in the face of a wall, don't line them up; plant in drifts from lower left to upper right, for example, so that they look as though they have self-seeded. To visually link the wall to the overall garden, plant the same perennials above and below the wall to enhance the illusion that they have all self-sown over time.

If you have an existing wall into which you want to set trailing plants and sempervivums, for example, look for small loose stones in the existing wall. Carefully extract them and excavate some of the backfill material with a trowel. Then fill the blade of a small shovel with sandy loam, backfill the hole halfway, plant the perennial, and then complete the planting. Then, as above, stuff hay or loose sphagnum moss around the crown of the plant to help hold the soil in place until the root system develops.

▦ FIGURE 6.18 If you want to plant some of the gaps between facing stones in a retaining wall, backfill with topsoil. Set two stones on the face 2 to 4 inches apart, backfill with topsoil, plant, and then place a bridge stone across the top to protect the plant while linking the two lower stones together.

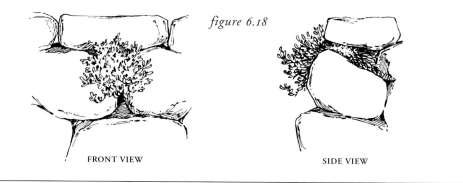

figure 6.18

FRONT VIEW   SIDE VIEW

Hearting To prevent slippage or subsidence due to internal hollows, you need to keep the interior of the wall firmly and fully stuffed. Hearting, which is that stuffing, is a collection of stones anywhere in size from a sliver up to 8 inches. Dan Snow either uses the rubble that results from trimming and shaping stone as he builds his wall, or he orders a few cubic yards of what is known as Gabion stone, that is, 3-to-8-inch stones, for the job. He will only use the small stones once he has filled as many gaps as possible with larger stones. He never uses peastone, gravel, or sand as hearting: what can pour in with a shovel can pour back out over time.

Hearting also keeps hollows out of the center that might eventually fill with organic matter such as leaves, which can decompose, hold water, and start the destructive freeze-thaw cycle. Hearting enables you to level the tails of facing stones and to fill the gaps between them so that a firm flat surface is ready for the next course.

Throughstones are those that are as wide or ever so slightly wider than the wall itself. They are put at random heights along the length of the wall and extend through the full thickness of the wall, tying the two faces together for greater wall stability. These stones can be of any thickness, but be careful not to choose ones that are too thin, because they may snap under the weight of the wall built atop them. Don't be tempted to put a stone with its length along the face of the wall just for looks. Take full advantage of its construction potential by laying it through the wall. If you don't have any long throughstones, strengthen the wall by increasing the wall's batter to 2 to 3 inches for every vertical foot of wall height.

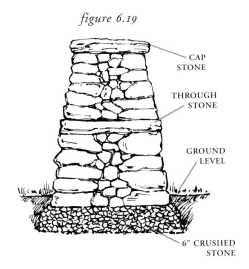

figure 6.19

CAP STONE

THROUGH STONE

GROUND LEVEL

6" CRUSHED STONE

▦ FIGURE 6.19 In well-draining gravelly or sandy soils, 6 inches of crushed 1½-inch stone suffices for a base. Through-stones and capstones solidify the wall by linking both sides of a freestanding wall to the center.

▦ FIGURE 6.20 Chinking can either be exposed or hidden, depending on the type of wall you want or the demands the stones place on you. Be certain to remain consistent along the full length of your wall once you choose which style to adopt.

▦ FIGURE 6.21 By slightly slanting the length of stones toward the center of the wall, you can use gravity to draw the weight of the wall toward its center, strengthening the construction.

DRY-LAID

WALLS

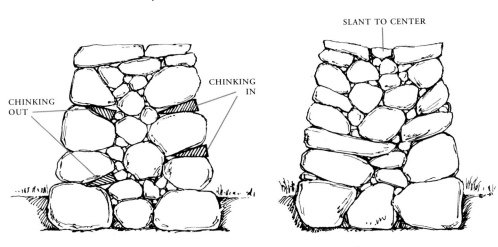

SLANT TO CENTER

CHINKING IN

CHINKING OUT

figure 6.20

figure 6.21

Capping The goal of any wall builder is to create a wall capping that is solid enough to stay in place if children climb on top of it. Safety, as well as longevity, are the central qualities of good capping. So the cap can be made of the same material as the bulk of the wall. It can be coped with stones set vertically and across the wall or set horizontally if the pieces are large enough to stay in place when a person sits on them.

It's best to decide before beginning construction what the top of the wall will look like. You will therefore want to taper the wall so that its top thickness will accommodate capstones that you set aside for that job as you work through the stockpile.

Given the specific dimensions and purposes for capstone, it is best to begin setting them aside right from the start. By knowing the dimensions of capping stone, and therefore the desired thickness of the wall top, you have another cue as to how wide to make the base. Finally, get as much of the surface of the capstones touching the hearting and facing stones as possible. A well-packed wall at that top surface is very important for safety, longevity, and appearance.

▥ FIGURE 6.22 Stiles allow people – not cows, sheep, or horses – to walk up one side of a freestanding wall and down the other. Stile steps can also be built into the exposed face of a retaining wall.

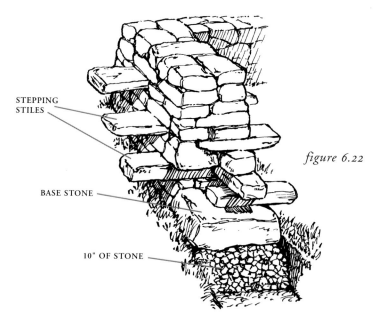

STEPPING STILES

BASE STONE

10" OF STONE

figure 6.22

GERTRUDE JEKYLL'S PLANTS FOR STONE WALLS IN A COOL PLACE

Saxifrages
Wall pennywort
Arenaria balearica
Corydalis
Erinus alpinus
Small Ferns

To Hang Down:
Rock Pinks
Iberis
Alyssum
Othonnopsis
Aubrieta
Cerastium
Mossy saxifrage
Arabis

In Sun or Shade:
Wallflowers
Snapdragons
Centranthus
Thrift
Dianthus fragrans

Shrubs to Hang Over from the Top
Cistus cyprius
Phlomis fruticosa
Santolina chamaecyparissus
Rosemary
Berberis vulgaris
Lavender
Pyrus japonica
Othonnopsis cheirifolia
Desmodium penduliflorum
Rosa arvense
R. lucida
R. sempervirens
R. wichuraiana

Gray-Leaved Alpine Plants for the Wall:
Cerastium tomentosum
Artemisia nana
A. sericea
Achillea umbellata

Plants for the Hottest Places
Campanula isophylla
C. fragilis
C. garganica
C. muralis
Stonecrop
Yucca gloriosa
Y. flaccida
Y. recurva
Opuntia

CHAPTER SEVEN

LAYING PATHS AND TERRACES

ROPERLY LAYING STONE YOURSELF IS QUITE SATISFYING, IN part because the stone paving will last for a very long time but also because any job well done is rewarding. I've restored many overgrown gardens, always knowing that somewhere in the chaos of neglected plants is an area of intact though messy stone paving. Stone stays.

Take 15 minutes to read this chapter and 15 more talking with a stone supplier to line up the materials, and you will be able to lay stone paving. As with all stonework, be patient. When you make a mistake, tear up the problem area and put it right, and in the process you'll learn a lot about how to avoid mistakes in the future. And because you'll find yourself on your knees a lot – a new position for most – pay attention to what amount of unusual physical effort your body can take. Don't push yourself. Stonework is not a competition between you and the rocks. It's a physical skill, and the skills gathered around stonework take time to master.

Visualizing the final shape and dimensions of your completed stonework is the first step, so lay out a variety of options for your path or patio at ground level using stakes with cord tied to them. As you lay out the edges with cord, keep in mind how the shapes and proportions of stonework near the house should relate to the lines and proportions of the house (see Chapter 2). For example, a path leading to a formal two- or even three-story home might be straight and 5 to 6 feet wide, while a path leading to a simpler one-story home might need to be only 3 to 4 feet wide and curve. If the ground slopes, you'll need to determine where steps will go or whether or not a gently sloping walkway will work.

To determine patio dimensions, measure the adjacent walls of the house or building to help you establish proportion. If the wall at the back of your house is 10 feet high, for example, take 1½ times that height, or 15 feet, as a possible distance your patio will be laid out from the house foundation. If the back wall is 24 feet wide, that might well be your patio width. Try out various options, and see if these measurements produce enough paved area

To lay out paths, first place goals at natural points of interest. Then connect the goals to one another to form the paths . . . their paving should swell around the goal.

Christopher Alexander
The Pattern Language (1977)

for gatherings of family and friends. And when it comes to positioning steps off a patio, line them up with any door that leads out of the house onto the patio, thereby establishing yet another relationship between house and paved areas and thus gardens.

■ Refine the Design on Paper

Once you've got a rough idea of what the path or patio will look like, refine the design on paper. Measure the area and make a number of alternative scaled sketches of the paved area until you get just the design you are after. For example, if you have a 12-by-18-foot patio in mind and you have an 8½-by-11-inch piece of graph paper, use a scale of ½ inch = 1 foot – that is, 6 inches will represent the 12-foot dimension; 9 inches will represent the 18-foot dimension. If your terrace is 18 feet by 24 feet, you'll have to drop down to a smaller scale (¼ inch = 1 foot, wherein 4½ inches represents the 18-foot dimension and 6 inches represents the 24-foot dimension), or you can

FIGURE 7.1 - Don't build retaining walls in places that will force you to cover roots of trees with even 2 inches of topsoil. This retaining wall, which we now use as a sideboard for serving food in our outdoor dining area, has been in place for decades, so the tree roots adapted themselves to the soil levels as they grew.

figure 7.2

■ FIGURE 7.2 This cut-stone sitting area, which is the same width as that of the wing of the house, is surrounded by stone wall capped with the same cut stone. Notice that the steps into and out of the terrace are of the same cut stone, lending unity to the design. Less formal fieldstone steps lead from the terrace and alongside an informal garden to a door on the other side of the house, linking separate areas into a uniform ground plan.

simply tape some sheets of graph paper together and stay with the ½ inch = 1 foot. The larger the scale, the easier the drawing is to work with, especially when it comes to laying out plantings at the edges of walkways or patios.

■ Choosing Cut Stone or Fieldstone

As you are developing your design, select the type of stone you'll use, for the stone will help determine the shape of the paved area. The first decision you have to make regarding stone is whether you want a patio or walkway of tightly fitting cut stone or more loosely fitting fieldstone. Cut stones foster straight lines, uniformity, predictability; cut-stone paving is the black tie and tails of the paving world. Fieldstones produce fluidity, curves, irregularities, creativity; they are the dressed-down denims of Saturday afternoon. Choose between these two, keeping the style of your nearby house and gardens in mind. Cut stone will help you produce a uniform, flat surface for walking and for setting chairs and tables on. Fieldstones will generally create a more organic, relaxed look – gaps between the stones can be planted with thyme and other plants – while still providing a reliable surface for furniture and feet.

A practical consideration regarding stone choice is snow removal. Shoveling snow from a tightly laid cut-stone terrace or pathway is eased by its uniform surface; fieldstones are rougher, their contours irregular, so shovels catch. Maintenance is another practical issue. Weeds have a tough time growing in the tight gaps between cut stones and an easier time setting roots in soil or sandy loam grouting between loosely laid fieldstones. You can choose either to keep that grouting weeded or to put some time into getting weed-smothering groundcovers to take hold in the gaps between the fieldstones, thereby reducing maintenance. To help you make a more informed decision regarding these two types of stone, let's take a closer look at each.

CUT-STONE PATHS AND TERRACES

■ The Stone Itself

Several types of cut stone are available across North America. In the Northeast, Pennsylvania or New York bluestone and gray New Hampshire granite are readily available. In the mid-Atlantic states, you'll find a lot of limestone as well as bluestone that is trucked in from the Northeast; and in the Midwest and West, you'll find a lot of sandstones and limestones.

Bluestone is blue-gray, sometimes streaked or washed a rusty red from

figure 7.3

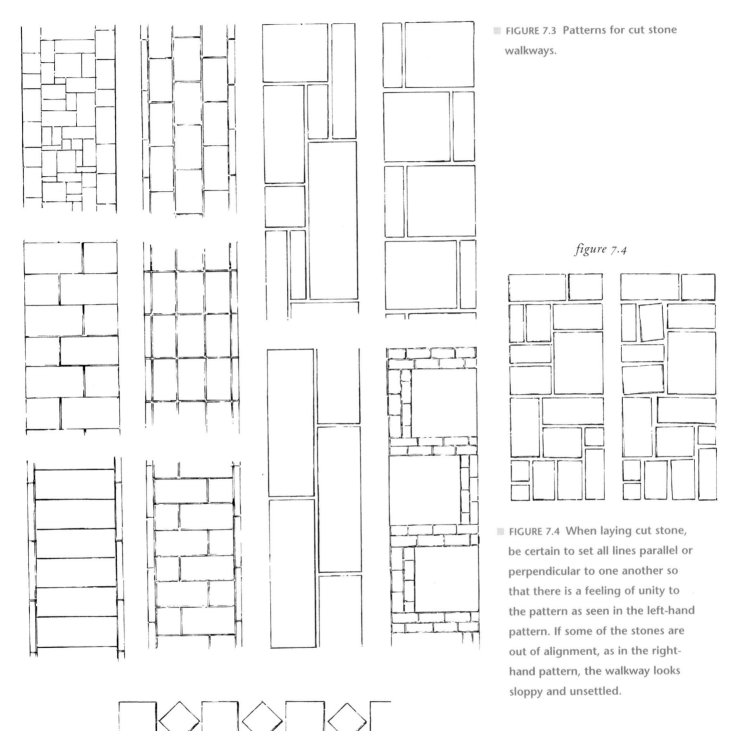

FIGURE 7.3 Patterns for cut stone walkways.

figure 7.4

FIGURE 7.4 When laying cut stone, be certain to set all lines parallel or perpendicular to one another so that there is a feeling of unity to the pattern as seen in the left-hand pattern. If some of the stones are out of alignment, as in the right-hand pattern, the walkway looks sloppy and unsettled.

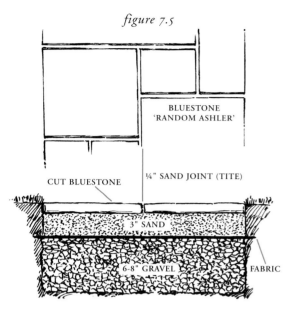

figure 7.5

BLUESTONE 'RANDOM ASHLER'

CUT BLUESTONE

¼" SAND JOINT (TITE)

3" SAND

6-8" GRAVEL

FABRIC

■ FIGURE 7.5 If the soil in which you want to lay a cut stone path is sometimes wet, make a base to increase drainage while forming a solid, stable base. The fabric between the sand and gravel prevents fine sand from filling the voids between the gravel particles.

iron oxide (hematite) within it. Bluestone and a number of pink, beige, red, and brown sandstones from Arizona, Utah, and other western states have a texture that assures a good grip by the sole of your shoe. Designers in the Southeast often use Crab Orchard limestone from Tennessee, which comes in browns and beiges, with striking graining and striations. Slate, polished marble, or polished granite are also available as cut stone, but while all three make handsome paved surfaces, they are so slick when wet or frosty that they are dangerous to walk on. Sawn or polished granite can be professionally flamed, a process that creates tiny pockmarks for good traction. Rough-surface marble is sometimes available. Slate is never safe; avoid it.

Another consideration when choosing cut stone is its color as it relates to heat absorption. If you're going to construct a patio in full sun, dark colors will absorb the heat of sunlight; light colors will reflect sunlight and stay cooler. White marble or light sandstones and limestones stay cooler during the day, whereas darker bluestone absorbs and holds heat. Bluestone and other dark stones, therefore, are best in areas shaded at least part of the day.

Of course, you can manipulate the amount of shade that falls on a patio by planting one or two shade trees right in the patio before you build it or near its edges after construction. Awnings, umbrellas, and rolled canvas covers of all sorts can also help provide cooling shade.

Choose the color of the stone in light of adjacent buildings. Gray granite and gray mica schist terraces, for example, will look good next to a white or gray Colonial in New England, whereas a chalky red sandstone path will look appropriate leading to a doorway through an adobe wall in New Mexico. Faux coquina stone, made to look like sawn reef stone, will look best in a garden in Florida, whereas Crab Orchard stone from Tennessee will look terrific around any swimming pool in the Southeast. And once you have completed the stone-paved area, you can choose flowering perennials to plant along its edges taking into consideration the color of the stone.

Once you have chosen the stone and are ready for its delivery, consult Chapter 11 before making arrangements, since heavy trucks will have to come to your home. The information there will help you prevent damage to your lawn and driveway and save you a lot of work.

■ Preparing the Base for Cut Stone

The first job is to create a well-draining base for the stone paving. Information regarding the standard base for a walkway or patio is included in a sidebar in this chapter; it will work in most cases irrespective of the nature of your soil. Follow that information closely, and you won't have any problems.

However, if you are going to construct a patio or walkway in a region of the country where soil freezes and thaws (roughly the northern third of the U.S.) or gets sodden in the winter and bone dry in the summer (as in parts of the West), here is a heftier alternative so that you can be absolutely certain that your stone surface will stay in place for a long time. Excavate and remove the organically rich topsoil until you reach the gravel or clay subsoil, perhaps 12 to 18 inches down. Fill the resulting area with 1½-inch-diameter crushed stone to within 6 to 8 inches of the finish grade. Then lay down 3 to 4 inches of ⅜-inch crushed stone or crushed gravel, and cover that with landscape cloth or filter fabric. Atop the cloth, lay 2 to 3 inches of sand or crusher dust (a by-product of crushing stone) on which you'll lay the 2 to 3-inch-thick stone and then tamp it down.

It's easy to read the preceding paragraph, but it's another thing to do what it suggests. That's a lot of excavation, and crushed stone is difficult to shovel. If you need to create such a sound base for your walkway because the soil is poorly draining, hire a contractor with a small backhoe and dump truck to do the trenching and the backfilling with the crushed stone, drainage fabric, and sand. Then you lay the stone, the easier, fun part of the job.

When laying stone, keep drainage in mind. Cut-stone patios and terraces "sheet drain" – rainwater drains off the surface as a very thin sheet of water. (In fieldstone patios, water seeps down into the grouting between individual stones.) It is important, therefore, to slope the patio away from the foundation of your house ¼ inch for every foot.

■ Peastone at the Dripline

You can use another form of stone – ⅜-inch peastone, or its equivalent – to solve another problem. If your house has no gutters to catch and drain away rainfall on the roof, water drips in a line from the edge of the roof to the ground below. You may have a problem with muddy water splashing up onto the house siding, which looks unsightly and causes that 36 inches of lower wooden siding to rot away prematurely. To solve this problem, as I did at our place, excavate 2 feet out from your foundation (or at least 6 inches beyond the existing dripline) and 8 inches deep. Then line the trench with 8 inches of peastone, which breaks the force of the falling water and significantly reduces the backsplash onto your foundation and siding. If the amount of water is considerable and you want to drain it away from the foundation, line the trench with stout plastic sheeting. Then lay a 4-inch-diameter PVC perforated pipe in the bottom – with the holes down – and drain it to daylight somewhere away and downhill from the house.

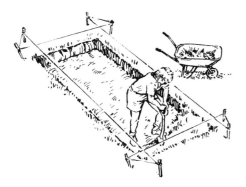

figure 7.6

■ **FIGURE 7.6 The three steps in laying a cut-stone walkway: excavate the area to a depth of around 8 inches; backfill with finely crushed gravel to within 1 inch of the adjacent grade and tamp down; lay the stones, in this case so that they are just as wide as the landing by the door to which the path leads.**

■ Laying Geometric Cut Stone

If your stone paving is adjacent to the house, lay the first stones next to the building or the peastone dripline edge and work away from it. If paving is going between the garage and house, or between two buildings, start by the most important building and work toward the other. If the site requires steps along the way, start constructing the steps at the bottom and work toward the top.

When constructing a path, begin by choosing one of the largest stones to form the threshold, or first stone, one that will promise sound footing as well as visual emphasis. Roughly place the large stone first, and then try out a few other stones near it to get the feel of how they will look together and how far apart they should be. If you want a tight fit, butt one to the next, but don't feel you have to be too Type A about it. Manufacturers rarely produce perfect uniformity stone to stone, so it is best to leave ¼ to ½ inch between them to assure room for adjustment and drainage.

Once you have roughly set five or six stones, twist them down into the sand or crusher dust until they are level and in their final positions. Tap each stone several times in several places with the rubber mallet to set it firmly, and check with a spirit level. Don't step on the stones until they are completely supported underneath; many kinds of 1-to-2-inch-thick stones snap underfoot if not uniformly supported.

As you progress, continually use your spirit level atop a 5- or 6-foot perfectly straight 2-by-4-inch board laid across several stones. Use this same method to check that you have a slight slope on your patio so that water will drain away from the house. When you are finished, spread sand over the whole walkway or terrace and sweep it into the joints. Then set an oscillating sprinkler on the stone surface, and let it run for half an hour to settle the sand between joints. You may have to backfill the gaps a few times before everything is finally settled. Leave about a ½-inch gap between the top of the stone and the sand so that the sand won't scatter onto the surface of the stone, end up on the soles of people's shoes, and thus onto your floors and carpets.

Whatever you do, don't set small 12-by-12-inch or even 12-by-18-inch stones on the edge of the path or patio; they more easily dislodge underfoot than do large stones. Use smaller stones in the interior of the patio or terrace, where they will be supported on all four sides by larger stones. It is also important to note that no cut stones should be laid so that their joints form a cross, because the design will appear to "break" at that point. Lay stones so that their joints from a T or an L, and the design will remain coherent.

Cutting the Stone

If you find it necessary to cut stones, use a circular saw equipped with a masonry cutoff wheel, or a diamond blade and a board as a cutting guide. You don't have to cut all the way through. Score the stone with the radial handsaw to a depth of about ¼ to ½ inch. Then lay the stone atop the board so that the cut is just above and parallel to the edge of the board underneath. Push on the center of the section you want to remove with the heel of your hand, and it will snap clean along the score line. When cutting, be certain to wear a dust mask and eye and ear protection.

Another way to cut the softer stones is to use a mason's scribe. This is a light, sharp, carbide-tipped, two-bladed instrument. Scribe a line three or four times across the stone by pressing down firmly as you draw the instrument across the stone. Use a piece of 2-by-4 as a straightedge. Then set the score line above and parallel with the edge of a board underneath, lightly rap the piece you want to break off with a blunt cold chisel at various places along the score line, and it will snap.

Edging Cut-Stone Walkways and Terraces

If the cut-stone path or patio runs along the edge of a perennial bed, set the same or complementary stone, such as granite cobble or brick, on edge or end to separate the soil of the bed from the paving surface. On 3 to 4 inches of compacted crushed gravel, set the edge of 12-inch-wide cut stones tight up against the edge of the patio or walkway surface. Depending on the look you want, keep the top of the edging material flush with the top of the adjacent surface, or have the upper edge of the edging stone 3 to 4 inches above finish grade. Then backfill with crushed gravel, compact, and backfill with 6 inches of topsoil for planting.

FIGURE 7.8 Cutting cut stone with a circular saw employs all the same principles as cutting wood. Draw a line with a ruler on the stone itself as a guide. Pass over that guide lightly with the blade and then go back and slowly cut through the depth of what is normally 1-to-1½-inch-thick stone.

figure 7.8

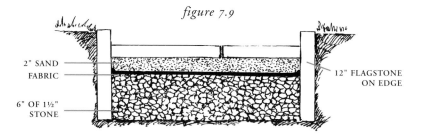

figure 7.9

2" SAND
FABRIC

6" OF 1½"
STONE

12" FLAGSTONE
ON EDGE

■ FIGURE 7.9 Edging a cut-stone walkway with the same material used for the surface helps create a refined look. Choose 1½-inch crushed stone under the layer of fabric rather than finely crushed gravel if you want to increase drainage in areas that are sometimes or often quite wet.

■ FIGURE 7.10 If you want to build a mortared base for your cut-stone walk, excavate down 12 inches, backfill with 6 to 8 inches of gravel, lay down metal reinforcing mesh and then pour in 4 inches of concrete and let it harden. The next day, put down a 1-inch layer of fresh mortar, and lay your cut stones on top of it, using the same mortar for grouting between the stones.

Paths and patios of one type of stone can be edged with a different stone. Blue-gray rounded river stones that edge a path of cut bluestone relaxes the look of the path a bit; a light red sandstone used to edge beige sandstone paving would be attractive because of the shared texture and color. The best way to decide whether to mix materials or not is to obtain samples of those you are considering from a stone supplier. Lay them out in your garden to see how they look, all the while paying attention to other nearby materials, such as brick walls, wooden or stone outbuildings, or fieldstone walls.

■ Setting Cut Stone on a Concrete Base

Thin, soft, or brittle stone is best laid on a mortar pad with mortared joints. If you decide to lay your cut stone in mortar for whatever reason, excavate the soil to at least 10 inches and put in a 6-inch layer of crushed stone or quickly draining gravel. Cover with wire reinforcing mesh, and then pour a 3-inch layer of concrete atop it. A good proportion for such a foundation would be 1 part cement, 3 parts sand, and 5 parts crushed gravel. The next day, spread a thin coat of concrete over the cured pad, and set the cut stones on that thin layer. When the mortar on which the stones are sitting has hardened, the joints can be mortared. When laying a colored stone, such as bluestone, Arizona sandstone, or a reddish Colorado sandstone, tint the concretized grout with a coloring agent to blend the color of the grout and the stone. That way the gaps will not be in stark contrast to the stone itself.

figure 7.10

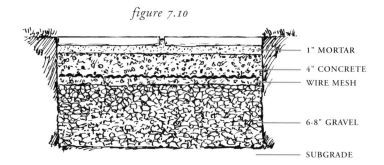

1" MORTAR

4" CONCRETE

WIRE MESH

6-8" GRAVEL

SUBGRADE

FIELDSTONE PATHS AND TERRACES

RANDOMLY SHAPED FLAGSTONE, SUCH AS QUARTZITES, MICA schists, limestones, and sandstones, are the best to use when you want a paved surface that has a lively, varied look, one punctuated here and there by plants. These flat stones that have either angular or curved edges can have anywhere from 2 to 12 square feet of surface and be 1 to 3 inches thick. They don't fit tightly together the way geometric cut stones do. To give you a clearer idea of your options among the many stones now available, turn to the photographs in Chapter 11 or visit a local supply yard where you can see the stone firsthand.

A stone-carpet path is made up of randomly shaped fieldstones laid atop sand or finely crushed gravel. While the outer edges of the walkway can be straight, thereby increasing formality, they can also be much looser. Stones can flow from the body of the path toward or out and around the trunk of a tree near the edge of your walk, or surround a nearby boulder, thereby creating a link between the walkway and naturally occurring elements of the landscape. The edge can also bulge out to form the base for a stone bench or sculpture or even a water feature. At some points along the path – or along the whole path, for that matter – you might want to fit stones tightly together like a completed jigsaw puzzle. You can do this by shaping and forming each stone with a hammer and chisel, thereby creating a tighter look that requires less maintenance. This is often the style I use when designing a curving path to the front door for easy and relaxed clients who would feel a perfectly fitted and straight cut-stone path would be too formal.

■ Choosing the Stone

The best materials for walkways are the uniformly flat mica schists, bluestone, limestones, or sandstones. Quartzite is another frequently used paving stone, but often the surface is irregular and bumpy, with quite jagged edges. Thickness of stone is another issue, because it bears directly on weight, something you need to keep very much in mind if you are going to lay the stone yourself. To make a paved surface look settled, safe, and visually attractive, you want to use the largest stones you can manage. But the thicker a stone is, the greater its weight and the less surface area it can have and still be manageable. So you have to decide what amount of weight you can handle: this will help you determine the appropriate thickness and therefore

FIGURE 7.11 At the entrance to informal homes, you might want to enclose the entrance garden with a 24-inch-high freestanding wall and then pave the resulting space with fieldstones out of which two trees might grow. The result is a welcoming and generous space, around the perimeter of which you could create a lush garden. Gaps between the stones could be planted with ground-hugging perennials.

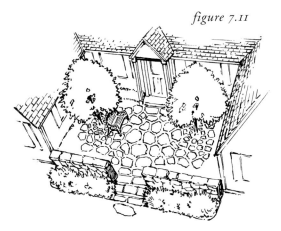

figure 7.11

FIGURE 7.12 Patterns you
can use for your fieldstone
walkways, terraces, or patios.

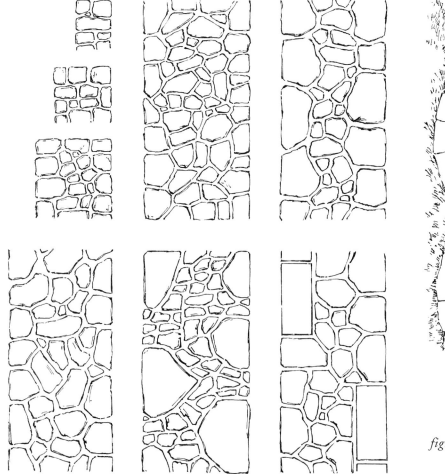

figure 7.12

surface area for the individual stones you'll order. Choose too many small pieces, and the walkway will look busy and be unsafe. Choose pieces 2 to 3 or even 4 feet across and 2 to 3 inches thick, and the walkway or patio will look terrific.

■ Laying the Stones

The most important element of laying these fieldstone paths or patios is to be sure the shapes of the stones speak to one another: fit the convex of one into the concave of the other. Lay lots of stones on the nearby lawn or on tarps so that you can see all their shapes, and then experiment with the convex/concave fits. Start by roughly setting the stones closest to the house or at the beginning of the path to get a feel for how they will look; shape stones that need it for a better fit with hammer and chisel at this point. Once

figure 7.13

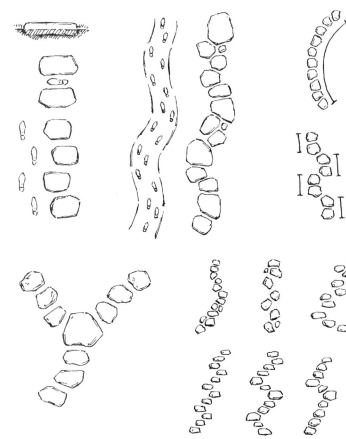

FIGURE 7.13 Patterns for stepping-stone paths. Notice that the first and last stones, as well as any stones at the junction of paths, should be the largest.

FIGURE 7.14 Keep an eye on the shape of the crevices as you lay a fieldstone walkway. Don't let long uninterrupted crevices develop and don't use too many small stones, giving a busy, unsettled look.

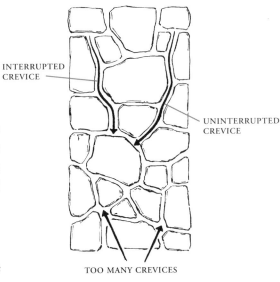

INTERRUPTED CREVICE

UNINTERRUPTED CREVICE

TOO MANY CREVICES

figure 7.14

satisfied with the appearance of the first five or six stones set them permanently into the sand an inch or so above the grade of adjacent soil for good drainage. Then tap them with a rubber mallet to settle the stones in place. If you are using uniformly flat stone, consult your spirit level frequently; if it's a rougher fieldstone, eyeballing usually suffices.

■ Gaps and Grouting

If you lay stones 2 to 3 inches apart to allow for plants between them, fill the gaps with sandy loam 6 inches deep. Then set out ground-hugging plants in the gaps, using *Mazus reptans, Phyla nodiflora, Sagina subulata* (Irish moss), saponaria, thymes, *Ixeris dentata* var. *stolonifera,* or mosses, depending on the hardiness requirements of your area. (See the list of plants appropriate for planting within the gaps of stone walkways and terraces at the end of this chapter.)

LAYING PATHS
AND TERRACES

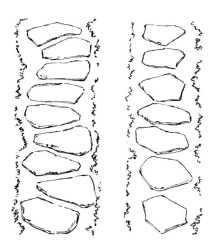

figure 7.15

▥ FIGURE 7.15 When laying a stepping-stone path, pay attention to the space between the stones. Those on the left are generally uniform, so the path reads as a whole; those on the right lack uniformity and so the stones read more as individual shapes on the ground.

▥ FIGURE 7.16 Try to keep the spaces between the stones flowing (right), rather than breaking the flow (left).

figure 7.16

STONE

IN THE

GARDEN

If you don't want plants between the stones, finely crushed gravel is an alternative, but if you do make this choice, fit the stones as tightly together as you can. Gravel grouting can migrate onto the surfaces of the stone, look unsightly, and track into the house. Choose grouting gravel that is as close to the color of the paving stone as possible. If you choose a dramatically different grouting material, you create a very busy look on the ground which distracts from nearby gardens and views. Keep it simple.

▤ Laying Stone Carpets in Concrete

Because smaller stones set in sand or crusher dust create an unstable walkway, it is best to lay walkways made of small 12-to-18-inch stones in mortar. Depending on the ability of your soil to drain, excavate to a depth of around 1 foot and lay down 6 inches of 1½-inch crushed stone. Then set thin edging wood in place, held by stakes pounded into the outside of the wood. Pour a 3-to-4-inch concrete slab, leaving the uppermost surface rough. When set, 24 hours later, remove the wooden forms and lay down ¾ inch of wet concrete on which you lay the walkway stones. Fill the joints with mortar colored with a pigment that blends with the color of the stone. The grout surface should be at least half an inch below the surface of the stone to create well-defined shadows.

LAYING A STEPPING-STONE PATH

T
O DETERMINE WHERE INDIVIDUAL STEPPING-STONES SHOULD be placed, rake the area where the path will be and then walk it at a comfortable pace. Each footprint you leave marks the center of each 18-to-20-inch diameter stone. Since your gait isn't everyone's, ask your spouse to walk the raked area as well and find a comfortable compromise. Regarding the size of the stones, keep in mind that the dimensions of the stones themselves should always be larger than the spaces between them. And always place the length of the stone across, not parallel with, the path. Following these rules ensures that the individual steps will read as a group rather than as isolated stones.

The distance between stepping-stones determines the pace at which the walker moves, so if you want to slow guests down to observe special plants, details, or distant views, create gaps no greater than 3 to 4 inches between stones. If you want to increase the pace, as you might from the garage to the

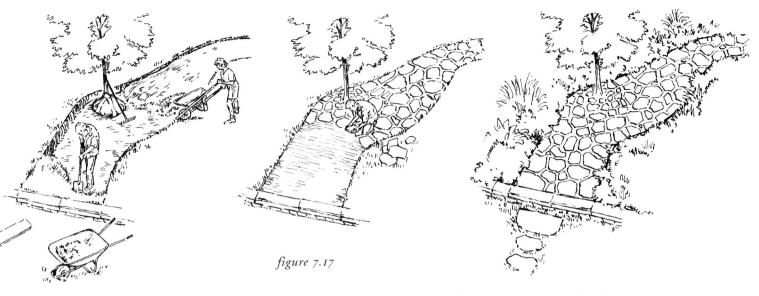

figure 7.17

kitchen door, place them 8 to 12 inches apart. Remember, however, that the faster people move, the surer the footing required, and thus the larger the stones should be. If you place stones any farther than 12 inches apart, you are running the risk of causing people shorter than you to have to stretch.

Stones at the beginning and end of a path are called threshold stones; those at the juncture of paths are called junction stones. Both types need to be one-third larger than all other stones in the path to emphasize their importance.

Determine the nature of the base for stepping-stones by the nature of your soil. If you plan to lay stepping-stones on dry or gravelly soil, there is no need to lay a base; the soil under the stone will remain stable throughout the year. If soil where your path will go is moist for even six to eight weeks a year, create a well-draining foundation for each stone by digging down 6 to 8 inches below each stone and backfill the area with crushed gravel. In wetter soils, the larger the stone the better, as they spread the pounds-per-square-inch load farther, reducing the possibility of them settling into the ground over time. The final position of all stepping-stones should be about ½ to 1 inch above adjacent grade to allow for good drainage off the stone.

▪ Laying Stepping-Stones in Turf

As with a path through a garden, roughly lay all stepping-stones on your lawn. Then study them, move them, and try different combinations so that when you find their final position on top of your lawn, their shapes relate to one another and the path feels like a whole unit rather than a line of separate stones. Then with a straight-nosed spade or a turf knife, cut down through

▪ FIGURE 7.17 The three steps for laying a fieldstone walkway are much the same as those for a cut-stone walk: excavate down 8 to 12 inches; perhaps plant a tree to one side of (but in) the path, and then backfill with finely crushed gravel; lay the stones, constantly checking for level as you proceed.

LAYING PATHS
AND TERRACES

■ FIGURE 7.18 Gravels or fine crushed stones can be successfully combined with fieldstones or cut stone to create attractive paths through your garden.

the roots of the lawn following the outline of the stone. Lift the stone out of the way, being careful to set it down nearby in the same alignment that it will have in the path. With the straight-nosed spade, excavate the turf and topsoil to the thickness of the stone plus 1 inch. Shovel in 1 inch of sand to ease setting the stone. Then place the stone atop the sand so that it fits into the shape you cut in the turf for that particular stone and settle it into place. Its surface should be about ½ inch or so above adjacent topsoil level to ensure drainage yet not interfere with a lawn mower passing over it. Work topsoil around the edges to settle the stone firmly into place, and stand on all its edges to be certain it is uniformly supported before setting the next stone.

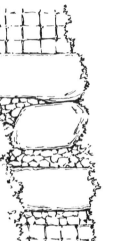

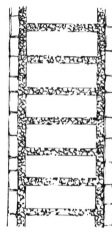

figure 7.18

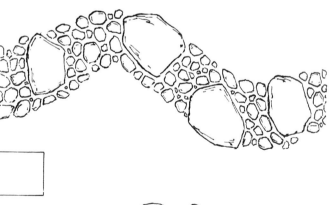

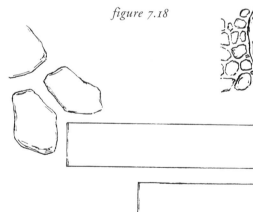

THE BASIC FOUNDATION

Preparing the base is one of the most important parts of creating a path or patio. While never seen, it assures a long-lasting trouble-free base for the surface on which you walk or set furniture. If the base is carefully established with crushed stone, gravel, and sand, fewer weeds intrude, the area drains well, and stones stay in place.

Dig a hole 12 inches into the soil where you will set your paving, and fill the hole with water. If it has not drained away in half an hour or so, then you will need to create a well-draining base as outlined below. But before deciding how serious to get with base preparation, consider a few other issues. How frequently will you and others walk the path or be on the patio? What kind of maintenance equipment, if any, will the surface have to support? Will the path be built in sun or shade? Are there any erosion or drainage problems near the area that need addressing first? Once you have answered these questions, decide how much of a base you need to construct under your patio or path. If you want the high-performance solution, here it is.

First, excavate to a depth of 10 to 12 inches and 3 to 4 inches wider than the desired width of the paved area. Shovel the soil right into a wheelbarrow so that you can use it elsewhere in the garden: to fill low spots in the lawn, to build up the compost pile, or to store under plastic for later use in transplanting. Backfill the resulting hole with gravel or, if the drainage is really poor, 4 to 6 inches of 1½-inch crushed stone. If the area is sometimes sodden in the spring or fall, first lay PVC perforated pipe at the center of the bottom of the trench, with the holes down and the blue line of print up. The end of the drain can come out to daylight somewhere along the side of the path with a 45- or 90-degree angle section; a grating piece should be put on the open end of the pipe to prevent small animals from crawling inside.

If you simply backfill the hole with gravel, you then wet, tamp, and lay over it whatever thickness of sand will be necessary so that the surface of your paving material will be flush with, or just slightly above, the adjacent grade. If you put down large crushed stone, lay porous ground cloth over it and then spread 2 inches of gravel on top of the cloth at the bottom of the hole, wet, and tamp. Then spread a bed of sand to whatever depth will be necessary to bring the surface level of the paving material flush with, or just slightly above, existing ground levels.

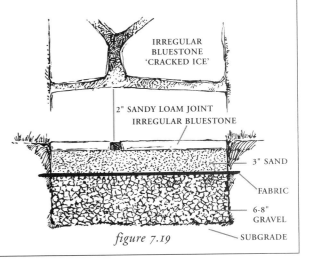

▓ FIGURE 7.19 Irregular bluestone or fieldstone indigenous to your area can make an attractive surface for your walkway. Excavate 12 inches or thereabouts of soil from the walkway area, backfill with 6 to 8 inches of crushed gravel, lay down a layer of woven black plastic landscape cloth, and then 2 to 3 inches of sand on which to set your stones.

IRREGULAR BLUESTONE 'CRACKED ICE'

2" SANDY LOAM JOINT IRREGULAR BLUESTONE

3" SAND

FABRIC

6-8" GRAVEL

SUBGRADE

figure 7.19

MAKING STONE STEPS

START WITH THE BOTTOM STEP. First, follow directions for the standard base, just as you would for a walkway or patio. Steps need excellent drainage so that they aren't undermined by seeping water or heaved by the freeze/thaw or wet/dry cycle. Build risers and treads with the same stone used for paving the walkway, or use other complementary

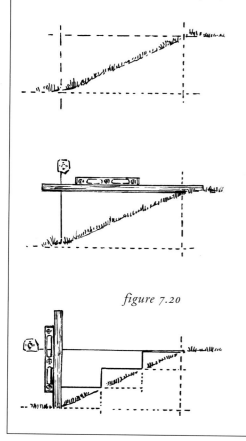

figure 7.20

stone or brick. But be certain to follow one simple rule that will assure you that people won't trip: twice the riser (the height you have to lift your foot to get onto the next step) plus the tread (what you put your foot on) must equal 27 inches: $(2xr) + t = 27"$. Here's an example. A standard 7-inch riser requires a 13-inch tread: $(2 \times 7") + 13" = 27"$. If you want a shallower riser and a longer tread, use the same formula: $(2 \times 3\frac{1}{2}"$ riser$) + 20"$ tread $= 27"$. Employ this formula, one that reflects the human gait, and people won't trip on your steps.

Start by building the base for the lowest step atop the well-draining foundation you have already laid. Lay stone to form the face and sides of the riser by following the mason's dictum: one stone on two, two stones on one. Once you have built up a solid base for the tread, chink the stones to be certain they are all resting one on another to form a solid support, then backfill any space with crushed stone – not sand or crusher dust, because rainwater will wash it out. Use your level to be sure the step slopes ever so slightly forward to ensure drainage: ⅛ to ¼ inch per foot will suffice. Cut-stone steps should have a slight overhang or nosing where riser meets

tread so that a shadow forms just under the edge of the step. This shadow emphasizes the horizontal and safely highlights each step.

By laying the front of each upper step on the back of each lower step, you knit all steps together. If laying steps within a retaining wall, build the wall and steps simultaneously so that the tread stones are laid into the wall and held in place by its weight.

▦ FIGURE 7.20 Once you have chosen the site for cut-stone steps, use a level on a 2-by-4-inch board to determine the height the steps have to climb. This figure will help you determine the dimensions of risers and treads. The riser is the height of the step and is normally around 7½ inches; the tread is surface on which you place your foot and is normally around 12 inches. Start with the bottom step and work your way up.

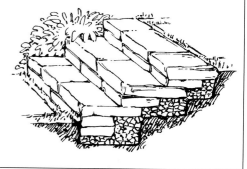

PLANTS FOR PATHS

Acaena 'Blue Haze' (New Zealand bur): Low silvery green creeper with pointed, serrated leaves. Light traffic. Height 1". Sun/part shade. Zone 5.

Anthemis nobilis (Roman chamomile): Soft-textured, light green aromatic foliage with small yellow flowers in summer. Light traffic. Height 2"–3". Sun/part shade. Zone 5.

Arenaria balearica (Corsican sandwort): Dense mat of mosslike foliage with small white flowers. Good for wet areas. Moderate traffic. Mounds to 3". Part shade/shade. Zone 5.

Bellis nitidum (miniature daisy): Mat-forming with small, pink daisies on 1" wiry stems. Height 1"–2". Zone 7.

Bolax glebaria nana: Glossy tight rosettes with yellow flowers in summer. Height 1". Zone 4.

Cotula squalida (New Zealand brass buttons): Evergreen creeper with soft gray, hairy foliage and small yellow flowers. Height 1"–2". Zone 5.

Eleocharis radicans (miniature rush ornamental grass): Tiny grasslike blades form a deep green deciduous lawn. Height 1"–2". Zone 7.

Erysimum kotschyanum (dwarf wallflower): Light green jagged leaves with deep yellow flowers in spring. Excellent for crevices. 1"–3". Zone 4.

E. kotschyanum 'Orange Flame': Mat-forming with orange flowers.

E. kotschyanum 'Yellow': Yellow flowers in early spring.

Euonymous fortunei 'Kewensis': Tiny evergreen leaves; nice trailing habit. Slow grower to 2". Zone 5.

Glechoma hederacea 'Variegata' (ground ivy): Dense creeper with white variegation on green leaves, small blue flowers in spring. 3". Zone 5.

Herniaria glabra (green carpet, rupturewort): Tiny, tight green leaves form a very dense groundcover. Turns bronze in winter. 1"–2". Zone 5.

Hypericum empetrifolium: Tiny green/bronze leaves with yellow flowers summer to fall.

1"–3". Zone 7.

Laurentia fluviatilis (blue star creeper): Low groundcover with star-shaped, light blue flowers blooming spring through summer. 3". Zone 5–10.

Linaria lobatus (toadflax): Tiny green shamrock-shaped leaves with white flowers in spring/summer. 1"–2".

Lindernia grandiflora (blue moneywort): Moisture-loving creeper with light green leaves and deep blue flowers. 2". Zone 7–10.

Lysimachia japonica 'Minutissima' (miniature moneywort): Slow growing with bright green and tiny yellow flowers. 1". Zone 4–9.

L. nummularia (creeping Jenny): Moisture-loving with small green leaves, crawling rapidly. 2". Zone 4–9.

Mazus reptans: Bright green, low mat that rapidly spreads. *M. r.* 'Alba' has white flowers; *M. r.* 'Purple' has abundant purple flowers spring to fall.

Mentha requienii (Corsican mint): Forms a tight green, mint-scented mat 3". Zone 7.

Muehlenbeckia axilaris nana (creeping wire vine): Tiny, dark green leaves on wiry stems to 4". Zone 4.

Nierembergia repens (white cup): Aggressive-rooting creeper; deep green, oblong leaves with buttercup flowers in spring and summer. 2"–3". Zone 5.

Potentilla verna: Fast-spreading runners covered with dark green leaves. Yellow flowers in summer. 2"–6". Zone 5.

Pratia angulata (white star creeper): Bright green succulentlike foliage. Can be invasive. Profuse white flowers spring through frost. 2"–3". Zone 7.

Raoulia australis: A dense mat of tiny, gray leaves; for dry locations. 1". Zone 6.

Sagina Subulata: Dense mosslike tufts form a carpet of green (*S. s.* 'Irish Moss') and gold (*S. s.* 'Scotch Moss') with small star-shaped flowers in late spring. 1'. Zone 5.

Sedum (stonecrop): Indestructible, low-maintenance succulent. Zone 4.

S. hispanicum var minus 'Purple Form' (blue carpet): Tight blue foliage, light pink flowers. ½".

S. requienii (miniature stonecrop): Tiny green leaves grow to form tight mat; white flowers in summer. 1".

Soleirolia soleirolii (green baby's tears): Dainty, creeping leaves forms lush mats of green carpet. 1". Zone 9.

S. soleirolii 'Aurea' (gold baby's tears): Tiny gold leaves. 1". Zone 9.

Thymus (thyme): Aromatic, sun-loving herb that forms a mat. Zone 4.

T. pseudolanuginosus (wooly): Dusty-gray foliage; pink flowers. 3".

T. serpyllum 'Albus' (white creeping): Emerald-green leaves with white flowers. 2".

T. serpyllum 'Coccineus' (red creeping): Small, dark green leaves with red flowers. Turns bronze in fall.

T. serpyllum 'Elfin': Slow-growing miniature thyme with pink flowers. 2".

Veronica (speedwell): Great drought-tolerant plants that thrive on sun and heat. Fast-growing.

V. liwanensis: Tiny, glossy oval leaves form a mat with blue flowers in late spring. 2". Zone 6.

V. repens (creeping speedwell): Shiny small leaves with white to lavender flowers in spring. 1"–3". Zone 4.

V. repens 'Sunshine': Brilliant gold foliage. 1". Zone 7.

V. surculosa 'Waterperry Blue': Creeping, shiny green foliage turns bronze in winter. Large sky-blue flowers. 4"–6". Zone 5.

Viola hederacea (Australian violet): Extremely fast-spreading mini viola. White and purple flowers spring to fall. 2".

V. labradorica: Fast-spreading viola with rounded green/blue/black leaves and lilac flowers. 2"–4". Zone 5.

(This list is provided by Under A Foot Greenhouse and Gardens, Salem, Oregon. Go to stepabales.com for a further list or call 503-581-8915.)

CHAPTER EIGHT

BOULDERS AND BEDROCK

NO MATTER WHAT SIZE YOUR HOUSE AND GARDEN, ONE of *the* goals of good design is to make a graceful transition from the house to the gardens and out to the natural landscape, integrating all three into a seamless whole. Because boulders, whether naturally occurring or trucked in, and bedrock, whether real or faux, are such strong structural elements in the garden, they can be a major unifying element. Some people are lucky that nature provided both on their property.

Years ago, I was in a garden up in the hills outside Scottsdale, Arizona. The backdrop to the house, built upon bedrock, was a sheer red sandstone bluff. Great boulders twice as high as I am tall were here and there throughout this hilltop garden, interplanted with creosote plants and foothill palo verdes, brittlebrush, and jojoba, all planted in existing native soil. I couldn't tell where the garden ended and the natural landscape began.

But not everyone has such a dramatic landscape. Even if you have just a few boulders out in the garden or woodland, or one shoulder of bedrock, you can use them to advantage. And if you have neither, you can truck in large stones and build up faux bedrock following the sequence I outline later in this chapter.

BOULDERS

■ Finding the Face of a Boulder

Every time I position a boulder in a garden, I recall a lecture in Boston many years ago given by the now late Professor Kinsaku Nakane, a Japanese garden master from Kyoto. He, with landscape architect Julie Messervy, designed and oversaw the installation of the Japanese Garden Tenshin-En (The Garden of the Heart of Heaven) at the Museum of Fine Arts in Boston. Professor Nikane was standing before an audience of 500 garden designers

". . . trees and rocks will teach you things not to be learned elsewhere. You will see for yourselves that honey may be gathered from stones and oil from the hardest rock . . . "

From St. Bernard of Clairvaux (1091–1153)

and avid home gardeners in Gund Hall at Harvard University's School of Design; on the desk in front of him was a roughly 12-by-18-inch stone on a stout turntable.

As he ever so slowly turned the stone, he talked to us about finding its face. He said that every stone was like a human being, with a face, a torso, arms, and legs. He said that if we paid attention, we would know when we saw its face, and he encouraged us to say when we did. (This is something you can do just as well as we did, for he never once told us how to find what we were looking for. He simply assured us we would know the face when we saw it.)

He slowly turned and turned the stone and shifted its angle this way and that and slowly turned the stone and slowly, slowly shifted its position, and then, as the stone came round just so, in unison, the entire audience said, "That's it!" He beamed. We were right. If you were in that audience, you would have been right too.

FIGURE 8.1 Massive bedrock in this garden just outside Dublin, Ireland, was carefully exposed (or covered with topsoil) here and there to form the foundation – the theme – that runs throughout this woodland garden.

■ FIGURE 8.2 In classic Japanese garden design, the upright stone symbolizes heaven, the horizontal stone symbolizes earth, and the diagonal stone symbolizes man. By placing these three closely together you set up a visual relationship between the three. A small tree planted among them (the yin) complements the strength of the stones (the yang).

■ FIGURE 8.3 A boulder will look settled into the earth if you bury at least a third of its mass. If you simply set the rock on top of the ground, (top), it will always look temporary and unrelated to the earth on which it sits.

figure 8.2

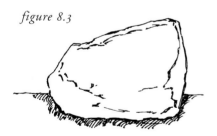

figure 8.3

STONE

IN THE

GARDEN

Walking around and around each boulder about to be set in the garden, I look for the face and align it toward a specific vantage point along a path or from chairs in a sitting area. The convex of one boulder should answer the concave of another so that what the Japanese call the "ma," that is, the shape of the space between the two, is in proportion with the boulders. Mounding boulders should contrast gently with horizontal and vertical ones. Boulders need to "speak" to one another to create an interplay of shapes, forms, and volumes, developing coherence and relationship among them. Then paths, trees, shrubs, and groundcovers can be related to them to produce a whole. I also want to create a pleasing sets of contrasts by juxtaposing organic and inorganic, vertical and mounding. In this way, the boulder is fused into the overall design and does not stand apart like a sentry.

■ Moving and Setting Boulders

Given that 1 cubic yard (3 by 3 by 3 feet) of stone very roughly weighs 4,000 pounds and 1 cubic foot weighs about 200 pounds, depending on density, you must move boulders with a front loader, a backhoe, or with ingenuity. The best boulders come from your own property, and we're fortunate here in the Northeast to have an abundance of them left behind by retreating glaciers.

Before transporting a boulder from a woodland edge or a meadow to its position in the garden, I dig a depression in the ground where the boulder will go that is roughly twice as wide and long as the boulder and between one-third and one-fifth its depth, all the while being careful not to disturb the earth deeper than that to prevent the boulder from settling farther into the earth. That gives us plenty of room to try out various positions for the boulder before finding its final alignment.

172

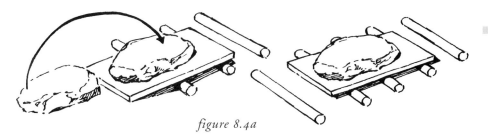

figure 8.4a

We then drive a backhoe to the place where the boulder lies in the ground. Before the backhoe operator gets his machine into position, I place an old rug or blanket over the boulder and then set 2-by-6-inch boards along the ground where the bucket of the backhoe will make contact with the boulder. (Sometimes, when moving a 4-to-5-foot boulder, we wrap nylon straps around it and suspend it from the front bucket.)

Once the boulder is protected, the operator carefully drives the bucket of the backhoe down into the ground about a foot back from the stone and then levers the bucket upwards. The 2-by-6-inch boards take the force exerted by the bucket, while the blanket or old rug prevents the boards from scratching the rock. Once the boulder is held firmly in place by the hydraulics of the backhoe, we set off for the garden. We move one boulder at a time; but if a boulder hanging off the rear backhoe is sufficiently heavy it can tip the front of the backhoe, including the motor and front tires right off the ground, we load a large boulder in the front bucket first as a counterweight.

When we get back into the garden, we set the stone down into its hole so that at least one-third of its mass will be below ground and it is resting on the bottom it had in the field or woods from which it came. We then go back and, one or two at a time, bring the remaining boulders to the garden and set them roughly in their holes.

Once all the boulders are roughly in place, I work with the operator to

▥ FIGURE 8.4A-C **Three ways to move rocks too heavy to lift:**
FIGURE 8.4A **Flip the stone onto a board that is resting on two or three 3-to-6-inch wooden dowels or metal pipe. Then push the stone along the ground, leap-frogging the dowels as you go.**
FIGURE 8.4B **Lay the utility cart on its back, and roll the rock into its cradle. Strap the rock to the cart framework, and then you have put wheels under your stone.**
FIGURE 8.4C **To flip a stone over, use a timber or another rock as a fulcrum that will enable you to get leverage with a crowbar. Or, you can tie the crowbar and the rock together with stout rope that will increase your leverage.**

figure 8.4b

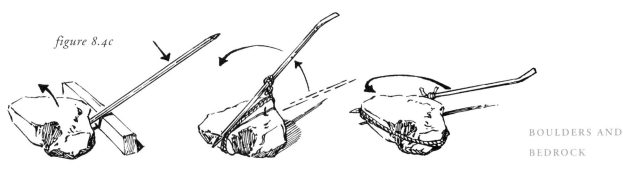

figure 8.4c

BOULDERS AND
BEDROCK

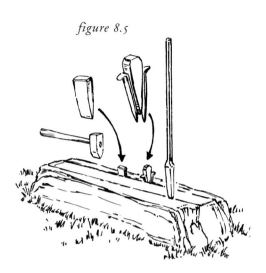

figure 8.5

■ FIGURE 8.5 Splitting stone is easy
if you work with the right tools.
The bedding planes of stone will
show you where to set your wedges.
To open a gap in the stone, use a
mash hammer to drive the wedge
(or a series of feathers and wedges)
between two bedding planes. You
might find that a crowbar will be
helpful to further open the gap,
breaking one large stone into two
or more pieces.

twist and turn the stones to create a unified relationship among them. All the time I keep in mind the dominant vantage point from which the boulders will be seen: a window of the house, a patio or terrace, a bench along a stepping-stone path. And always, when I need the bucket to push the boulder, I place a rug or folded cardboard or a board between the rock and the metal bucket to protect against scratching. Only when I have all the boulders arranged do we begin the process of backfilling the boulders with the topsoil necessary to give rise to the gardens around the boulders. When placing boulders within what will become a garden, keep the eventual growth of plants in mind; the danger is that you will put too many small stones too close together. Far better that you choose fewer but larger stones and set them far enough apart to allow for plant growth.

Positioning stone is a very satisfying, even exhilarating, experience. I once worked for the first time with a great burly mountain of a man who was running the backhoe as I placed boulders for a client in Massachusetts. At first, he thought I was truly, certifiably nuts. I fussed and fussed and shifted this boulder over a foot and that one a one-eighth turn, and he could not for the world fathom what I was about. Once we completed positioning the first grouping and had backfilled them, we set a stepping-stone path, which wound among them from the driveway to the side door, and then planted birches, yews, azaleas, European ginger, and ferns among them to create a woodland entrance garden. When the operator saw that garden at the end of the day, he understood what the fuss was all about.

The next day he came back to the site to help me place the last grouping, and he looked really tired. I asked him if he was okay, and he said that he and his wife had been up until almost midnight. They had been working in the light of car headlights as well as those on the backhoe he had at home, AND the floodlights on the side of the house, to place boulders in their front garden.

BEDROCK

Y EARS AGO, CLIENTS PHONED ASKING FOR HELP TO SOLVE A problem they had with a weedy mass of bedrock only 15 feet from the side entrance to their home here in southern Vermont. An account of what I did for them will give you a picture of how to think about and prepare bedrock for planting, and therefore, how to integrate bedrock into your garden.

Very simply, my clients asked, could I make their mass of bedrock beautiful? I found they had a shoulder of bedrock some 30 feet wide and 50 feet long that sloped up out of lawn to a maximum height of 6 feet and then sloped down on all sides back into lawn. Further up into the woods were other outcroppings and exposed bedrock, so this one down on the lawn would give me the opportunity to link it visually with others in cleared woodland.

While the boulders in the woodland were kept clear by sheep, the one down in the lawn was covered with grasses, weeds, and saplings and appeared as a large unkempt island in otherwise pristine lawn. Here and there were patches of exposed granite. Because the house and adjacent barn were three stories high and therefore in scale with the massive bedrock, I felt it would be appropriate to make a feature out of this large outcropping. Had the house been smaller and the barn not been there, I might have created retaining walls nearby and buried some of the bedrock to reduce the visual weight of the massive outcropping to bring it into scale with the existing and nearby architecture. However, given its size and importance right there by the front door, I decided to clean off the rock to see what I had to work with.

Three men spent two days carefully clearing the rock of all grasses, weeds, and debris. We used shovels at first to get the mass of grass roots and weeds off the surface of the rock, throwing the clods directly onto the beds of pick-up trucks. Next we used sharp trowels and sharply pointed hoes to get the roots out of the crevices in the rocks; we threw this smaller debris onto tarpaulins, which then were dragged up onto the trucks via wooden ramps.

Throughout the process, I set aside moss and was especially careful not to damage the lichen that had grown over the decades on some of the soil-less vertical surfaces. I wanted as few scratches on this bedrock as possible so that when finished, the bedrock would look as though it had been in just that condition for decades.

Once the bedrock was stripped of all weeds and roots, I searched for decomposed areas of bedrock that we could chip away with pickaxes and found several areas perhaps 2 to 3 feet across and 6 to 8 inches deep. The best area, because it added so much space for a garden on the rock, was a depression about 5 feet wide and 18 inches deep. After cleaning out these depressions, we filled them with water, which quickly seeped away through crevices. Because all the depressions drained quickly, we knew we could garden in them. So we backfilled them with organically rich soil that would support small woody shrubs such as dwarf azaleas and herbaceous peren-nials, albeit drought-tolerant ones. We also found that there were some

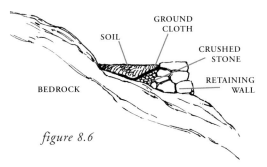

figure 8.6

FIGURE 8.6 In the cooler, moister parts of North America, you can build small retaining walls directly onto flat areas of bedrock so that you can plant drought-tolerant groundcovers and perennials. Position such a retaining wall to take advantage of water running down a sloping section of bedrock as well as shade from overhead that will help keep the soil cool and moist.

BOULDERS AND
BEDROCK

places that would allow me to build 12-to-18-inch-high retaining walls 3 to 4 feet long right on the rock to help create other planting pockets.

Running up through the center of the bedrock and down the other side was a 4-to-6-inch deep cleft in the rock that was, in places, as much as 24 inches across. We filled that cleft to within 3 inches of the top with crushed gravel to which I added ¼ part topsoil. Then we installed stepping-stones atop this mix the full length of the cleft. This pathway encouraged our clients and their guests to walk up, across the top, and down the other side of the bedrock. The changing vantage point added a lot of interest to the garden from up there on the bedrock.

Having completed the planting pockets and the stepping-stone path, we planted drought-tolerant plants. In the sunny areas, we set out semper-vivums, sedums, *Arctostaphylos uva-ursi*, deciduous azaleas, and *Juniperus procumbens* 'Nana'. In shadier areas, we planted rooted cuttings of *Vinca minor* 'Bowles' and 'Alba', European ginger, moss in crevices, and Christmas fern transplants from nearby woodland.

To link the bedrock to the landscape even further, I designed a spur in an already-existing stone wall, which was some 35 feet away to the west side of the bedrock and separated the sloping cleared woodland from the flat pristine lawn. Made of stone to match the existing wall, this new linking wall ran perpendicular from the old wall to the bedrock 35 feet away, with a 3-foot-wide gap in the middle for access. The result of this stone wall was to draw the new bedrock garden into a firm relationship with its surroundings in as natural a way as possible. After all, the beauty of the image was in the planted bedrock, not in architectural features we could add.

To give a visual center to the bedrock garden, my clients later put a 4-foot-high pair of metal crane sculptures in the largest planting bed and among the azaleas as a Japanese touch to this otherwise New England bedrock garden.

During the first winter, we mulched the entire planting with straw held down with plastic deer netting because of the possibility that the evergreen plants would not be able to replenish moisture lost to transpiration in such an exposed site. In subsequent years, as the plants established sufficient roots, this precaution became unnecessary.

▪ Creating Faux Bedrock

Over the years, I have had occasion to work with landscape architect Patrick Chassé, a graduate of the Harvard Design Program. On two occasions, Chassé built up faux ledge for two different purposes. In a Vermont garden in which we were working together, a sloping panel of lawn some 30 feet long and 10 feet wide separated an upper stone terrace from a swimming pool surround about 5 feet lower than the stone terrace. He wanted to turn this sloping area of lawn into a transition area that would relate pool to terrace, and he decided to do this by creating faux ledge.

To get stone for Chassé to work with, we scoured the nearby woods and old stone walls and gathered 30 or so lichen-covered stones ranging in size from 5 feet long by 2 feet by 18 inches down to jagged stones 2 feet by 1 foot by 1 foot. We transported them to the side of the swimming pool with a front loader of a backhoe, wrapping each stone with old blankets before loading them into the bucket.

We excavated the sod and took out about 10 inches of topsoil, which we stockpiled nearby on tarpaulins. Chassé began to set the stones on the earth, marking with a yellow piece of chalk the eventual grade to be around each stone. In some cases, two-thirds of the stone would be buried in compost-enriched topsoil. Some boulders doubled as steps along a rugged stepping-stone path up through the garden to the upper stone terrace.

Chassé set the length of each stone on line with every other stone so that they all ran, as they do in nature, with a grain. (The glacier that scoured bedrock in southern Vermont did so in such a way that stones in the whole region were scoured in a north-south direction.) By setting all the stones on this line, but setting some more deeply than others, he created a natural rock

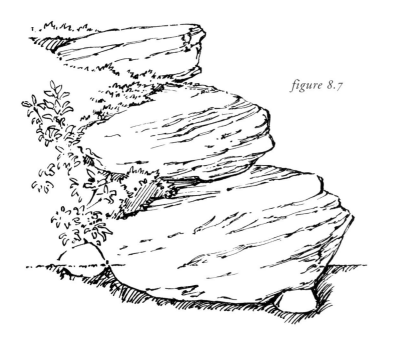

figure 8.7

▦ FIGURE 8.7 When creating faux bedrock, set the planes or grain of the rocks parallel to one another and be certain to use only one kind of rock. Be certain to bury at least one third of each rock back into the slope as well as in the ground at the bottom of the slope.

BOULDERS AND
BEDROCK

177

outcropping that looked as though it had been there for ages; also enhancing this effect was the lichen that we had left intact on all the stones. Once all the rocks with chains, nylon strapping, and the front bucket were set, we backfilled with compost-enriched topsoil up to the yellow chalk lines.

We then went up onto nearby land our clients owned to find a sunny site that would match the very sunny conditions by the swimming pool. There we gathered low-bush blueberry, hayscented fern sods, and any low-growing sods with lichen and sun-tolerant ferns within them and brought them down to the new garden site.

Over the next day, we patched in these sods and planted containerized native species of sheep's laurel (*Kalmia angustifolia*), grasses, and other sun-tolerant indigenous plants we had purchased. The result of all this was a garden that looked like a natural rock outcropping.

In another garden Chassé worked on in the suburbs of Boston (see figure 3.6), he found decomposed bedrock when excavating for a stone path between a steeply sloping area and the side of the garage. Using shovels as well as the backhoe, he pulled the bedrock apart about 6 feet farther than he needed to for an opening to the back gardens. He then used the resulting chunks of stone to rebuild the face of the excavated bedrock in such a way that he could backfill with soil for plants, thereby softening what might be a rugged-looking area in an otherwise refined garden.

He then took the remaining chunks of bedrock and carried them farther into the garden, replicating the look of existing bedrock. Thus, he was able to visually tie the first part of the garden to another part of the garden 30 feet away. In doing so, he created coherence and made a feature of the existing bedrock in not one but two places in the garden. By planting richly in both areas, he was able to cover most of the rugged bedrock and yet leave just enough showing to achieve the effect he was after: bedrock as the visual foundation of his garden.

Chassé then brought a geometric bluestone patio up to the base of the bedrock, scribing some of the square or rectangular cut stones so that the two materials met. In other places where there was a gap a few inches wide between the bluestone and the faux bedrock, he backfilled the space with soil and planted it with a ground-hugging plants as an intermediary between the two materials.

CHOOSING BOULDERS IN A STONE YARD

To find stone supply yards near you, go to Appendix A in this book for a list of suppliers nationwide. If you don't see one listed near you, ask a local landscaper or building supply yard where to find a source for boulders. Before going to the yard, take samples of stone from your own property so that you can match old to new.

When you get to the yard, be imaginative. You'll see rocks sitting one way, but you need to imagine all the possible ways that rock could be positioned. A long, narrow rock could stand on end or become a bench or step, or it could rest diagonally against other mounded stones. Keep the scale of your garden in mind, and choose as wide a variety of stone shapes and sizes as you can. Stones also have per-sonalities, so choose ones that are con-sistent with the mood of your garden: brazen and bold, smooth and gentle, rounded and calm, jagged and wild.

Prices vary widely across the coun-try, but generally local fieldstone and large slabs might cost around $125 per ton. Granite boulders might cost $150 per ton, while basalt columns might cost more. Lichen- or moss-covered stones might cost a bit more than those without either, but the lichen or moss will not necessarily survive in the climate and exposure in your garden as it did when the rock was high in the moun-tains, or wherever it came from.

Many stone supply yards have equipment that can shape, cut, polish, or flame stones for greater texture. Some have large bandsaws that can cut through boulders to make many free-form stepping-stones; others can shape smooth water basins in boul-ders, and still others can drill a hole down through a stone so that it can be used as a bubbler. (See Chapter 10 for details on how to make a water stone.)

Finally, ask about delivery and costs involved, and if you need a hand placing the boulders, ask whether they know of designers who could help.

FIGURE 8.8 Boulders are available in stone yards in any number of shapes and dimensions. The mistake most of us make is to choose boulders that are too small. Think big, especially given that one third of their bulk will be buried. And think about the mood or feeling of individual rocks: upright ones are strong, forceful, energetic; horizontal boulders recede, are at peace and feel restful; jagged rocks are unsettled, aggressive, sharp. Choose boulders to support the atmosphere of your garden.

figure 8.8

CHAPTER NINE

BUILDING POOLS AND FOUNTAINS

NATURALISTIC POOLS

I F YOU WANT TO BUILD YOUR OWN NATURALISTIC POOL, USE A RUBBER liner rather than plastic or concrete to make your pool watertight. Synthetic rubber, the only liner I use, offers great flexibility regarding the shape of your pond, because the material itself is so malleable and long-lasting. Using a flexible hose, try a variety of shapes and sizes until you develop a pleasing outline. Consult Chapter 4 for specific information regarding how to site a small pool and Appendix E for information you can get on the Internet or directly from water garden supply houses. Be certain to check with local authorities regarding codes regulating the construction of small pools. You may find that you'll have to put a fence around a naturalistic as well as a formal pool, but unsightly fences can often be hidden well back within gardens and attractive gateways can be built into them for access.

■ Digging the Hole for the Pool

Once you have chosen the site and design, dig a hole in the ground that is 22 to 28 inches deep; given the amount of work this entails, hiring someone with a small tractor-based backhoe is a good idea. This depth will enable you to grow water plants, especially water lilies, in what will become an 18-to-24-inch-deep pool once you have installed the liner and put soil or gravel on it. Anything shallower would preclude growing the bulk of water-loving plants. The sides of the hole you dig should be vertical, stepped, or very slightly sloping, though the slope of the pool sides will depend on the nature of the soil in which you are digging. Clay soil will hold a vertical edge far better than sandy or gravelly soils. As you dig, keep safety in mind. There will be times when you'll need to get into a pool for planting and maintenance;

Fountains and

waters are the

soul of the

garden.

Pierre Husson
*La Theorie et la Pratique
du Jardinage* (1711)

FIGURE 9.1 With a rubber liner, we turned this abandoned 18-foot-diameter concrete silo base into a pool and fountain. The addition of a simple pump under the antique marble wellhead allowed us to introduce the sound of plashing water into this corner of our garden.

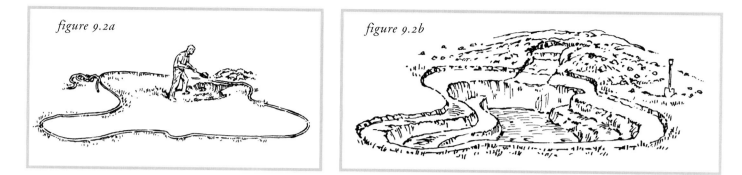

figure 9.2a

figure 9.2b

FIGURES 9.2A-F (pages 182-188)

Steps in creating a pond:

FIGURE 9.2A Use a hose or clothesline to create a curvilinear outline; create bays and inlets to provide interest.

FIGURE 9.2B Excavate the pond and a waterfall area if you want one, leaving the soil on which the liner will eventually rest undisturbed; create shelves for boulders, rocks and container plants leave ramps for falling water.

vertical sides with ledges ease stepping in and out, as do gentle slopes with gravel atop the liner. Steep slopes prevent access and it's more difficult to cover the liner as gravel slides to the bottom.

The bottom of the pool, no matter what its shape or diameter, should slope ever so slightly toward a single low spot 12 to 18 inches in diameter. Because it will invariably become necessary to drain the pool with a small pump for maintenance purposes, it is helpful to have this low spot on which to set the pump while it empties the pool. The last of the dirty water and detritus can gather at that spot, making its removal simpler than if it were evenly spread over the entire bottom.

As you dig the pool, periodically stretch a straight 2-by-4-inch board across two points of the outer rim, and then check with a spirit level to be certain the rim of the pool will be level. What you want to avoid are high points that will expose the liner above water level later. If you find the rim edge is not level, use soil that you have excavated to berm up and feather out the soil on the low side to bring it up to appropriate grade.

Also consider creating shelves at various depths around the perimeter for underwater potted plants, such as papyrus or other annual or perennial plants. Many water lilies left in their plastic pots require 18 to 24 inches of water depth, while other perennials might require only 6 inches; shelves at various depths will accommodate the requirements of a broad range of water plants. A shelf or shelves can also support rocks or boulders of varying sizes around the rim or stones for a waterfall. As you excavate soil, prune the ends of protruding tree roots or remove angular rocks that might puncture the liner.

When excavating the pool, use the soil to form a berm that embraces the back and part of the sides of the pool, and then set boulders and stones within the soil, again consulting Chapter 4 on how to design the layout for stones around a naturalistic pool.

If you dig your pool partway down or even at the bottom of an existing slope, build up even more of a slope on the uphill side of the pool with the excavated soil to provide a place for a simple rubber-lined waterfall of boulders and flat stones. To understand better how soil can be used to create mounds that appear natural and right, look closely again at the photographs of pools in Chapter 4.

■ Lining the Pool

The strongest liners on which to set boulders and rocks are made of two types of synthetic rubber: butyl rubber made from butyl polymer, and EPDM (ethylene propylene diene monomer polymer). Butyl rubber is sold in 30-to-45-mil thicknesses and is black; EPDM is usually sold in 45-mil thickness and is charcoal gray. One mil equals one-thousandth of an inch, or one-fortieth of a millimeter; 45 mils roughly equals the thickness of 10 to 12 pages of this book. Thickness has a significant impact on the ease of installation. The thinner the liner, the easier it is to form and fold over the shaped bottom and sides, but the more susceptible it is to puncturing. The thicker it is, the bulkier the folds become and the less tightly it fits into corners, but the less susceptible it is to punctures. Rubber liners pose no threat whatsoever to fish or plants that you might eventually include in your pool.

There are two main alternatives to rubber liners – plastic liners and concrete – but I don't recommend either. Plastic liners have three major drawbacks: when temperatures drop below freezing, plastic often becomes brittle and cracks; many plastic liners are not long-lived because they are susceptible to ultraviolet rays that break down the structure of the material; PVC plastic liners are not nearly as elastic and stretchable as rubber liners, and so they tend to split and crack more readily. Concrete-lined pools might crack over time as the soil under them shifts from frost, excessive moisture, or drought, whereas synthetic rubber liners stretch and mold to fit shifting soil without cracking or splitting. You have to know what you're doing with concrete. I avoid it.

Given that you will be resting stone on a rubber liner, buy the thicker,

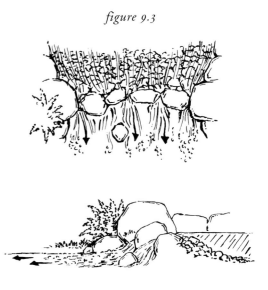

figure 9.3

■ FIGURE 9.3 A waterfall is simple to make. Set large boulders at either side of the water flow; then create a dam with middle-sized rocks infilled with smaller rocks to help dam up the water.

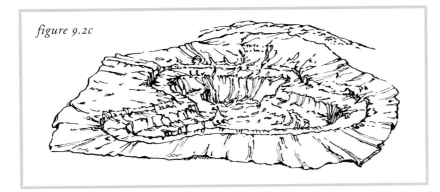

figure 9.2c

■ FIGURE 9.2C Lay the liner protection fabric first and then the liner itself over the excavated area.

more puncture-proof 45-mil material. Keep in mind that although 45-mil material is more puncture-resistant than is 30-mil liner, it is definitely less pliable. When developing the shape and surfaces of the bottom of your pool, create broad curves and sweeping lines, shapes to which the thicker liner will readily conform. If you try to mold this heavy-duty liner around complex forms, such as promontories or sharp angles, you will find the material will bunch up and remain conspicuous underwater.

Purchase rubber pond liners through mail-order for $1.00 to $1.25 per square foot. (See Appendix E for sources.) To determine the square footage of the liner you need, measure your pond's maximum length, width, and depth. To calculate the length of the liner to order, add the maximum length of your pond plus 2 times the depth plus 2 feet of overhang. To calculate the width of the liner, then, add the maximum width of the pool plus 2 times the depth plus 2 feet for overhang.

For example, if you have a pond that is 15 feet long, 7 feet wide, and 2 feet deep, you would calculate the dimensions of the liner you need to order as follows: length – 15 + (2x2) +2 = 21 feet; width – 7 + (2x2) + 2 = 13 feet. So you would need a piece of synthetic rubber liner 13 feet by 21 feet. Many suppliers (listed in Appendix E) suggest that you round those figures off to the nearest 5 feet. Always round these numbers up. As with this example, round off 13 by 21 feet to 15 by 25 feet, which should cost around $375.

One way to save money – but limit your design options somewhat – is to design a pool that can be lined with standard-size liners. One company sells these for ponds 18 inches deep in the following standard dimensions expressed in feet: 3 by 6, 6 by 6, 6 by 11, 6 by 17, 11 by 11, 11 by 17, 11 by 22, 17 by 17. If you want to take advantage of this saving, look into standard pool liners before making a final decision regarding pond size and shape.

Given that you will be placing rocks and boulders on this liner and then covering the liner itself with 3 to 4 inches of gravel or soil, you should also purchase liner protection fabric, which you can place on top of as well as under the rubber liner. This ⅛-inch-thick tough, polyester fabric readily conforms to all the same shapes as the rubber liner does. It is typically sold in standard sizes (5 by 100 feet, 7.5 by 100 feet, 10 by 100 feet) and generally costs about 20 cents per square foot – a roll 5 by 100 feet would cost around $100. This textured fabric will also help keep the gravel and topsoil that you will put on the sloping areas of your pool as well as over the entire surface of the bottom in place .

As you are excavating, lay the rubber liner in sunlight to make it pliable. Once you have excavated the pool, spread 2 inches of sand on the bottom.

figure 9.2d

FIGURE 9.2D Place a few of the main boulders (set on a second protective piece of liner) on the bottom of the pond. Once the main boulders are in place at the bottom, fill the pool. Then place the boulders and stones around the water line.

Put down liner protection fabric evenly on top of the sand, and then the rubber liner on top of the protection fabric. Fold it where necessary into corners, and be certain that the liner extends at least 1 foot beyond the top of the rim on all sides. Don't cut the liner to fit yet. Next put down a layer of protection fabric on top of the liner, and you are ready to fill the pool.

As inconvenient as this sounds, it is best to fill the pool with water before putting any stones or gravel atop the liner and its protective cover. By filling the pool first, you allow the water's weight to settle the liner into all nooks and crannies. If you put heavy stones in first and then fill the pool with water, the weight of the water will cause the liner to settle into depressions and cracks and corners. However, because the weight of boulders holds the liner in place at specific points, something has to give, and that something is the liner. It may stretch to the point where it is weakened or torn.

Once the pool is filled with water, you may find that you have a high spot where too much liner is showing. Pull out excess soil from under the liner at that high spot to lower the liner to the appropriate height. Then let the water and liner settle for 24 hours before setting any stones on the liner.

■ Setting Rocks Around the Edge

Turn back to the photographs in Chapter 4 to see how rocks have been placed with an eye to their relationship to the water's edge as well as to one another. Rocks should hide the pond liner in a way that appears natural and uncontrived. Rocks, plants, and water should be in harmony, with no one material overwhelming the others. Also refer to Chapters 3 and 9, both of which address the use and setting of boulders in garden soil, because you may well want to set these larger rocks outside the perimeter of the liner as well as in or at the edge of the water.

If you want to be able to see the pool from a bench or a terrace some distance away, build a level panel of fieldstones from the edge of the pool out

figure 9.2e

FIGURE 9.2E **Build the waterfall if that is in your plan. Only when all boulders are in place, trim the excess liner away. Fill between gaps with bank run gravel to cover level areas of the liner between stones.**

perhaps 6 to 8 feet and on line with the distant vantage point. In this way, you invite people to the pool's edge and keep a sight line open to it. The reflection of sunlight on the pool, in concert with plantings and perhaps a fountain, will act as a visual magnet to draw people to one of your garden's most important destinations. A stone bench or 24-inch-high sitting boulder set on this fieldstone pad will provide them with places to sit once they have arrived at the pool's edge.

Upon deciding what the surround of the pool will look like, position stones atop the liner, but herein lies one caveat. To reduce damage to the liner, limit your choice of stones and boulders to those with rounded edges and surfaces, rather than sharp, edgy corners and protrusions. Start by laying the biggest stones throughout the whole pool garden, keeping in mind that you should have one very big stone to anchor the others and to act as the visual center around which all others gather. Place one or two boulders on the bottom of the pool so that only the top one-third or even less shows above the water's surface, thereby defining the pool's depth. (Really large stones might have to be lowered into the pool by backhoe and nylon strapping wrapped around a boulder.) Next set a few of your largest stones on any shelves you have made for them, and then lay the last large stones on the perimeter of the pool.

If you have chosen smooth, weathered river stones that have a grain in them, be certain that they are positioned so that the grain of each one is facing in the same direction. The photographs in Chapter 4 will be helpful in seeing how to relate these largest of stones to middle-size and small stones. They will also show you how to contrast horizontal stones with mounding ones so that pleasingly contrasting shapes and forms are next to each other.

Then decide how to cover the balance of the liner not covered by stones.

figure 9.4

FIGURE 9.4 **Three boulders along with several smaller stones can be set in the pond. The space between them could then be backfilled with topsoil to support a small tree or herbaceous plants.**

STONE

IN THE

GARDEN

FIGURE 9.5A-G Covering the edge of the liner is always a problem. Here are several ways to use stone to help hide that black liner:

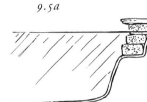

9.5a

a) Build a flat shelf on which to rest flat rocks. Above the water line, lay a long think rock to establish a refined look at the pond's edge.

9.5b

b) Slope the liner gently to dry land; cover that liner with small rocks and bank run gravel and even some larger rocks for variety.

9.5c

c) Build a solid concrete rim around the pool set atop crushed rock. A shelf in the crushed rock could support flat stones onto which you could cantilever a larger rock that juts out over the water's edge.

9.5d

d) A sloping edge is also an alternative with a small cup-shaped depression below water's edge to receive the end of a small stone.

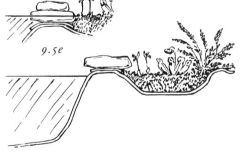

9.5e

e) Use the liner to create a boggy area adjacent to the pond, one that you can periodically water with a hose to keep it wet.

9.5f

f) A broad shelf with stones acting as little retaining walls will enable you to create under-water soil pockets for edge-of-pond plants.

9.5g

g) If you build in a shelf at the water's edge that slopes gently enough to hold soil, then you will be able to support plant life in different depths of water. Such plants could be supplemented by others growing in containers. Waterlilies are a natural for container growing.

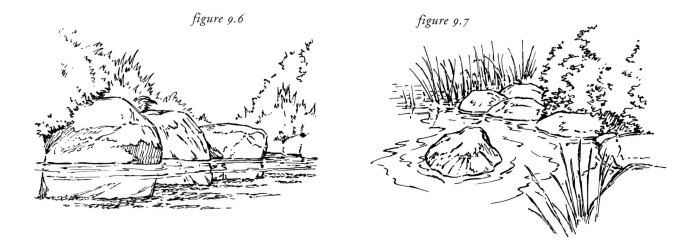

figure 9.6 *figure 9.7*

FIGURE 9.6 Large boulders set so that a third of their bulk is underwater make for a solid and dramatic edge. They would have to be strapped and carefully lowered into place with a backhoe or carefully rolled down a ramp. Use old rugs or blankets to protect the liner as you proceed. Set such large boulders before filling the pool with water.

FIGURE 9.7 Boulders also make wonderful islands in shallow ponds.

FIGURE 9.2F Plant around the perimeter of the pond using a variety of foliage forms for interest.

We covered our 18-foot-diameter pool solely with about 2 inches of pebbles, leaving plants that we wanted to grow in the pool, such as *Acorus gramineus* 'Variegatus', in the pots in which we purchased them. Over time we divide and transplant them into larger pots. In this way, we introduce only topsoil that is contained in pots.

Another method is to cover the liner with a combination of small and medium stones, with one or two larger ones poking above the water's surface. You can then cover the balance of the liner with bank-run gravel, that is, gravel that has a variety of sizes and different-colored stones in it. Finally, you could combine any of the above approaches with lots of topsoil so that you can grow plants directly in 4 to 6 inches of soil in the bottom of the pool rather than in soil contained in pots. It all depends on the look you want.

figure 9.2f

STONE

IN THE

GARDEN

188

FOUNTAINS

A SIMPLE FOUNTAIN CAN ADD THE SUBTLE MOVEMENT AND sound of water to your garden. Such a small water feature is best located in an intimate setting where people will sit nearby. Mine, which took about three hours to create (not including the electrician's time), is near our outdoor dining table, but it could also be in the corner of your back terrace or in the center of a small herb garden.

While the following example centers around a cast-stone urn in our garden (see figure 4.4), you could also use any stone artifact, such as a figure made for a water fountain. I have also used the same system as outlined below, but rather than using a cast-stone urn, I placed an 18-to-24-inch boulder atop the basin and then drilled a hole down through its center to create a bubbler. Water is pumped up through the hole in the stone, and then it flows down all sides of the stone before falling back into the basin below. If you turn on the fountain at least two or three times a week for a few hours, moss begins to form on the stone, creating a very old appearance in remarkably little time. Here's how to put one of these simple small fountains together.

■ Electricity

Before deciding where to locate your small fountain, keep in mind that you will need an electrical line (but no water line) nearby. Get an electrician to install the line and switches. My electrician buried 12-gauge UF direct burial cable 6 to 8 INCHES deep in the lawn from a ground-fault circuit interrupter switch in the garden shed to a switched power outlet near the dining area. He mounted the power outlet at the garden end of the cable on a 30-inch piece of 2-by-6-inch pressure-treated lumber buried 12 inches into the ground and within just a few feet of the fountain, hidden within shrubs and perennials. Where I might hit the cable with a shovel (especially within the garden itself), the electrician buried 1-inch-diameter PVC schedule 40 conduit and then passed the 12-gauge cable through it.

■ Gather the Materials

■ One Pondmaster filter/pump item 34140 from Lilypons Water Gardens (1-800-999-5459) or a comparable Little Giant Pump PE-2F-WG from Lilypons, which would pump about 200 gallons of water an hour to 1 foot of height (around $100)

■ 24-inch-diameter, 15-inch-deep molded plastic tub – Lilypons item 40437, or a similar-size Duraflex 15-gallon rubber tub (around $25)

■ 36 inches of tubing for the pump – Pondmaster 34140, for example, requires ¾-inch interior-diameter tubing. Purchase with the pump.

■ One 2-inch-by-8-inch-by-6-foot piece of pressure-treated lumber

■ One stone urn no wider than 20 inches in diameter, with a hole up through its base and stem and into the water basin. We used a cast-stone urn decorated around the water basin with a 20-inch-diameter urn on an 8-inch-by-8-inch base. (Around $100)

■ One 48-inch-by-48-inch piece of hardware cloth with ¾-inch gaps between the wires, which you could purchase at any hardware store

■ Two 5-gallon buckets of rounded river stones from 1-inch to 5-inch

■ Two 5-gallon buckets of ⅜-inch peastone

■ Preparing the In-Ground Basin

Measure the outer diameter of the water basin you will set in the ground, and then cut a 2-by-8-inch pressure-treated board to that dimension. Drill two holes in the lip of the plastic basin that will line up with two holes you'll have to drill at either end of the pressure-treated board. Pass bolts down through the holes in the board and basin, and fasten tightly. Then drill a 1-inch hole in the exact center of the board to receive the tubing that will connect the pump to your urn. To prevent water from running the length of the board and draining the water away, cut two ¾-inch-wide, ½-inch-deep notches near the outer ends of the board to direct water atop the board back into the in-ground water basin. These notches need to be outside the dripline of the urn.

Now dig a hole in the soil that is 3 to 4 inches wider and deeper than the receptacle you will set into it. Line the bottom of the hole with peastone, and then set the water receptacle onto it, making certain that the lip of the

■ FIGURE 9.8A-C A small fountain is very simple and inexpensive to make. By recirculating the water, you don't need complex piping but just a hose to periodically top up the water level in the in-ground basin. The above-ground basin (or boulder, through which a hole has been drilled) can then provide you with the sight and sound of running or dripping water.

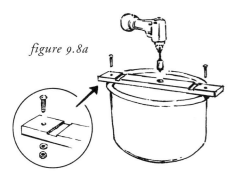

figure 9.8a

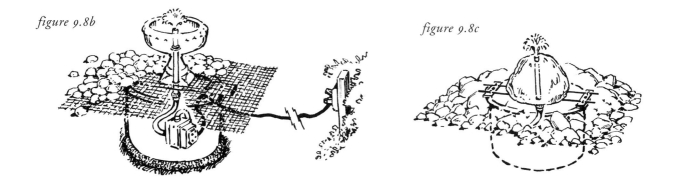

figure 9.8b

figure 9.8c

receptacle is about 1 inch above the adjacent grade. Sift the remaining peastone around the sides of the receptacle to backfill the gap between the undisturbed earth and the sides of the basin completely. Use a spirit level to make certain the board affixed to the receptacle is level.

▪ Setup

Now set the pump in the bottom of the receptacle, attach the tubing to the pump outlet, and run the balance of the tubing up through the hole in the 2-by-8-inch board, leaving it longer than will be necessary for the moment. Leave extra tubing below the board so that you have room for corrections in the future.

Find the center of the 48-by-48-inch hardware cloth, and open a hole at its center with a screwdriver so that you will be able to pass the tubing through the hole. Slide the hardware cloth down the tubing until it comes to rest on the board, the edges of the water basin, and the existing grade of the soil.

Place the cast-stone urn atop the board to enable you to determine where you should cut off the excess length of tubing. Cut the tubing, and then slip it up into the hole at the base of the urn. Seal the junction of these two materials with hydraulic cement, and set the base of the urn down on the board, making certain you don't pinch the tubing closed as you do.

With a hose, fill the in-ground water basin two-thirds full, and then plug in the pump. Water should fill the urn, drip over its entire outer edge, and fall back into the basin. Once you have everything in working order, place the river rocks atop the hardware cloth to mask the underground workings.

▪ Maintenance

I have to top up the in-ground water basin with a hose about once a month, depending on evaporation rates from usage and the heat of summer days. In midsummer, I lift one edge of the hardware cloth, take out the removable filters, and clean them with soap and water. Before winter, I reach in to remove the pump and bail out the water. Then I place a 30-by-30-inch piece of plywood atop the urn and set a stone on that to keep it in place during the cold season.

CHAPTER TEN

SETTING
SCULPTURES
AND BENCHES

J UST BECAUSE GRANITE STANDING STONES, SCULPTURE, AND benches in your garden will last forever doesn't mean they'll stay put forever. All kinds of forces are at work to disrupt their placement: drought and downpours, frost 4 feet into the ground, erosion, soil settling, and ever-expanding tree roots are just a few of the problems. The main culprit is water in the soil and the effect fluctuating temperatures have on it.

Let's look at a pair of 6-foot-high 6-inch-square granite fenceposts I set in the ground on either side of an entrance to our herb garden. Wanting 4 of those 6 feet above ground, I buried one-third of each post for a solid setting. I dug holes three times as wide as the posts – that is, about 18 inches in diameter – and 2 feet deep, being certain to leave the soil in the bottom of the holes undisturbed. After placing the fencepost into the hole, I surrounded the bottom 20 inches of it with 4 to 6-inch rocks and tamped them strongly into place against the stone and the outer soil with a sledgehammer. I then filled the remaining 4-inch hole with topsoil to hide the rock backfilling and planted *Iberis sempervirens* in nearby soil, plants that would shortly grow around the base of the fenceposts to integrate them better into the garden. Now those two firmly set standing stones mark one entrance to our herb garden; at 4 feet high, they also act like the top of newel posts on a staircase banister, where you can rest your hand. The rocks not only support the standing stone, but they keep water from gathering in the soil next to it.

You will notice that I did not use concrete to hold the stones in place. I simply would not pour concrete against those lovely old stones that André Bernier brought us from Martha's Vineyard.

Here's what happens underground to disrupt the position of standing stones that are set only in existing topsoil, with no small stones to hold them

He builded better

than he knew –

The conscious

stone to beauty

grew.

Ralph Waldo Emerson
(1803-1882)

■ FIGURE 10.1 I marked the entrance to our woodland garden with two antique granite fence posts. Stepping-stones set horizontally at ground level among plants often don't clearly announce the beginning of a path, even from a few feet away. Vertical stones help send a signal, even from a distance, that this is where you enter the garden.

firmly in place. As soil gets wet, it expands; as it dries, it shrinks, just as you've seen in photos of cracks in soil in drought-stricken areas. Any stone object you put in or on soil has to move with it. As wet soil freezes, it expands; as it thaws or dries, it shrinks. Ask any farmer who works in the colder regions of North America, and he'll tell you that this action can literally bring buried rocks to the surface of his fields. My father was certain that one of the best crops we grew in our orchards in gravelly, stony northwestern Connecticut was rocks.

To counteract these fundamental laws of physics, you have to pay attention to good drainage around any stone artifacts you want to set on or in your garden if you want them to stay in place. The first step is to gain an understanding of the nature of your soil vis-à-vis drainage. And don't assume that because one area of your garden has 12 inches of native topsoil that your whole property has the same. It might, but it also might not. I garden 1½ acres and have run into those 12 inches of topsoil as well as hardpan, gravel, muck, and even a bit of decomposed ledge. The only way you'll be able to determine what you have to do to make an appropriate base is to see what's there first.

Dig a hole 1 foot deep where you will set your stone artifact, then fill the hole with water from a hose, stand back, and watch what happens. If it's gravel or sand, the water will drain out within a few minutes, and you've learned that you will not need to go to a great deal of effort to set a base. If the water takes as much as 15 to 30 minutes or more to drain, your soil probably has a lot of slow-draining clay in it, or is hardpan; you'll need to put some work into creating a well-draining base.

Here's another way to look at soil. If you garden in Zones 2 to 6, where soil freezes and thaws throughout the winter, or you live in a warmer area where there are long periods of very wet followed by very dry weather, as in parts of California, you need to create a proper base.

SETTING SCULPTURE

AS WITH ALL STONE ELEMENTS, YOU WANT TO PLACE THEM properly from both a design as well as a practical point of view. Benches and sculpture are best set on cut-stone or fitted fieldstone bases, which in turn sit atop a crushed-stone and gravel base, much like the base described for the pathways in the previous chapter.

For help with the details for this chapter, I turned to Dieta Matthiessen, an artist living in Upstate New York. She has been importing and professionally installing fine European and English garden sculptures, urns, and benches for many years throughout the Northeast, and she shared her experience with me.

Moving Heavy Stone Objects

One of the most useful pieces of equipment for moving heavy sculpture in the garden is a dolly that has inflatable rubber tires, a ground-level frame onto which you can slide the artifact, and a vertical 4-foot open metal framework with handles. This simple piece of equipment essentially puts wheels on a heavy object. You can rent them from U-Haul or many equipment rental agencies or perhaps borrow a ballcart from a landscaper (figure 10.1). Before loading the sculpture onto the dolly, Dieta recommends that you drape a thick blanket or padding over the back of the dolly. Then wrap the artifact as well. Tip the sculpture so that you are able to slide the dolly base under the sculpture, and then carefully rest the piece against the dolly's frame. Lash it to the dolly with canvas or nylon straps or rope to be certain it won't fall off as you wheel the dolly across dry lawn. (If the lawn is wet, you might have to set down four 2-by-8-inch planks on which to run the dolly wheels, and you'll need to leapfrog the back pair of planks forward as you work your way across the lawn.) If you are not going to wrap the artifact itself, then put a blanket or some other soft fabric between the canvas strapping and the sculpture to avoid friction marks. Dieta feels that the most important things of all are to be careful, to be patient, and to take your time to do every step correctly. When dealing with heavy stone objects, things can go wrong very quickly.

The Base for Carved or Cast-Stone Pieces

Once you decide on the site for the sculpture, you need to determine the shape and dimensions of the stone pad on which it will sit. And stone it should be. Never place a stone artifact on bare earth. Moisture will wick up into cast stone, and eventually pieces will slough off; solid stone will discolor and, if soft enough, pieces will slough off as well. Furthermore, rain will fall and splash soil particles up onto the artifact.

A geometric pad is always the best: circular, square, rectangular, though irregular pieces of irregularly shaped fieldstone can also be used to good effect if used to create a base with a geometric outline. A single piece of irregular stone is too distracting. The dimensions of the sculpture will help you determine the dimensions of the pad, but be generous. A large

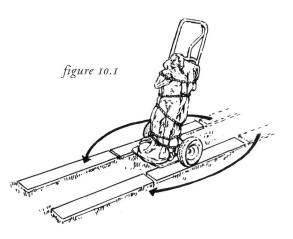

figure 10.1

■ FIGURE 10.1 Four boards and a ball cart borrowed from a landscaper will enable you to move heavy stone sculptures. By leap-frogging the boards you can go anywhere on your property. If you need to go uphill or down, tie a rope to the bottom center of the frame of the cart. Someone can then help pull the weight up a hill or hold it back from going too fast down a hill.

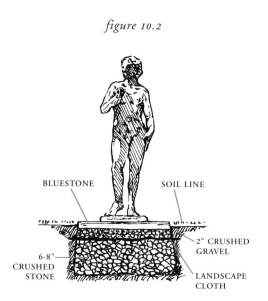

figure 10.2

BLUESTONE   SOIL LINE

6-8"
CRUSHED
STONE

2" CRUSHED
GRAVEL

LANDSCAPE
CLOTH

▦ FIGURE 10.2 Never set a stone or cast stone sculpture directly onto topsoil. A beautiful stone garden ornament deserves to be properly supported and displayed on stone. That way water will drain away from the base, keeping it dry and intact.

sculpture on a small base will look out of scale. Take the widest dimension of the piece (which will likely not be the base), and add 4 to 6 inches to that figure to give you the width of the base. Rain dripping from any part of the artifact should fall onto the stone base. If the piece is easy to move around, set it where it will eventually go, and then with colored tape or string, outline a variety of pad shapes and dimensions to determine which will look best.

Once you have decided on the dimensions of the stone pad, dig down 8 to 10 inches or more, depending on the ability of the soil to drain freely, and backfill the hole with ¾-to-1½-inch crushed stone to allow for good drainage under the piece. Cover the crushed stone with a porous geotextile such as DeWitt Weed barrier, and then cover that with 2 to 3 inches of finely crushed gravel, which you will in turn cover with a piece of cut stone (figure 10.2). But which stone?

You basically have three options: loosely or tightly fitting fieldstones, freely draining gravel, or tightly fitting cut stones. Make this decision in light of the sculpture or artifact itself, as well as the garden in which it is being set. If the stone artifact is formal, and the garden is too, then setting it atop tightly fitting cut stone is most appropriate. I did just that for a client in Peterborough, New Hampshire. At the four corners of a formal garden, with a bluestone-edged reflecting pool in the center, I designed four 10-inch-high boxwood squares and set one 3-by-3-foot bluestone square within each. That bluestone became the base for four formal 24-inch-square stone pedestals, atop of each of these sat a 30-inch-diameter lead urn.

However, if the garden and sculpture are much less formal, a base of large fieldstones grouted with moss or other ground-hugging perennials would be more appropriate. For a Vermont garden, a client purchased a lovely cast-stone sculpture 3 feet high of a little girl holding a basket of flowers. We set her in the corner of a stone wall (that acted as the backdrop for a lush perennial garden) on three fieldstones that matched the color and texture of the stone wall. Those 20-inch-diameter fieldstones sat atop 8 inches of gravel. This cast-stone sculpture brings up an important point – there are good castings and a lot of very bad castings. Here's how to tell the difference.

▦ Selecting Cast-Stone Pieces

Dieta Mathiessen, who has visited many English and European casting workshops, told me that stone-cast artifacts are made by mixing stone dust and minute stone chippings in a concrete slurry. This slurry is poured into the bottom of an upside-down latex mold. Air bubbles released from this slurry rise to the top – that is, the base of the piece. When selecting a cast-stone piece, turn it upside down to check on the density and uniformity of the base, for that is its most vulnerable point.

The quality of detail in the rest of the cast-stone artifact loses its refinement for a number of reasons, all of which gather around the latex mold itself. Each time the two halves of a mold are removed from a hardened casting, bits and pieces – and therefore detail – adhere to the stone casting. Over repeated castings, more and more details get lost as the latex mold gradually wears out.

Manufacturers might also make new molds from old molds that have lost their detail, or from subsequent, and therefore inferior, castings rather than from the original piece. Check the detail in a casting carefully before purchasing a cast-stone piece. Quality is apparent in crisp, sharp lines and clear definition. Lack of quality lies in concrete repair patches or in the damaged or badly finished seams where the two halves of the mold met. Check for deterioration and irregularity along these mold lines, for it is on those lines, or at the base, that cast-stone pieces usually begin to deteriorate. Feel free to ask the salespeople to point out perfect and imperfect pieces so that you learn to see the difference clearly.

Finally, some large cast-stone artifacts come in several pieces. Check to be certain the colors of the various pieces match, that the solidity and quality of casting is consistent across all pieces, and that the joint where the pieces meet allows for a tight fit. These cautionary notes also hold true if you are buying a pair of artifacts, for you will want symmetry and a mirror image.

▦ Winter Care of Cast-Stone

If you have cast-stone planters that are too heavy to take in under cover in the winter, remove the plants and soil, and then elevate the planters off the ground with bricks or rectangular granite cobbles. Cover a planter or urn that could hold water with a sheet of heavy-gauge plastic or plastic tarpaulins, and then tie the plastic firmly in place. Check the placement of large cast-stone sculptures that you will have to leave out over the winter to see if they are in full view from windows of the house. If they are, you may want to leave them uncovered. If they are out of sight from the house or walkways you use in winter, check to see whether any elements of the piece will hold water that might freeze and snap that part of the piece. A bowl held aloft by a figure, for example, would be vulnerable to being damaged. Either cover it with a flat piece of cut stone, wrap just the bowl, or cover the entire piece with heavy gauge plastic and tie it tightly.

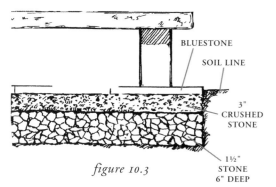

BLUESTONE

SOIL LINE

3" CRUSHED STONE

1½" STONE 6" DEEP

figure 10.3

Sculptures and stone artifacts made of limestone, sandstone, or cast stone do slough off bits and pieces over time, especially in sites where the freeze-thaw process goes on throughout the winter, so apply a clear silicon sealant to prevent them from absorbing water.

SETTING STONE BENCHES

The Base for a Bench

Like stone garden ornaments, a bench is best set either on a platform of tightly fitting and therefore more formal cut stone, on loosely fitting field-stones with groundcovers growing between them, or, most informal of all, on the crushed gravel itself. As with other stone artifacts, the degree of formality of the bench and the garden in which it is set will give you clues as to the degree of formality its base should have.

Whatever the base material – gravel, fieldstone, cut stone – it should be extended at least 1 foot behind, 2 feet on either side, and perhaps as much as 3 feet in front of the bench to provide room for the feet of those sitting on it. Don't set a stone bench on lawn; a bench needs a context, and a base helps establish that. You will also create a maintenance problem in that you'll have to move it out of the way every time you mow the grass. Anyway, people love to have their feet resting on a solid stone surface; a stone bench set on lawn looks temporary at best.

One way to determine what material to use for the base of the bench is to look around to see what stone is already underfoot in that part of your garden. If you have a bluestone walkway, a panel of the same stone under the bench would look right and lend another element of coherence to the garden. If you site the bench along a stepping-stone path, lay a fieldstone

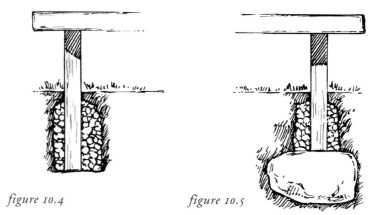

figure 10.4   *figure 10.5*

carpet under the bench made of the same stone as those used to make the path. If there is no stone path nearby to give you a cue, look to the color and material of the stone bench itself for the color, texture, and degree of formality of the stone you will choose for its base.

SETTING STANDING STONES

WHEN SETTING STANDING STONES SUCH AS GRANITE FENCE-posts or ornamental upright stones in your garden, don't take shortcuts and don't use concrete. Dig a hole that is a third of the length of the standing stone and twice as wide as the end of the stone you will bury. As with my example in the early part of this chapter, don't dig the hole any deeper than you will set the stone. In that way, your standing stone will rest atop undisturbed earth and therefore not settle.

Once you have the hole dug to the right depth, have a helper hold the stone, checking its verticality with a spirit level as you throw larger stones down into the hole. Then tamp them home with a sledgehammer or the tamping end of a large pry bar. It is important to tamp these supporting stones tightly into place as you fill the hole. When within 6 inches or so of the very top, backfill the rest with topsoil. You may have to adjust the stone over the years as weather, water, and frost shift the stone, but this is a small price to pay for such a dramatic addition to your garden.

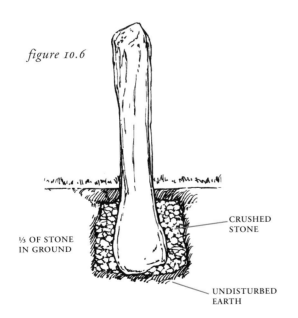

figure 10.6

⅓ OF STONE IN GROUND

CRUSHED STONE

UNDISTURBED EARTH

FIGURE 10.6 Digging a hole twice the diameter and one-third the depth of a standing stone is the first task in properly setting a stone. Crushed stone or smaller stones from your property can then be tamped around the standing stone with the head of a sledgehammer. A few inches of topsoil can be set atop the tamped stones to support groundcovers.

CHAPTER ELEVEN

THE GEOGRAPHY OF STONE

EFORE CHOOSING STONE AT A SUPPLY YARD OR GARDEN center, look around your own property and your own neighborhood. What stone already exists naturally or is already a part of your garden? What you see will help you narrow the choices when you get to the stone yard. In fact, take along samples of the existing types of stone in your garden. This will help you and anyone you work with be clear as to what new stone will complement it.

Also keep in mind that mixing two or, at most, three types of stone in a patio or wall can sometimes be a good thing, as long as they share a common color or range of colors. Consult with people at the yard regarding which stones have similar properties and would weather and work well together over time. When creating a wall or patio, you are creating background, not foreground, for your garden, so be careful not to mix too many materials in a self-conscious way. A tour de force of hard materials in a garden demands a lot of visual attention, taking interest away from the plants or views.

DELIVERY OF STONE

NCE YOU ARE READY TO PLACE AN ORDER, ASK THE SUPPLIER, who will also see to delivery, how best to determine where the stone should be dumped on your property. Describe your property and where you intend to use the stone, and ask the delivery people if they foresee any problems with the location. If you're ordering a lot of stone, you may even suggest the delivery people visit your place ahead of time. Many people don't have the foresight to get all these details ironed out ahead of time, and costly problems can quickly arise, particularly if you are not at home during delivery. Having to move tons of stone even 20 feet on your own is a daunting task indeed. Think ahead.

To help you do that, I spoke with Fran Judd, a quarryman from Goshen,

Are we to make

this day with a

white or a black

stone?

Don Quixote de la Mancha
by Miguel de Cervantes
(1547–1616)

Massachusetts, who delivers hundreds of truckloads of stone he quarries annually and then delivers throughout the Northeast, eastern Canada, and the Mid-Atlantic states. I have chosen to cite an example that illustrates how to arrange for the arrival of the largest delivery truck that might arrive at your place. Smaller trucks will pose fewer problems.

A three-axle dump truck, the kind you so often see on the highways, weighs around 15 tons. It has one front axle for two wheels and two back ones for four wheels each. A full load of around 800 square feet of 3-inch-thick landscape flagging for patios and walkways (enough for a large 20-by-40-foot paved surface) weighs around 15 tons, for a total of about 30 tons, or 60,000 pounds. Given this considerable weight, the truck driver would have to know ahead of time about weight limits of any bridges (as well as town or village roads) he might have to drive over. These limits are posted in full view at either end of bridges and at the beginning of roads.

FIGURE 11.1 We have consciously left the wall on the east and south boundaries of our garden rough to honor the practical role the wall would have played over the last 200 years on what was a Vermont hill farm.

QUESTIONS TO ASK
AT THE SUPPLY YARD

- Which stone in your yard is indigenous to the immediate area? The state? The region?

- Which stone is best for edging? For terraces and patios? For walls?

- Which two or three types of stone lend themselves to being mixed in a wall or terrace?

- How many square feet of surface will a ton of this stone produce for my patio?

- How much does this stone cost per ton? Per cubic yard?

- What are the delivery costs, per ton, to my home?

- Is there a separate loading and/or unloading charge?

- Is there a volume discount if I order a larger amount?

- Can this stone easily be shaped with hammer and chisel, or is it very difficult to shape?

- What equipment do I have to provide at my home for off-loading the stone?

- How much room do I need to provide for the unloading?

- Can you recommend professionals who could lay this stone?

This tri-axle dump truck, which is 30 feet long, needs 12 feet of width on a straight road or driveway; it needs 20 feet of clearance to negotiate most driveway curves. Before the driver backs the truck into your property, he wants to know whether you have a leach field for a private septic system and, if so, where it is. He also wants to know where heating oil or other tanks are located, as well as where sprinkler system lines and television cables are placed. He will also look for a level place to park and set his brakes before raising the body of the truck to dump the load. If you are asking a driver to back over part of your lawn, don't call for a delivery on a rainy day, because the ground will be too slippery; and be prepared to have to backfill 6-to-8-inch-deep ruts his tires will leave.

Before the driver raises the bed of the truck to dump the load, he will look for limbs and power lines overhead. Because the headboard at the front of the bed of a dump truck will be raised anywhere from 20 to 25 feet above ground level before stone slides off the bed, your choice of a delivery spot will have to provide adequate room overhead. When he dumps a load of stone flagging, it spreads over an area as large as 15 by 25 feet.

The delivery costs for a load of this dimension would be about $55 to $75 an hour, round trip. You would expect to pay just slightly more an hour for a backhoe to move the stone from the dumpsite to where you are building your patio or wall.

STONES FROM ACROSS NORTH AMERICA

FOLLOWING ARE PHOTOGRAPHS OF A WIDE, BUT BY NO MEANS all-inclusive, range of landscaping stones available across North America. These photographs which represent a broad cross-section of landscaping stones, were taken at the supply yard of Interstate Rock Products, Inc. at 9921 NE 72 Avenue in Vancouver, Washington. The photos will introduce you to some of the varieties and textures available so that when you do go to a supply yard, you will have some background information with which to make informed choices. Prices listed are approximate and may vary widely according to supply and demand.

▣ DRY-LAID WALLS

1. Montana Mossy

This stone with many flat surfaces comes from the face of ledges and has moss attached to it, thereby adding the impression of age to any wall; $310/ton for 45 square feet of surface.

2. Glacier Green Boulders

A hard quartzite that breaks along many angles, so it will be difficult to shape. This stone will produce a rough-looking but serviceable wall; $270/ton.

3. Mica Lime Light (Green Ledge Stone)

This stone has many flat surfaces. The green looks good associated with chartreuse, blue, and white in plants or other stone; red is very dramatic against the green; pink would not look good; $250/ton for 100-125 square feet of surface.

4. Split-faced roughly squared granite in coursed rubble

This is the handsome look of a wall in the Northeast of the US. With its many flat surfaces, a wall of this stone can be readily dry-laid.

5. Roughly shaped fieldstone in a dry wall

This is also what many of the walls in the Northeast look like; such a neutral-colored wall is a fine backdrop for virtually any plantings.

▣ MORTARED WALLS

6. Black Basalt

This is a blocky stone with many flat faces, but some stones may be hexagonal and therefore tough to fit into a wall. One ton will cost around $75 and will provide about 18 square feet of wall surface.

1

2

3

4

5

6

7. **Thin-Split Basalt**

   This grayish stone has many flat surfaces and faces 2 to 3 inches thick, but the individual stones will be relatively small, from 12 to 18 inches at their largest dimension; $160/ton; 1 ton will provide 50 to 60 square feet of surface in a veneer wall.

8. **Quartzite set in random ashlar pattern**

   This blocky stone provides you with the material to make a tightly fitting wet- or dry-laid wall.

9. **Split-faced Vermont Danby Marble in an ashlar pattern**

   This stone is actually cut and shaped by machinery and so may well prove very costly. Price varies widely according to the market at the time.

10. **Granite set in coursed random ashlar pattern**

    Dressed granite blocks will fit tightly together and could be used in either a wet- or dry-laid wall for a formal look.

11. **Rusticated granite set in coursed ashlar bond**

    Flamed or snapped faces of rusticated granite create a less formal look and provide more texture and shadow on the stone's surface. This could be used to make a dry-laid wall, because it is so blocky.

12. **Split-faced, rusticated granite set in random ashlar pattern**

    Using different dimensions of granite creates a random and varied look to a wall, a style that enables you to use a variety of sizes, all of which have a single, and therefore unifying, color.

13. Random Rubble

Such a wall of randomly sized stones can look unsettled. Be certain you have a good mason who can make such a style of wall look coherent.

14. Uncoursed rubble, some split-faced

Using rubble stone like this, with many rounded shapes that don't fit together well, will mean that a good deal of mortar will show. The stone can be fit more tightly together than is shown here.

15. Mixed stone in mosaic or cobweb pattern

Many similarly sized jagged stones in a wall have the potential of creating a busy, fractured look. Try for more varied sizes of stones than are shown here.

16. Coursed Granite Fieldstone

Small, medium, and large stones used in the same wall set up an interplay of shadow and light that makes for an interesting image. Granite offers good flat surfaces to work with.

17. Coursed roughly squared rubble bordered by dimension stone

Coursed rubble of similar sizes can be used to advantage at the ends and caps of walls when contrasted with stones of much larger dimension.

▨ PAVING STONES

18. Sunset Gold

A mica slate stone 2 to 3 inches thick, flat top and bottom, with a gold and reddish tone to it; $265/ton. Excellent warm-looking stone for paving, walkways, or stepping-stones through a garden of yellows, reds, blues, lavenders.

THE GEOGRAPHY
OF STONE

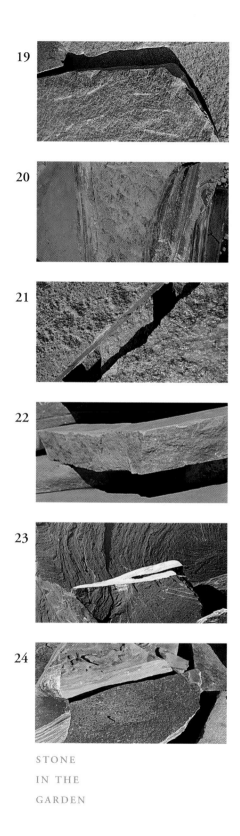

19. Lime Green Mica
A mica slate of uniform thickness, flat top and bottom; grout with light gray gravel or crusher dust; good near a gray garden; $250/ton.

20. Iron slabs
Reddish iron oxide is very much a part of the surface of these large paving stones. Good near a gray garden that would calm the red down.

21. Silver Mica
This mica schist comes in uniform 2-to-4-inch-thick stone; excellent for patios and stone walkways; $440/ton.

22. Rosewood
A sandstone; around $265/ton for 80-90 square feet, excellent for paving walkways and patios, especially in the Southwest, where these colors occur naturally in indigenous rock. This is a beautiful uniformly flat stone that, when wet, turns a much deeper red.

23. Buckingham Black
Can be used as stepping-stones or in a patio, although it is decidedly rougher than Rosewood; $265/ton.

24. Iron Mountain Flagstone (2 to 3 inches thick)
A finely textured surface, but the edges break irregularly down through the ½-inch bedding planes making for a somewhat rough edge; $240/ton for 75-100 square feet of surface.

25. Blue Mountain

This stone looks similar to the New York and Pennsylvania bluestone, but it has large patches of reddish iron oxide coloring its surfaces; beautiful when wet. Good for walkways or terraces; $470/ton.

26. White Mica

Breaks along bedding planes to create oblique angles as well as many edges that will need to be trimmed; used for wall veneer or paving. One ton, at $435, covers 175 to 200 square feet of surface.

27. Lavender Flagstone

Uniformly flat surfaces of sandstone; easily worked to create a tightly fitting patio or walkway. One ton, at $385, provides 100 to 125 square feet of paved surface for a path or terrace.

■ CUT STONES – GRANITE SETTS, COBBLE

28. Flecked Granite Setts

Excellent for creating a driveway apron or edging for a walkway or patio; these have a clear rectangular shape so that they can also be fitted close to one another.

29. Black Granite Cobble

Combine with Black Buckingham Slate; use the cobble as an inlay laid flush with the surface of the slate and around the perimeter of each slate slab in a stone patio; keep out of direct sunlight, for it readily collects heat; also good for edging gravel walkways. ($395/ton for 30 square feet.)

30. Granite Setts

Given their edges are rounded and won't fit tightly together, this stone is good for creating cobble patios or walkways, between which plants can grow. Also good for edging beds. About $8 to $10 each.

31. Granite Blocks

Good for forming a uniform, predictable surface for a patio or terrace. 7" x 10" blocks; $395/ton for 30 square feet.

32. Rose Granite Cobble Block

A warmer-colored rectangular cobble than the gray granite; around $12 per square foot of top surface.

33. Green Tumble Cobble

Good as edging for an informal gravel walkway as well as in a mortared wall; 1 ton, at $445 covers about 75 square feet; especially nice cut stone as its edges are rounded.

▪ RIVER ROCKS, ROUNDED COBBLE

34. Brown Cobble

Especially good as a surround for a pond, because rounded rock is associated with water and its ability to erode and to make rock smooth.

35. Sunny Cobble

This type of cobble is less reliably rounded and has a higher percentage of iron oxide, thus giving it the redder look.

36. Rainbow Cobble

From Montana; set in gravel for a cobble walkway; set in mortar in a wall. One ton, $100, provides 35 to 45 square feet of surface.

37. Oregon Moss Cobble

The moss and lichen on the surface will give any wall or walkway an immediate impression of age. One ton will cost around $195. Good for setting in a dark, finely crushed gravel of a similar color for a walkway, or set in mortar in a wall.

■ VOLCANIC ROCK

38. Oregon Moss Volcanic Rock

This lightweight rock is good for casual retaining walls into which pockets of soil can be set for plants; you can also use these for rock mulching. Set one-third its bulk in soil, and it will wick up water and soon be covered completely with moss; $195/ton.

39 and 40. Featherrock (large pieces/boulders; smaller pieces)

These are rough boulders for edging a walkway or for creating mossy accents at entrances to a garden. Set one-third its bulk in soil, and it will wick up water and turn mossy; $465/ton.

■ STANDING STONES AND BENCHES

41. Columnar Basalt

Can be used horizontally for low retaining walls; used vertically as a pair of standing stones to mark an entrance, or singly to add a vertical accent in a garden. 5-foot-long boulders, $120/ton; 10-foot + boulders, $160/ton; 18-inch-thick columns, $185/ton.

■ PEBBLES FOR IMBEDDING IN CEMENT

42. Mexican Pebbles (1 to 2 inch; 2 to 3 inch)

These gray pebbles look wonderful in a slightly gray-tinted cement; 31¢/pound or $515/ton for 85 square feet.

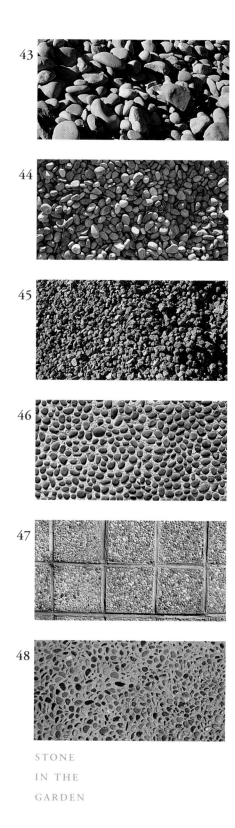

43. Larger River Rock

Set these in a bed of brownish crushed gravel or a brown-tinted cement to create a walkway; set three-quarters of the thickness in the gravel or cement. Typically sold as 2 to 6 inch or 4 to 10 inch; $35/ton.

44. River Rock (1½ to 1¾ inch)

Set within a slightly gray-tinted cement for a walkway or patio. $35/ton.

45. Red Rock (1½ to 1¾ inch)

Use this dramatically colored gravel in tinted cement of roughly the same color, but only if the color approximates that of indigenous stone in view from your home. One ton, at $80, provides about 80 square feet of finished surface.

46. Exposed pebble aggregate concrete

One ton, at $35 to $65 per ton, depending on the nature of the pebble, provides about 100 square feet of finished surface. This is what the Mexican pebble would look like in place.

47. Pea Gravel in fine aggregate concrete

Score lines set in the concrete add form and pattern to a walkway or patio of this material. One ton, at $20, provides about 100 square feet of surface.

48. Beach Pebble aggregate in tinted concrete

The river rock above looks much like this beach pebble. Use this style of embedding, especially if the pebble is indigenous to your area.

■ INSCRIBED STONE

49. Weathered carved marble
Calling on the help of a monument maker would enable you to get any stone inscribed with the name of your garden, home, or any inscription that echoes the mood of your garden.

■ ARTIFICIAL STONE (concrete)

50. Precast Concrete "stone" units set in mortar
You can purchase concrete "stones" that are surprisingly convincing. Set into mortar, they take on the look of a real wall.

51. Precast concrete artificial stones
Artificial stones come in a wide variety of shapes, colors, and sizes. Choose them according to what looks most like the stone indigenous to your area.

52. Stamped and tinted concrete paving
Professionally installed concrete such as this can be made to look like real stone.

53. Composite stone at the Chilstone Manufactury, England
Many stone artifacts for the garden today, including benches, statuary, and dimensional stone, are actually made up of finely pulverized stone that is bound together in a mortar mix and then cast in forms.

GLOSSARY

(With help from The Dry Stone Waller's Association Publications)

A-frame – A wooden or metal frame used as a guide when building.

Ashlar – Any kind of cut and shaped rectilinear stone used in walls.

Basalt – A fine-grained igneous rock, strong and weather-resistant, used in garden walls and as stepping-stones and standing stones.

Batter – The backward slope or taper of a wall.

Belgian blocks – Paving units, often approximately the size and dimensions of a large brick. They are made of granite or other durable stone and are used to construct or edge paths and terraces.

Berm – A low, artificially made mound of earth that adds height and depth to a flat landscape.

Bond – The arrangement of stones in a wall, designed to increase the wall's strength as well as to enhance its appearance.

Boulders – Boulders are large fieldstone or quarried rocks and are sometimes described as "one-man" or "two-man" rocks to indicate size.

Chinking – Small stones used to pack the heart of a dry-laid stone wall.

Chisel – A steel tool with a wedge-shaped or pointed cutter, made in a range of sizes and used with a hammer to cut and shape stones.

Cleavage – The fault line at which certain metamorphic rocks split most readily.

Cobblestones – Naturally rounded stones with dimensions between two and 12 inches; used in paths, terraces, and water features.

Coping – The line of stones along the top of the wall that protects the structure beneath.

Course – A layer of stones in the face of a wall.

Crushed rock – Stones approximately ¼ inch to 2 inches in size that have been mechanically crushed; characterized by sharply angled corners and irregular planes, crushed rock packs together well and is useful as a foundation material for stone construction.

Dressing – The process of shaping the faces of a stone.

Dry stone wall – A wall built without mortar.

Face – An exposed side of a stone wall.

Face stone – A stone whose outer surface forms part of the face of the wall.

Featherrock – A natural volcanic rock quarried in the High Sierra country of California. Robust and heavy in appearance, this exceptionally strong and enduring stone is, in fact, light in weight.

Fieldstone – Fieldstone is gathered from fields, prairies or even deserts, where it has lain for many years and, depending on locale, will show a weathered effect on the exposed side, usually a covering of moss and lichens.

Fillings – Small, irregular stones placed between the two faces of a wall to pack the space between them. Also known as hearting.

Flagstone – Any kind of stone that splits into shallow slabs suitable for paving.

Footing – Stone at the base of a wall or the foundation of a wall.

Gneiss – A medium to coarse-grained metamorphic rock; strong and weather-resistant, it is most often used in garden walls and rock gardens.

Grain – The lines of natural stratification in sedimentary rocks.

Granite – A fine to medium coarse-grained igneous stone; dense and water-resistant, it is often used in garden walls and as stepping-stones and specimen rocks.

Gravel – Naturally rounded or mechanically crushed stones ranging in size from ¼ inch to 1½ inches. Often used in gravel gardens, paths, terraces, and water features.

Hearting and heartstones – The small stones used as filling or packing in a stone wall.

Igneous rock – Rock formed from solidified minerals and gases originally found within the Earth's crust.

Joint – In walling, the crack between two adjacent stones in a course.

Limestone – A fine- to coarse-grained sedimentary rock; often used as ashlar or flagstone because it splits easily.

Marble – A fine-grained metamorphic rock that is strong and weather-resistant; more often used in indoor than outdoor paving and walls because of its cost and its slickness when wet.

Metamorphic rock – Igneous, sedimentary, or other metamorphic rocks that have been transformed by heat, pressure, or chemical action into other kinds of stone.

Mortar – A mixture of cement and fine aggregates, such as sand and lime, that is used to bind paving and wall stones together.

Outcrops – Bare rock formations protruding from the surrounding soil.

Pea gravel – A fine grade of naturally rounded stones ⅜ inch in diameter.

Random paving – Paving consisting of irregularly shaped pieces set on a mortar bed.

Retaining wall – A wall built across the face of a bank or slope to hold soil back, thereby creating a level place behind the wall.

Round rock or river rock – Rock that is always rounded and smooth from being tumbled in streams or by glacial action over many centuries.

Sandstone – A fine- to coarse-grained sedimentary rock that splits easily.

Scree – An accumulation of angular rock fragments found at the base of a cliff or steep slope; often replicated in rock gardens, where its stony "soil" accommodates a variety of alpines and rock plants.

Sedimentary rock – Rock composed from the consolidated debris of igneous, metamorphic, and other sedimentary rock; because they split easily, sedimentary stones, such as limestone and sandstone, are used extensively in garden constructions.

Sett – A small square block of stone, usually granite, used for paving.

Slate – A fine-grained metamorphic stone that is highly weather-resistant; sometimes used as flagstones in constructing garden paths and terraces.

Stile – A set of steps over a wall, designed to allow passage to pedestrians, but not livestock.

Throughstones – A large stone placed across the width of a wall to tie the sides together.

Tie stones – Long stones laid across the width of the wall to add lateral stability.

Weep holes – Through-wall drainage holes used to prevent water from backing up behind mortared retaining walls.

APPENDIX A
Sources of Stone Across North America

Internet Searches

Initiate a search using such key words as "quarried stones," "wall stone," "paving stones," "stone walls," "fieldstone," and the like.

Go to the stone search resource tool: natural-stone.com
This site offers a vast range of information on locating natural stone, including information on ordering a $50 CD Rom that will give you more than 1,100 stone images. Many are for interior use, so pick and choose carefully as you move through the site.
OR
Go to constructionnet.net, a comprehensive directory of materials for the construction industry. This directory will send you off in many directions in your search for stone suppliers.
OR
Go to thebluebook.com, The Electronic Blue Book for Building and Construction. Choose your region, and then type your keyword search for such topics as "flagstone suppliers," "cut stone suppliers," "wall stone suppliers," etc. Many names and addresses tailored to your region of the country will appear.

A Mail-Order Source for Stoneworking Hand Tools

Trow and Holden Company
  45-57 South Main Street
  Barre, VT 05641
  PH: 800-451-4349
  PH: 802-476-7221
  FX: 802-476-7025

Sources for Stone

A.A. Will Materials Corp.
  168 Washington Street
  Stoughton, MA
  PH: 617-344-0300
  PH: 800-4AA-WILL
  FX: 617-341-0300
  E: aawill@thecia.net
Adam Ross Cut Stone Co.
  1003 Broadway
  Albany, NY 12204
  PH: 518-463-6674
  FX: 518-463-0710
  Web: adamrosscutstone.com
Adventure Stone, LLC
  9830 Isabelle Road
  Lafayette, CO 80303
  PH: 303-664-8390
  FX: 303-665-6448
  Web: adventurestone.com
Allegheny Mountain Flagstone Quarries
  1400 Gardner Street, NW
  Ellerslie, MD 21529
  PH: 301-777-5069
Alpine Stone Co.
  3505 Carpenter Pond Road
  Durham, NC 27703
  PH: 919-596-4649
  PH: 800-315-7227
  FX: 919-596-2922
American Slate Group
  1328 4th Avenue SE
  Decatur, AL 35601
  PH: 256-350-9888
  FX: 256-350-2856
American Stone
  4040 South 300 West
  Salt Lake City, UT 84107
  PH: 801-262-4300
  OR
  3616 Spring Mountain Road
  Las Vegas, NV 89102
  PH: 702-876-6749

OR
  17603 NE Union Road
  Vancouver, WA 98642
  PH: 360-573-8055
Annandale Rock Products Offices
  12128 State Highway 55 NW
  Annandale, MN 55302
  PH: 612-274-3037
Ashfield Flat Stone
  (Jerry and Johanna Pratt)
  Hawley Road
  Ashfield, MA 01330
  PH: 413-628-4773
Bergen Bluestone
  404 State Highway
  Paramus, NJ
  PH: 201-261-1903
Brock White Stone
  580 41st Avenue North
  St. Cloud, MN 56303-2026
  PH: 320-251-5060
  PH: 800-892-8589
  FX: 320-251-2763
Butler Stone Quarry
  15027 Falls Road
  Butler, MD 21023
  PH: 410-771-4200
  FX: 410-771-4320
Bybee Stone Co.
  P.O. Box 968
  Bloomington, IN 47402
  PH: 800-457-4530
  FX: 812-876-6329
  Web: bybeestone.com
China Stone, International –
  Granite and Marble Manufacturing
  Call 734-996-8051 for nearest distributor
  Web: constructionstone.com
  E: lumber@earthlink.com
Clifford Stone and Material Co,
  2900 North Campbell
  Valparaiso, IN
  PH: 219-462-4055

Connecticut Stone Supplies
311 Post Road
Orange, CT 06477
PH: 860-795-9767

Courtland Industries
P.O. Box 32
Courtland, MN 56021
PH: 507-359-2570
PH: 800-422-0751
FX: 507-354-7320

Decorative Rock Network
639 East Lockford Street
Lodi, CA 95240
Web: decorock.com

Elliott Stone Co.
(Mr. Bill Rhode)
P.O. Box 4220485
Summerland Key, Fl 33042
PH: 800-234-6227
FX: 305-745-2160
WEB: www.elliottstone.com

Endless Mountain Fieldstone Supply
2 Willow Street
Tunkhannock, PA 18657
PH: 717-836-3573
WEB: pafieldstonesupply.com
E: stone@epix.net

Environmental Aesthetics, Inc.
(faux boulders)
7525 Ethel Avenue, Unit B
North Hollywood, CA 91605
PH: 818-255-1355
FX: 818-255-1360
E: info c rockwork.com

Fletcher Granite Company
(Dimensional stone and hand-carved
ornaments)
275 Groton Road
North Chelmsford, MA 01863
PH: 978-251-4031
FX: 978-251-8773
E: ward@fletchergranite.com
Web: www.fletchergranite.com

Gerten's Boulders
5500 Blaine Avenue
Inver Grove Heights, MN 55076
PH: 651-450-0277
WEB: gertengreenhouses.com

Goliath Stone Sales, Ltd. (Wholesale)
739 Park Avenue
Huntington, NY 11743
PH: 888-423-5175
FX: 516-427-5419
Web: goliathstone.com

Goshen Stone Company
(Fran and Linda Judd)
164 Berkshire Trail West
Goshen, MA 01032
PH: 413-268-7590
FX: 413-268-3261

Halquist Stone
23654 West Lisbon Road
Sussex, WI 53089
PH: 800-255-8811
FX: 414-246-7148

High Plains Stone
P.O. Box 100
Castle Rock, CO 80104
PH: 303-791-1862
E: stone@hplains.net

Hilltop Quarries
(Brad Simpson)
Piermont, NH
PH: 603-989-5558

Interstate Rock Products, Inc.
(Jerry Cates)
9921 NE 72nd Avenue
Vancouver, WA 98686
PH: 360-573-3410
PH: 503-285-4142

Johnston and Rhodes Bluestone
1 Bridge Street
P.O. Box 130
East Branch, NY 13756
PH: 607-363-7595
FX: 607-363-7894
E: pjohnston@citlink.net
Allen Sherburne or Peter Johnston.

Lang Stone Co.
707 Short Street
Columbus, OH 43215-5618
PH: 614-228-5489
PH: 800-589-LANG
FX: 614-224-LANG
E: contact@langstone.com

Morrison Natural Stone
P.O. Box 817
Highway 271 West
Wister, OK 74966
PH: 800-430-4455
FX: 918-655-7740

Old World Stone, Ltd.
1151 Heritage Road
Burlington, Ontario
Canada L7L 4Y1
PH: 905-332-5547
FX: 905-332-6068
OR
300 Pearl Street
Suite 200
Buffalo, NY 14202
PH: 800-281-9615
FX: 716-842-3038
Web: oldworldstone.com

Oregon Decorative Rock Co.
11050 SW Denney Road
Beaverton, OR 97005
PH: 503-646-9232
OR
1716 NE Columbia Boulevard
Portland, OR 97211
PH: 503-289-7407

Pavestone Plus (Concrete pre-cast
paving materials to look like natural
stone)
In the US:
PH: 1-800-265-6496
FX: 1-800-276-3091
E: sales@pavestoneplus.com
In Canada:
519—740-2543

Phillips Stone Co., Inc.
7850 Ute Highway
Longmont, CO 80500-9201
PH: 800-820-6095

RMG Stone Products
P.O. Box 807
East Hubbardton Road
Castleton, VT 05735
PH: 802-468-5636
FX: 802-468-8969
Web: sales@rmgstone.com

Rock Specialties
P.O. Box 230120
Tigard, OR 97223

Rocky Mountain Stone Co., Inc.
4721 Pan American Freeway, NE
Albuquerque, NM 87109
PH: 505-345-8518
Web: rmstone.com

Rolling Rock Stone Company
RD 4
Boyertown, PA 19512
PH:215-987-6226

Santa Fe Stone, Burke Denman,
President
Santa Fe, NM 87502
PH: 800-484-5673
FX: 505-983-7450
Web: santafestone.com

Scotia Slate Products. Ltd.
Box 12 – Comp 3
Kennetcook, NS
BON 1PO
Canada
PH: 902-632-2989
FX: 902-632-2290
E: slate@fox.nstn.ca

Select Stone
John P. Mills, Geologist
P.O. Box 6403
Bozeman, MT 59771-6403
PH: 888-237-1000
FX: 406-582-1069
Web: jmills@selectstone.com

Sierra Nevada White Granite
90 Gault Way
Sparks, NV 89431
Rick Cline: PH 702-356-5351

Sierra Boulder
Yard is at:
3293 Taylor Road
Loomis, CA
OR, for mailing:
P.O. Box 2863
Grass Valley, CA 95945
PH: 530-265-4873

611 Stone
P.O. Box 292
Route 611
Pipersville, PA 18947
PH: 215-766-2882
Web: 611stone.com

Sticks and Stones Landscaping
Materials
Northampton, MA
PH: 413-584-2813

Stone Stackers
RR1, Box 1094
Sweet Valley, PA 18656
PH: 717-477-0989
FX: 717-477-5552
WEB: stonestackers.com

Texastone Quarries
P.O. Box 38
Garden City, TX 79739-0038
PH: 915-354-2569
FX: 915-354-2669
E: TEXASTONE@aol.com

Tri-State Stone
P.O. Box 34300
Bethesda, MD 20827
PH: 301-365-2100
FX: 301-365-5524

Vegas Rock
11635 Bermuda Road
Las Vegas, NV 89123
PH: 702-791-7625
FX: 702-896-4533
Web: vegasrock.com

Vengeance Creek Stone
P.O. Box 186
Murphy, NC 28906
PH: 800-295-6023
Web: natural-stones.com

Western Rock and Boulder
P.O. Box 2483
Fallon, NV 89407
PH: 877-289-2762
Web: westrocks.com
E: Sales@WestRocks.com

Wholesale Landscape Supply
(Tom Wilson)
102 South Elam
Peerless Park, MO 63088
PH: 314-861-3323
Web: infor@wlstw.com

APPENDIX B
Sources of Stone Benches, Sculpture, Garden Ornaments, and Details

Internet Research:
Type in such categories on your Web browser as: "stone benches," "stone garden ornaments," "garden sculpture," "garden ornaments."

Anavian Gallery (Arts of Islam and the ancient Near East)
160 East 56th Street
New York, NY 10022
PH: 212-319-7781
FX: 212-319-7784
Web: anaviangallery.com

Archiped Classics
315 Cole Street
Dallas, TX 75207
PH: 214-748-7437
FX: 214-748-7497
WEB: archipedclassics.com

Architectural Antique Warehouse
17985 Highway 27 (at Route 34)
Fairhope, AL 36532
PH: 334-928-2880
Web: architectural-antiques.com
Architectural Artifacts, Inc.
4325 North Ravenswood
Chicago, IL 60613
PH: 773-348-0622
Bates Architectural Collection
4238 North Craftsman Court
Scottsdale, AZ 85251
PH: 602-970-3025
FX: 602-970-4349
Web: batesarchitectural.com
Brock White Stone and Brick
580 41st Avenue North
St. Cloud, MN 56303-2026
PH: 800-892-8589
FX: 320-251-2763
Carved in Stone
Lee, NH 03824
(Custom stone carving and stone
sculpture)
PH: 603-659-4026
FX: 603-659-5642
Castique Garden Statues
Historic Pontiac Mills, Bldg S-1
334 Knight Street
Warwick, RI 02886
PH: 888-738-8866
FX: 401-738-0880
Web: castique.com
Cherry Blossom Gardens (Japanese-
style garden artifacts)
15709 North Lund Road
Eden Prairie, MN 55346
PH: 612- 949-3880
PH: 877-226-4387
FX: 612-975-0783
Classic Garden Ornaments
247 Glen Head Road
Glen Head, NY 11545
PH: 516-759-5601

Creations in Stone
Justin Rose, sculptor
4½ Catherine Street
Burlington, VT 05401
PH: 802-652-0730
E: info@creationstone.com
Dunn Mehler Gallery
337 Mirada Road
Half Moon Bay, CA 94019
PH: 650-726-7667
Web: elisha@dunnmehler.com
Eleganza Ltd.
Magnolia Village
3117 West Smith Street #316
Seattle, WA 98199
PH: 206-283-0609
Elizabeth Street
1176 and 1190 2nd Avenue
New York, NY 10021
PH: 212-644-6969
FX: 212-750-7048
Web: www.dir-dd.com/elizabeth-
street.html
Exotic Imports
5635 Snowdon Place
San Jose, CA 95138
PH: 408-274-7780
FX: 408-270-4001
E: artberman@aol.com
Web: exoticimports.org
Fine Garden Art and Ornaments
Fletcher Granite Company
(Dimensional stone and hand-carved
ornaments)
275 Groton Road
North Chelmsford, MA 01863
PH: 978-251-4031
FX: 978-251-8773
E: ward@fletchergranite.com
Web: www.fletchergranite.com
Garden Accents
4 Union Hill Rd.
West Conshohocken, PA 19428
PH: 610-825-5525

Garden of Distinction
5819 Sixth Avenue South
Seattle, WA 98108
PH: 206-763-0517
FX: 206-762-2002
Web: agardenofdistinction.com
Genuine Millstones
Anne Hathaway Shop
Tula at Bennet Street
Atlanta, GA 30309
PH: 404-352-4153
Web: millstones.com
Gifts OK
Route 5 Box 1630
Eufaula, OK 74432
PH: 918-339-2376
FX: 918-339-2376
Haddonstone (USA) Ltd.
201 Heller Place
Interstate Business Park
Bellmawr, NJ 08031
PH: 609-931-7-11
FX: 609-931-0040
Haddonstone (USA) Ltd.
5362 Industrial Drive
Huntington Beach, CA 92649
PH: 714-894-3500
FX: 714-894-5615
Web: www.Haddonstone.com
Lichenstone, Inc. (English stone garden
ornaments)
Dieta VonMatthiesen
Box 312
Center Cambridge Road
Cambridge, NY 12816
PH: 518-677-3754
FX: 518-677-2341
Limestone Concept
1438 S. Robertson Boulevard
Los Angeles, CA 90035
Web: limestoneconcept.com
E: stoneconcept@earthlink.net

Kenneth Lynch and Sons, Inc.
  Box 488
  84 Danbury Road
  Wilton, CT 06897-0488
  PH: 203-762-8363
  FX: 203-762-2999
  E: info@klynchandsons.com
Materials Unlimited
  Two West Michigan Avenue
  Ypsilanti, MI 48197
  PH: 734-483-6980
  FX: 734-482-3636
  E: materials@mat-unl.com
  Web: www.mat-unl.com
New England Garden Ornaments
  P.O. Box 235
  38 East Brookfield Road
  North Brookfield, MA 01535
  PH: 508-867-4474
  FX: 508-867-8409
  E: nego@bx.com
  Web: negardenornaments.com
Noble House and Garden (carved
granite)
  6408 Lakeside Drive
  Flower Mound, TX 75028-5834
  PH: 888-430-4455
  FX: 817-430-4455
  Web: granitesculpture.com
Jill Nooney
  Bedrock Farm
  45 High Road
  Lee, NH 03824
  PH: 603-659-2993
  FX: 603-659-6505
  E: zipity@aol.com
  Web: www.finegarden.com
North Canyon Stone Benches
  P.O. Box 129
  Aurora, UT
  PH: 435-529-1175
  FX: 435-529-4064
  Web: gbasin.net/~ncsi/index.htm

Pottery Row
  206 Northwest Tenth Avenue
  Portland, Oregon
  97209
  PH: 503-223-1600
  FX: 503-223-5120
Said In Stone
  8300 Douglas Avenue
  Suite 800
  Dallas, TX 75225
  PH: 214-363-6933
  FX: 214-363-6522
  Web: saidinstone,com
A. Silvestri
  2635 Bayshore Boulevard
  San Fransisco, CA 94134
  PH: 415-239-5990
  FX: 415-239-0422
  E: info@asilvestri.com
Soderback Gardens, Inc (fine
Japanese-style garden artifacts)
  1828 Anderson Creek Road
  Talent, OR 97540
  PH: 541-535-8887
  Web: olof@soderback.com
South Zenith Petroglyph
(Stone benches)
  RT 1 — Box 248
  Linside, WV 24951
  PH: 304-832-6459
  Web: homestead.com
Stone Forest (Japanese &
contemporary style — all granite)
  P.O. Box 2840
  Dept. WB
  Santa Fe, NM 87504
  PH: 888-682-2987
  FX: 505-982-2712
  Web: stoneforest.com
Stone Palace
  8936 Beverly Boulevard
  Los Angeles, CA 90048
  PH: 310-278-4165
  FX 310-278-9670
  Web: stone-palace.com

Stones Assembled
  (Jason Medland, sculptor)
  Box 73
  Peterborough, ON
  K95 6T5
  Canada
  PH: 705-749-0223
Urban Archaeology
  285 Lafayette Street
  New York, NY 10012
  PH: 212-431-6969
  FX: 212-941-1918
Vengeance Creek Stone
  9289 W., US Highway 64
  Murphy, NC 28906
  PH: 800-295-6023
  E: vcstone@grove.net
  WEB: vcstone.com

APPENDIX C
Associations

Building Stone Institute
  P.O. Box 507
  Purdys, NY 10578
  OR
  24 Yerkes Road
  North Salem, NY 10560
  PH: 914-232-5725
  They have many free booklets with
  titles such as "How to Build a Stone
  Retaining Wall," "How to Build
  a Patio," and other helpful
  publications.
Dry Stone Walling Association of
Great Britain
  c/o NFYFC, National Agriculture
  Centre
  Stoneleigh Park
  Warwickshire CV8 2LG UK
  PH: 011-44-121-378-0493
  Web: dswagb.ndirect.co.uk
  Good source for reliable how-to
  information on building dry stone

walls as well as information on dry stone wallers

Indiana Limestone Institute of America
400 Stone City Bank Building
Bedford, IN 47421
PH: 812-275-4426
Web: iliai.com

Marble Institute of America
30 Eden Alley
Suite 301
Columbus, OH 43215
PH: 614-228-6194
FX: 614-461-1497
E: miaadmin@marble-institute.com
Sources for information for supplies, masons, distributors

National Building Granite Quarries Association
1220 L Street, NW
Suite 100-167
Washington, DC 20005
PH: 800-557-2848
Information nationwide on the granite industry

APPENDIX D
Types of Stone from Across North America for Walls, Paving, and Standing Stones

WALL STONE

Cheyenne Autumn Ledge – linear, random-length cut; ledge stone; creamy color with brown and tan streaks

Kennesaw Mountain Moss Ledge Stone Dry Stack – blocky pieces with some moss on faces; dark brown and black; some with red, orange or gray streaking

Lompoc (California) Oatmeal Flagstone – extremely hard gray limestone; oatmeal color; moderately smooth surface

Wyoming Valley Ledge – angular, blocky, small stones for a small wall; gun-metal gray with brown and gold throughout

Colorado Water Wash Pink – water-worn appearance; pink; smooth faces

New England Wall Stone – rounded granite, often with moss or lichen

Sierra Nevada White Granite – white granite boulders and building stone; angular, with at least one flat face; from Washoe Valley, Nevada

Kootenai Ledge Dry Stack – from Montana; large, rectangular, lichen-covered fieldstones in light grays, reds

Mission Springs Dry Stack – from Montana; large tan-brown rectangular blocks

Eagle Moss Rock Dry Stack – from Montana; large, semi-rectangular, lichen-covered fieldstones

Limestone Outcropping – from Montana; large flat limestone slabs to make a massive retaining wall

Torrey Sandstone – from Utah; buff to light chocolate; rippled surface; good for wall capstone

PAVING STONE

Arizona Buff Flagstone – medium-hard Arizona sandstone; buff brown, tan to yellowish tan; smooth

Arizona Buckskin Flagstone – medium-hard sandstone; yellow-tan with some black running through it; smooth

Arizona Cinnamon Flagstone – very hard sandstone; light brown, true cinnamon color; with some red through it; very smooth

Arizona Rosa Flagstone – medium-hard sandstone; light to medium pink; smooth

Arizona Sedona Red Flagstone – medium-hard sandstone; red and smooth

Arizona Oak Flagstone – hardest of the Arizona sandstones; light brown to tan; very smooth

Arizona Peach Flagstone – medium-hard Arizona sandstone; mixed tan, yellow, pink, and peach; smooth

Idaho Quartzite Storm Mountain Select – extremely hard and thin quartzite; light earth tones; shiny flecks throughout; medium to smooth surface

Idaho Quartzite Gold – very hard; silver/gold blend; medium-smooth surface

New York and Pennsylvania Bluestone – a hard sandstone from the East Coast; blue and gray, sometimes with brown or copper color; also pure blue or gray; medium smooth

Arizona Chocolate Flagstone – brown to purplish brown sandstone; smooth

Mica Schist (AKA Goshen or Conway schist) – from the East Coast; light gray with flecks of mica; quarried in large 2-to-3-inch-thick sheets

Vermont Marble – white, or streaked with gray or black; very smooth

New Hampshire Granite – gray, very hard and uniform in color; typically available sawn or shaped for flagging

Indiana Limestone – from near Bloomington; light gray, almost white; AKA Indiana Buff or Sherwood Cut

Dolomitic Limestone (from near Lannon, Wisconsin); light gray to buff; orange, brown, gray or blue

Utah Sandstones – in browns, tans, creams; randomly shaped or cut

Texas Laredo Blend – a light gray, shiny, very hard quartzite

Old Spruce Mountain Quartzite (from Connecticut) – gray with sparkly flecks of mica and a copper wash on the surface

Silver Lakes Connecticut Quartzite – a very hard shiny dark gray surface with tiny black flecks

Crab Orchard Sandstone – from Tennessee; dark and light gray and buff
Battle Ridge Sandstone – from Montana; a tan to brown and red flagstone
Prichard Flagstone – from Montana; chocolate brown; very hard quartzite
Picture Rock Pavers – from Montana – multicolored limestone
Newcastle Sandstone – from Montana; gray to black sandstone
Aspen Frost Quartzite – from Utah; a white quartzite with golden highlights; flat, smooth, with mica flecks
Sunrise Sandstone – from Utah; a blonde sandstone with concentric veining of gold, rose, and lavender, giving the appearance of the light of the rising sun; very smooth
Cherokee Sandstone – from Utah; deep red with salmon-pink accents; smooth and flat

STANDING STONES
Columnar Basalt (often from the Columbia River Gorge near Portland, OR); roughly hexagonal, almost black, in columns
Granite fenceposts

APPENDIX E
Sources of Pool Liners and Stones, Real and Faux

For how-to videos for making pools, ponds, streams, and waterfalls:
Easyponds, Inc.
  51535 Bittersweet Road
  Granger, IN 46530
  PH: 219-277-3798
  FX: 219- 277-4279
  E: froggie@easyponds.com
  Web: easyponds.com
  At $29.95 each, this company provides videos on the basics of

creating water features; seasonal care of water features; how to create waterfalls, streams, and other attractions. Go to their Web site to preview the videos before purchasing.
Allscapes, Inc.
  4383 Saddlecreek Court
  Auburn, GA 30011
  PH/FX: 770-339-6655
  Web: allscapes.com
All South Stone and Water Garden Center
  2142 Stone Mountain Lithonia Road
  Lithonia, GA 30058
  PH: 770-482-6052
  FX: 770-482-3365
  Web: atl-watergardens.com
Aquascape Designs. Inc.
  1119 Lyon Road
  Batavia, IL 60510
  PH: 630-326-1700
  or 800-306-6227
Crary Waterfalls and Aquatic Nursery
  128 Narrows Road
  Ctr. Barnstead, NH 03225
  PH: 603-269-7769
  E: crary@worldpath.com
  Web: worldpath.net/~crary
Lilypons Water Gardens (plants, construction materials, and equipment)
  6800 Lilypons Road
  P.O. Box 10
  Buckeystown, MD 21717
  PH: 800-723-7667
  or 800-999-5459
  FX: 800-879-5459
  Web: lilypons.com
Paradise Water Gardens (a full range of pond and waterfall construction materials)
  14 May Street
  Whitman, MA 02382
  PH: 617-447-4711 or
  800-966-4591

Resource Conservation Technology (rubber and EPDM liners and other accessories)
  2633 North Calvert Street
  Baltimore, MD 21218
  PH: 410-366-1146
  FX: 410-366-1202
Rock and Water (cement and fiberglass rocks and water garden supplies)
  815 Fifth Street
  Fillmore, CA 93015
  PH: 805-524-5600
  FX: 805-524-7339
  Web: rock-n-water.com
Talavera Stone Company (waterfalls, boulders, fountains of faux stone)
  3831 E. Technical Drive
  Tuscon, AZ 85713
  PH: 800-737-5386
  FX: 520-790-7127
  Web: fallingh2o.com
Urdl's Waterfall Creations
  2010 Northwest 1st Street
  Delray Beach, FL 33445
  PH: 561-278-3320
  FX: 561-278-3320
  Web: urdls.com
Van Ness Water Gardens
  2460 North Euclid Avenue
  Upland, CA 91784
  PH: 800-205-2425
  FX: 909-949-7217
  Web: vnwg.com
Waterfalls, Etc.
  691 Larchmont
  Wood Ranch, CA 93065
  PH: 800-527-8363 or
  805-378-4690
  Web: waterfallsetc.com

BIBLIOGRAPHY

Allport, Susan, *Sermons in Stone: The Stone Walls of New England and New York.* New York: W.W. Norton & Co., 1990. (ISBN 0-393-31202-X)

Archer-Wills, Anthony, *The Water Gardener.* New York, Barron's Educational Series, 1993. (ISBN 0-8120-6332-5)

British Trust For Conservation Volunteers: *Dry Stone Walling.* Reading, UK: Wembley Press, 1978. (ISBN 0-9501643-5-6)

Goldsworthy, Andy, *Stone.* New York: Harry N. Abrams, Inc., 1994. (ISBN 0-8109-3847-2)

Jerome, John, *Stone Work: Reflections on Serious Play and Other Aspects of Country Life.* Hanover, NH: University Press of New England, 1989. (ISBN9 780874 517620)

Juracek, Judy, *Surfaces: Visual Research for Artists, Architects and Designers.* New York, NY: W.W. Norton & Co., 1996. (ISBN 0-393-73007-7)

Lawrence, Mike, *Outdoor Stonework: Twenty Easy-To-Build Projects for Your Patio and Garden.* Pownal, Vermont: Storey Communications, 1995. (ISBN O-88266-891-9)

Malitz, Jerome and Seth, *Reflecting Nature: Garden Designs from Wild Landscapes.* Portland, Oregon: Timber Press, 1998. (ISBN 0-88192-455-5)

McAfee, Patrick, *Irish Stone Walls.* Niwot, Colorado: Irish American Book Company, 1997. (ISBN 0-86278-478-6)

McRaven, Charles: *Stonework: Techniques and Projects.* Pownal, Vermont: Storey Books, 1997. (ISBN 0-88266-976-1)

Osler, Mirabel, *The Garden Wall.* New York: Simon and Schuster, 1993. (ISBN 0-671-79689-5)

Reed, David, *The Art and Craft of Stonescaping.* Asheville, North Carolina: Lark Books, 1998. (ISBN 1 57990 018 6)

Slawson, David A., *Secret Teachings in the Art of Japanese Gardens.* Tokyo and New York: Kodansha International, Ltd., 1987. (ISBN 0-87011-799-8)

Thomas, Charles B., *Water Gardens: How to Plan and Plant a Backyard Pond.* Boston and New York: Houghton Mifflin Company, 1997. (ISBN 0-395-81590-8)

Van Sweden, James, *Gardening With Water.* New York: Random House, 1995. (ISBN 0-679-42946-8)

Vivian, John, *Building Stone Walls.* Pownal, Vermont: Storey Books, 1976. (ISBN 0-88266-074-8)

Whitner, Jan Kowalczewski, *Gardening With Stone.* New York: Macmillan, 1999. (ISBN 0 780028 621340)

Whitner, Jan Kowalczewski, *Stonescaping: A Guide to Using Stone in Your Garden.* Pownal, Vermont: Storey Communications, 1992. (ISBN 0-88266-755-6)

Wilson, Andrew, *The Creative Water Gardener.* London: Ward Lock, 1995. (ISBN 0-7063-7290-5)

INDEX

Page numbers in *italics* refer to illustrations.

abelia, *101*
Acer campestre, 75
Alchemilla alpina, 68
algae, in pools, 104-5
"Anecdote of the Jar" (Stevens), 133
Anemone vitifolia 'Robustissima', 99
arabis, *24*
arbor vitae, 107
Arctostaphylos uva-ursi, 176
artifacts, cast-stone, 195-98
  selection of, 196-97
  winter care of, 197-98
artifacts, stone:
  drainage and, 192-94, *196*
  siting of, 125-27
  see also sculptures, stone; standing stones
Astilbe:
  'Fanal', 107
  'Professor Van der Weilen', 107
Austin, Alfred, 23

batter, 16, 146
bedding, 146
bedrock, *83,* 85-89, *171,* 174-79
  faux, *83,* 106, 176-78, *177*
  gardening on and around, 86-87, 89, *89,*
    174-76, *175*
  in natural gardens, 78-81, 85-87, *85,* 89
  not gardening around, 87-89, *88, 89*
  placement of, 85
  as pool edging, 105, *105,* 106
benches, stone, *28, 117,* 118-21, 128-33,
    128, 129, 131, 209
  roles of, 129-31
  setting of, 198-99, *198*
  siting of, 129-32
  wooden benches vs., 128-29
Berberis thunbergii 'Atropurpurea', *20*
Bernier, André, 121, 192
Betula japonica 'Whitespire', *20*
birch, *20,* 81-83, 84
  Heritage River, 34
birdbaths, 93-96
bluestone, *45, 46,* 49, 50, 72, 154-56

boulders, *23, 33,* 78-85, *80,* 170-74
  bridges and, *80, 114, 115*
  faces of, 170-72
  moving and setting of, 172-74, *173*
  in natural gardens, 78-81, *79, 84,* 89
  naturalistic pools and, 101, *101, 103,*
    104, 105, 106, *106,* 185-88,
    185, 186, 188
  paths and, 63, 82-83
  plantings around, 78-84, *79, 83, 84,*
    86, 87, 89
  positioning of, 81-84, *172*
  respecting shapes of, 84-85
  selection of, 81, 179
  splitting of, *174*
boxwood, *22, 54, 83,* 99
Brewer, David, *124*
brick, *63*
bridges, boulders and, *80, 114, 115*
Broughton Castle, 130

Camellia, *31*
Campanula formanekiana, 24
C. portenschlagiana, 22
capstones, 150
Cerastium tomentosum, 19, 24
Chamaecyparis pisifera 'Filifera', 75
channels, formal, 109
Chasmanthium latifolia, 107
Chassé, Patrick, *83,* 89, *106,* 121,
    127, 176-78
cobble, 207-9
coping, 99

dicentra, *54*
dry-laid walls, 16, 17-19
  bases of, 139-40, *139, 149*
  designing of, 138-39
  stone for, 138, 140-41, 203
  wet-laid walls vs., 141-42
dry-laid walls, building of, 136-51
  cautions in, 144
  questions to ask before, 136
  steps in, 143-46, *143*
  tools for, 147
dry stone wallers, 17-18

embedded-pebble paths, 64-66, *65, 66*
Epimedium sulphureum, 34

espaliers, *25*
Everts, Florence, 35, *35, 54*

Farrand, Beatrix, 43, 116
fenceposts, granite, 118, 123-25, *124,* 192
fencing, wooden, when to use, 39
fern, 28, *83,* 86, *89*
  Christmas, 78, 176
  hay-scented, *20,* 89
  maidenhair, *84*
  ostrich, 84
fieldstone, flagstone, *49,* 50-53, *50, 52,*
    54, 72-73, *83,* 161-62
  see also paths, fieldstone; terraces,
    fieldstone
fir, balsam, 78
Fothergilla gardenii, 107
F. major, 86
foundation plantings, 35-36
fountain grass, *101*
fountains, construction of, 189-91, *190,*
    191
freestanding walls, 14, 16, *18,* 20-26,
    26, 41, 42, 138, 145
  bases of, 18, 139-40, *139*
  designing of, 23-26
  intimate spaces created by, 22
  plantings on, *19, 25, 43*
  problems solved by, 20-22, *23*
  proportions of, 16, *18, 19,* 23-26,
    138-39, *138*

Gage Davis Associates, 89
Gainey, Ryan, 72
Galanthus nivalis, 36
garden design:
  Chinese rules for, 100
  principles of, 59, 96
  Zen, 96
Garden Wall, The (Osler), 14
Geranium macrorrhizum, 58
ginger, European, 86, 107, 176
granite:
  fenceposts, 118, 123-25, *124,* 192
  paving stones, 49, 50, 156, 207-8
gravel, *40,* 46, *73*
gravity, dry-laid walls and, 142

Hall garden, *48, 82, 91, 122,* 123

Hayward family garden:
  in England, 76-77
  in Vermont, 10-11, 75, *99*, 118,
    123-25, *181*
hearting, 149
hedge maple, 75
hedging, when to use, 39
Helictotrichon sempervirens, 108
herm, 116
heuchera, *74*
Highberg Garden, 112
holly, *23,* 34, 87, 99
hosta, 58
Hosta 'Betcher Blue', 107
H. plantaginea, 95
hyacinth, grape, *54*

Iberis sempervirens, 192
Ilex verticillata, 87

Jekyll, Gertrude, 151
joints, 146
Judd, Fran, 200
Juniperus conferta, 20
J. horizontalis, 28, 86

Kalmia angustifolia, 178
Kiley, Dan, 109

lady's pin cushion, 24
landings, *45,* 46, 59
Lavandula angustifolia, 108
lawn:
  drainage and, *107*
  laying stepping-stones in, 165-66
ligularia, 86
lilac 'Miss Kim', 107
limestone, 49, 72, 154, 156, 161
liners, pool, 183-85, *187*
liriope, 105
lobelia, *46*

maple:
  cut-leaf, *83, 110*
  hedge, 75
  marble, 49
Matthiessen, Dieta, 194-96
Messervy, Julie Moir, 96, 170
mica schists, 50, 72, 161

Miscanthus sinensis 'Gracellimus', *58*
mock orange, *22*
mosses, *81, 82, 89,* 176

Nakane, Kinsaku, 170-71
Nicolson, Harold, 74
nobedan path, 62-63, *66*

Oenothera speciosa, 108
oxalis, *67*

Pachistima canbyi, 86
pads, stone, 132-33, 195-96
pansy, *54*
paths, cut-stone, 154-60, *155*
  bases of, 156-57, *156,* 160, *160*
  edging of, 159-60, *160*
  laying of, 158-69, *158*
  plants for, *54, 55, 56*
paths, fieldstone, 154, 161-64, *162, 163*
  choosing stone for, 161-62
  gaps and grouting of, 163-64
  laying of, 162-64
  plants for, 54-56, 163-64, 169
paths, stone, 44-66, *47, 48, 49, 52, 53,*
    54, 56, 60
  boulders and, 63, 82-83
  curving, 49, *49,* 50
  designing and planning of, 44-48, 152,
    153-54
  laying of, 152-69
  mixed material, 53, 62-64, *62, 63, 166*
  planting of, 54-56, *55, 56,* 60, 163-64,
    169
  prioritizing of, 53-54, 57-62
  vs. paths of other materials, 46-48
  see also specific types of paths
patios, *see* terraces
Paul, Anthony, 118, *125*
peastone, 157
pebbles, for embedding in cement, 64,
  209-10
pennisetum, 107
Peschar, Hannah, 118
Phellodendron amurense, 104
Phlox divaricata, 123
P. stolonifera, 86, 123
P. stolonifera 'Blue Ridge', 107
P. subulata, 24

Picea pungens 'Glauca Procumbens', *89*
Pieris japonica 'Mountain Fire', 106
Pinus sylvestris 'Nana', *20*
plants:
  coordinating colors of paving stones and,
    36, 56
  when to use, 39
  see also specific plants; specific uses of plants
Platt, Jane, garden of, 87, *89*
pools, faux, 106-7
pools, formal, 96-100, *97, 99*
  installation and maintenance of, 100, 109
  placement of, 97-100
  proportions of, 97-99, 100
pools, naturalistic, *91,* 100-108, *108,*
    180-88, *182*
  digging hole for, 180-83
  formal pools vs., 100-101
  lining of, 183-85, *187*
  plantings around and in, *101,* 103, 107,
    182, *188*
  rocks and, 101, *101, 103, 104,* 105-7,
    106, 185-88, *185, 186, 188*
  siting of, 103-5
primary paths, 57-59

quartzite, 50, 161

Reflecting Nature (Malitz), 93
retaining walls, 10, 14, 16, *26,* 27-36, *27,*
    30, 31, 32, 38, *40, 42, 48, 83,*
    137, 145
  bases and backfill for, 18, *140*
  concrete, 39
  designing of, 32-36
  garden spaces created by, *23,* 28, 31, 34,
    35-36
  plantings and, *24,* 28, 31, *31,* 36, 148,
    153
  problems solved by, *23,* 27-28, 32, *32,*
    35-36, 59
  proportions of, 31, 32-34, *33,* 36
  steps and, *27,* 31, *32,* 34, *34,* 68
  wooden, 39
rills, *92,* 109
river rock, river stone, *41,* 53, *54,* 208-9
  in paths, *36,* 62, 64-66, *65, 66*
  water features and, *92,* 105
rodgersia, 86

rose, *24, 46*
Rose, James, 63-64
Rudbeckia 'Goldsturm', *58*

Sackville-West, Vita, 74
sandstone, *47, 49, 55,* 72, 154, 156, 161
Saxifraga fortunei 'Rubrifolia', *24*
Schultz, Michael, *84, 89*
sculptures, stone, 118, *121,* 125-27
  moving of, 195, *195*
  setting of, 194-98
  siting of, 125-27
  see also artifacts, cast-stone; artifacts, stone
secondary paths, 59-60
sedum, *36, 89, 110,* 176
Sedum acre, 19
S. spurium, 68
S. spurium 'John Creech', 106
Selaginella kraussiana, 110
sempervivum, 68, 176
sheep's laurel, 178
Sissinghurst, 74
Snow, Dan, *23, 26, 27, 31, 32, 36, 41, 58,* 136-50
snowdrops, 36
Solomon's seal, 78, *84*
Southwick, Clarisse, *124*
standing stones, 116-25, *122, 133,* 209
  large-scale, 121-23
  sacred and symbolic, 119, 120
  setting of, 199, *199*
  siting of, 116-18, 121-25
  small, 123-25
Steele, Fletcher, *88*
stepping-stone paths, 53, *54,* 56, 60-62, *60,* 127, *163*
  laying of, 164-66, *164, 165*
stepping-stones, 35, *46, 48, 49*
  individual, 62
  steps, *60*
  in streams, 111, *111*
steps, stone, *48, 58, 60,* 66-70, *67, 68, 70*
  construction of, 168
  degree of formality of, 67-68
  design principles for, 66-68
  plantings for, 68, *74*
  retaining walls and, *27, 31, 32,* 34, *34, 68*
  siting of, 66-67
  stepping-stone, *60*

Stevens, Wallace, 133
stiles, *23, 36, 150*
stone, artificial, 211
stone-carpet paths, *50, 52, 54,* 62-63, *66,* 161, 166
  see also paths, fieldstone
stones, cut, *45,* 49, 72, 154-60, 207-8
  cutting of, 159, *159*
  see also paths, cut-stone; terraces, cut-stone
stones, inscribed, 211
stones, landscaping, 200-211
  cutting and shaping of, 146, *146*
  delivery of, 200-202
  moving of, *144*
  North American, 202-11
  uses of, 9
  variety and availability of, 9-10
stones, paving, *73,* 205-7
  coordinating colors of plants and, *36,* 56
  designing with, 59
  drainage and, 156-57, *156, 160*
  hierarchy of, 48-53
  irregular, *46,* 50-53, *52, 54,* 72-73
  for patios and terraces, 72-73, 154-56, 161-62
  plant roots protected by, 74
  see also stones, cut
stonemasons, 17-18
Stone Work (Jerome), 20, *42*
stone yards:
  choosing boulders in, 179
  questions to ask at, 202
streams, *108,* 109-11, *110*
  informal, 109-11
  stepping-stones in, 111, *111*
  waterfalls and, 114

terraces, 71-73
  bases for, 156-57, 160, 167
  laying of, 152-69
  materials for, 72-73
  planning and designing of, 71-73, 152-54
  proportions of, 71, 152-53
terraces, cut-stone, 154-60
  bases for, 156-57, 160
  choosing stone for, 72, 154-56
  edging of, 159-60
  laying of, 72, 158-59

terraces, fieldstone, 154, 161-64, *161*
  choosing stone for, 72-73, 161-62
  gaps and grouting in, 163-64
  laying of, 72-73, 162-63
  plants for, 163-64, 169
tertiary stepping-stone paths, 60-62, *60*
throughstones, 149
Thuja occidentalis 'Smaragd', 107
thymes, 56, *67,* 68
Thymus pseudolanuginosus, 68
Tiarella cordifolia 'Slickrock', 78, 123
trellising, wooden, 39

Verey, Rosemary, garden of, 118
Verity, Simon, 118
viburnum, 58
Viburnum prunifolium, 118
Vinca minor 'Alba', 176
V. minor 'Bowles', *23, 34, 58, 99,* 176
volcanic rock, *110,* 209
Volk, Patricia, 127

walls, stone, 14-43, *16, 201*
  aesthetic and practical purposes of, 14-16
  costs of, 19-20
  good vs. bad, 37
  grown-in-place appearance of, 16, 18
  harmonizing of old and new, 16, 19
  house values and, 20
  Jekyll's plants for, 151
  softening of, 40
  when to use, 39
  see also dry-laid walls; freestanding walls; retaining walls; wet-laid walls
water, water features, 90-115
  appeal of, 90-92
  dry-laid walls and, 142
  nature-inspired, 92-93
  see also specific water features
water basins, 93-96, *94, 95*
waterfalls, 112-14, *112, 113, 114*
  creation of, 114, *183, 186*
wet-laid walls, 16-19, *141*
  drawbacks of, 16-17
  dry-laid walls vs., 141-42
  stone for, 203-5
Wheat, James, 78
winterberry, 87
witch hazel, 86